DENNIS HOPELESS
SERG ACUÑA
KENDALL GOODE
DOUG GARBARK

W9-CJF-997

WOMEN'S EVOLUTION

BOOM! STUDIOS

WWE

WWE BOOKS
Relive
Explore
Adventure
Discover

WWE Volume Four, December 2018. Published by BOOM! Studios, a division of Boom Entertainment, Inc. WWE is ™ & © 2018 WWE. All WWE programming, talent names, images, likenesses, slogans, wrestling moves, trademarks, logos and copyrights are the exclusive property of WWE and its subsidiaries. All other trademarks, logos and copyrights are the property of their respective owners. © 2018 WWE. All rights reserved. Originally published in single magazine form as WWE No. 14-17. ™ & © 2018 WWE. All rights reserved. BOOM! Studios and the BOOM! Studios logo are trademarks of Boom Entertainment, Inc., registered in various countries and categories. All characters, events, and institutions depicted herein are fictional. Any similarity between any of the names, characters, persons, events, and/or institutions in this publication to actual names, characters, and persons, whether living or dead, events, and/or institutions is unintended and purely coincidental. BOOM! Studios does not read or accept unsolicited submissions of ideas, stories, or artwork.

BOOM! Studios, 5670 Wilshire Boulevard, Suite 400, Los Angeles, CA 90036-5679. Printed in China. First Printing.

ISBN: 978-1-68415-283-4, eISBN: 978-1-64144-145-2

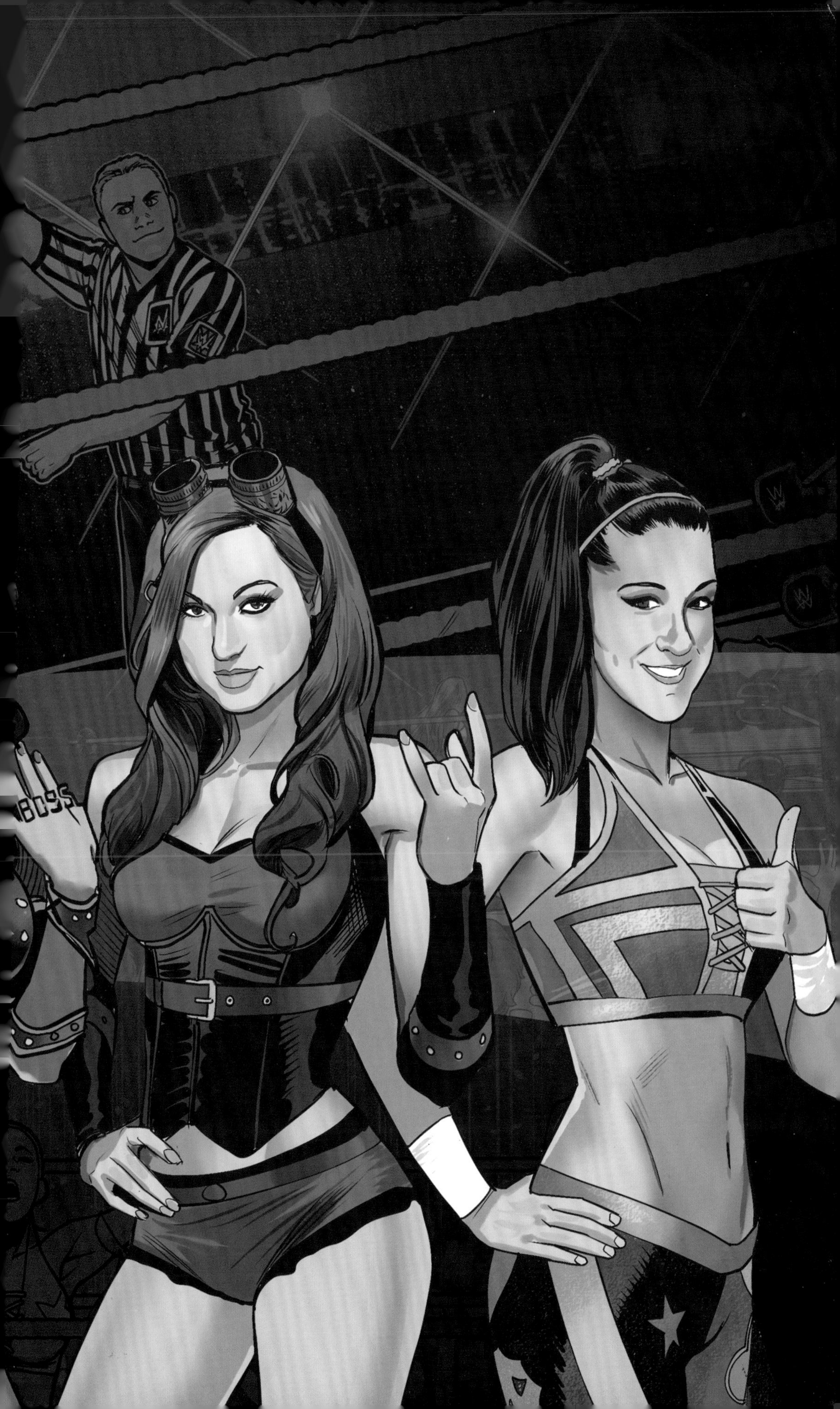

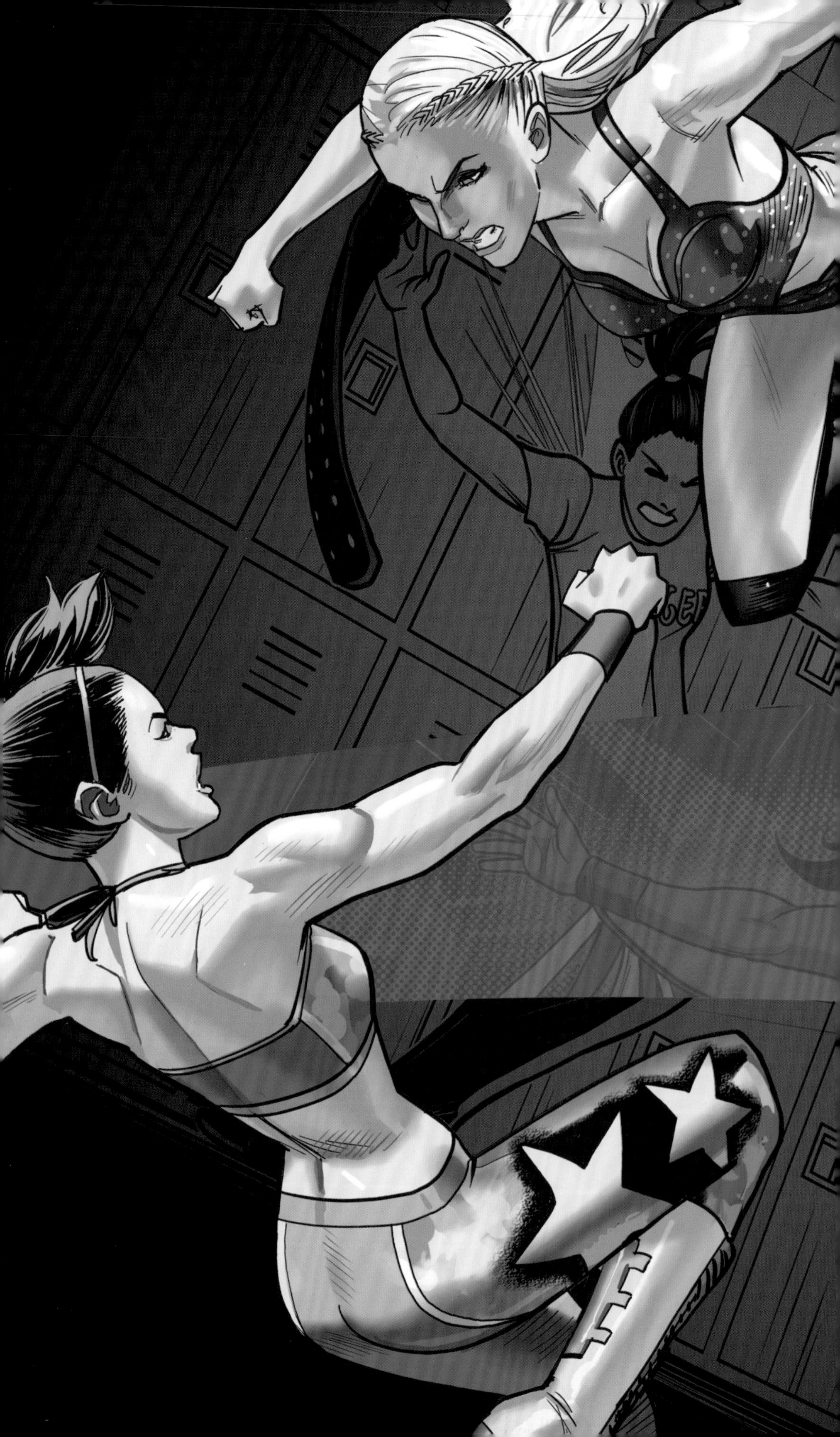

WOMEN'S EVOLUTION

WRITTEN BY
DENNIS HOPELESS

ILLUSTRATED BY
SERG ACUÑA

AND
KENDALL GOODE
(CHAPTER 3 PAGES 1-7, CHAPTER 4 PAGES 8-14)

COLORED BY
DOUG GARBARK

LETTERED BY
JIM CAMPBELL

COVER BY
DAN MORA

SERIES DESIGNER
GRACE PARK

COLLECTION DESIGNER
JILLIAN CRAB

ASSISTANT EDITOR
GAVIN GRONENTHAL

EDITORS
CHRIS ROSA
ERIC HARBURN

SPECIAL THANKS TO
STEVE PANTALEO
CHAD BARBASH
BEN MAYER
JOHN JONES
STAN STANSKI
LAUREN DIENES-MIDDLEN
AND EVERYONE AT **WWE**

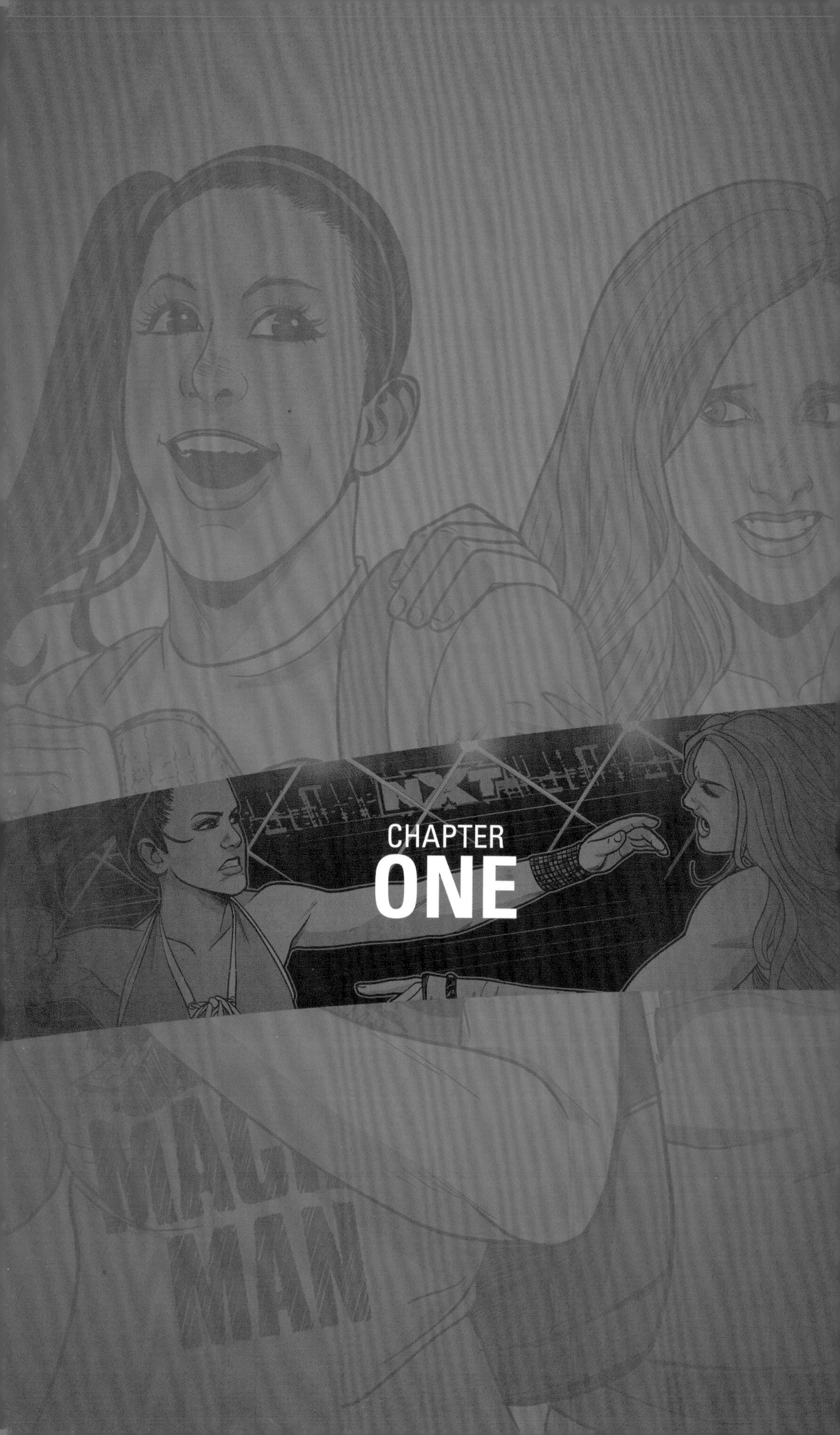

CHAPTER ONE

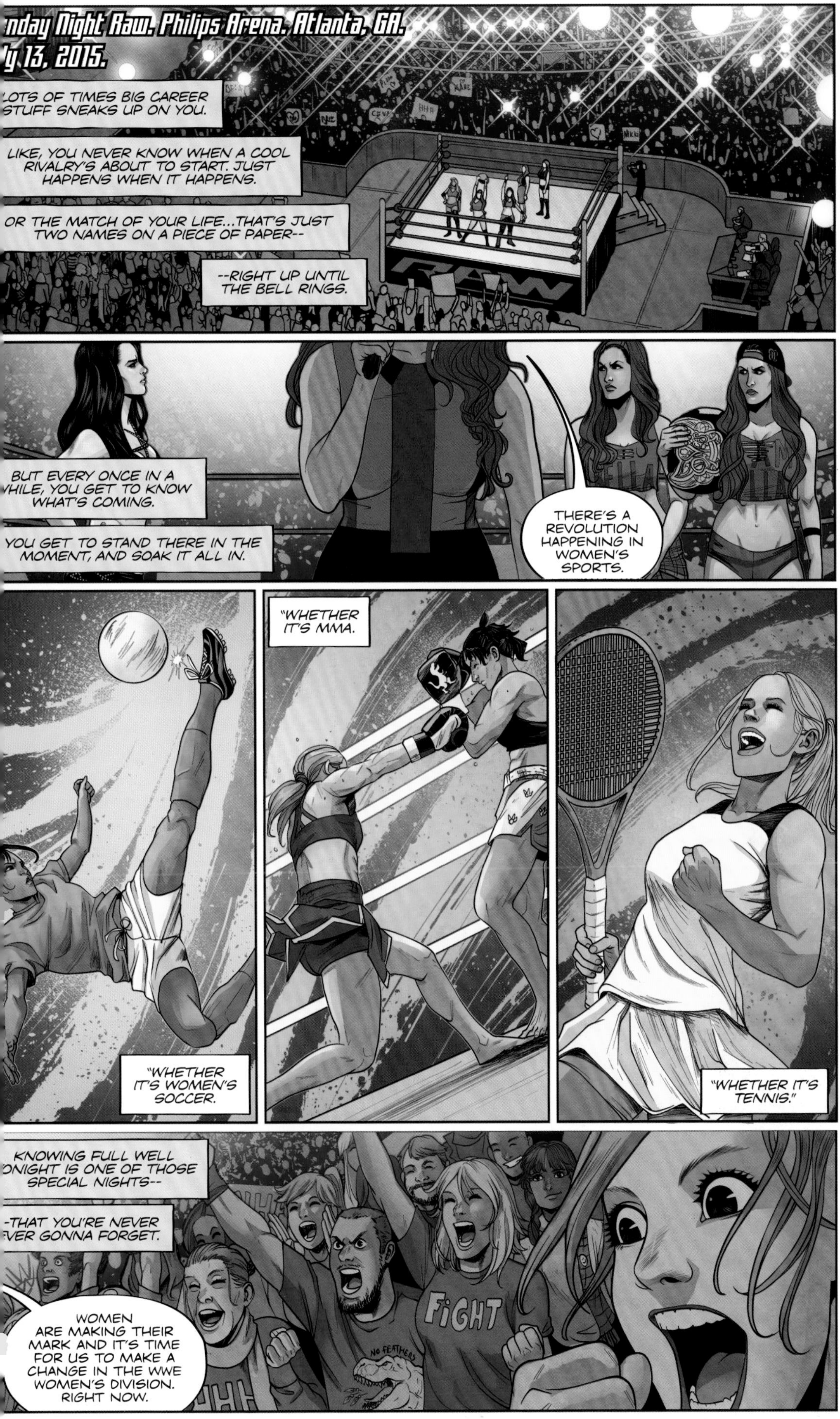

nday Night Raw. Philips Arena. Atlanta, GA.
y 13, 2015.
LOTS OF TIMES BIG CAREER STUFF SNEAKS UP ON YOU.
LIKE, YOU NEVER KNOW WHEN A COOL RIVALRY'S ABOUT TO START. JUST HAPPENS WHEN IT HAPPENS.
OR THE MATCH OF YOUR LIFE...THAT'S JUST TWO NAMES ON A PIECE OF PAPER--
--RIGHT UP UNTIL THE BELL RINGS.
BUT EVERY ONCE IN A WHILE, YOU GET TO KNOW WHAT'S COMING.
YOU GET TO STAND THERE IN THE MOMENT, AND SOAK IT ALL IN.
THERE'S A REVOLUTION HAPPENING IN WOMEN'S SPORTS.
"WHETHER IT'S WOMEN'S SOCCER.
"WHETHER IT'S MMA.
"WHETHER IT'S TENNIS."
KNOWING FULL WELL ONIGHT IS ONE OF THOSE SPECIAL NIGHTS--
-THAT YOU'RE NEVER VER GONNA FORGET.
WOMEN ARE MAKING THEIR MARK AND IT'S TIME FOR US TO MAKE A CHANGE IN THE WWE WOMEN'S DIVISION. RIGHT NOW.
FiGHT
NO FEATHERS

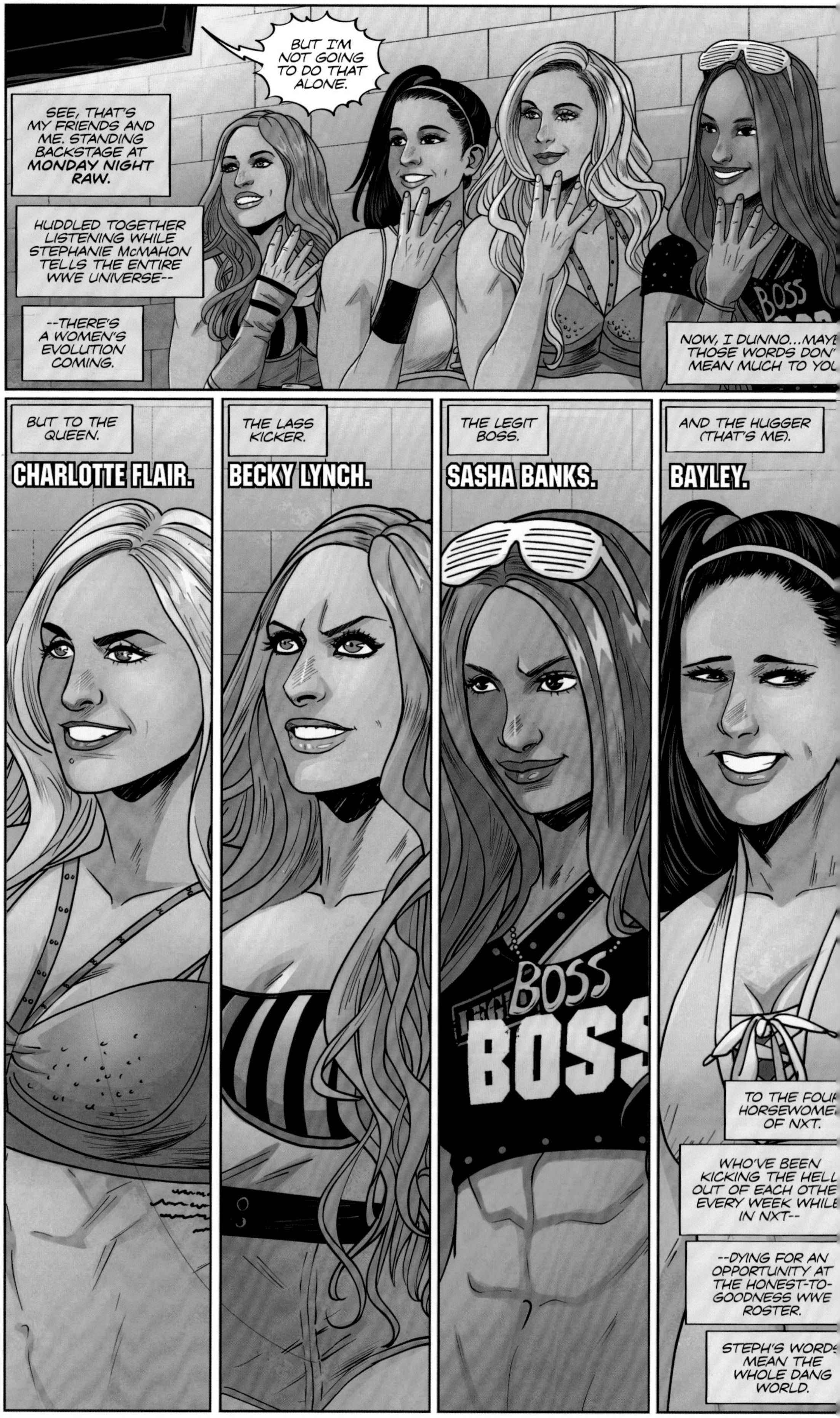
SEE, THAT'S MY FRIENDS AND ME. STANDING BACKSTAGE AT MONDAY NIGHT RAW.
HUDDLED TOGETHER LISTENING WHILE STEPHANIE McMAHON TELLS THE ENTIRE WWE UNIVERSE--
--THERE'S A WOMEN'S EVOLUTION COMING.
BUT I'M NOT GOING TO DO THAT ALONE.
BOSS
NOW, I DUNNO...MAY
THOSE WORDS DON'
MEAN MUCH TO YO
BUT TO THE QUEEN.
CHARLOTTE FLAIR.
THE LASS KICKER.
BECKY LYNCH.
THE LEGIT BOSS.
SASHA BANKS.
AND THE HUGGER (THAT'S ME).
BAYLEY.
BOSS
BOSS
TO THE FOU
HORSEWOME
OF NXT.
WHO'VE BEEN KICKING THE HEL
OUT OF EACH OTHE
EVERY WEEK WHIL
IN NXT--
--DYING FOR AN OPPORTUNITY AT THE HONEST-TO-GOODNESS WWE ROSTER.
STEPH'S WORD
MEAN THE WHOLE DANG WORLD.

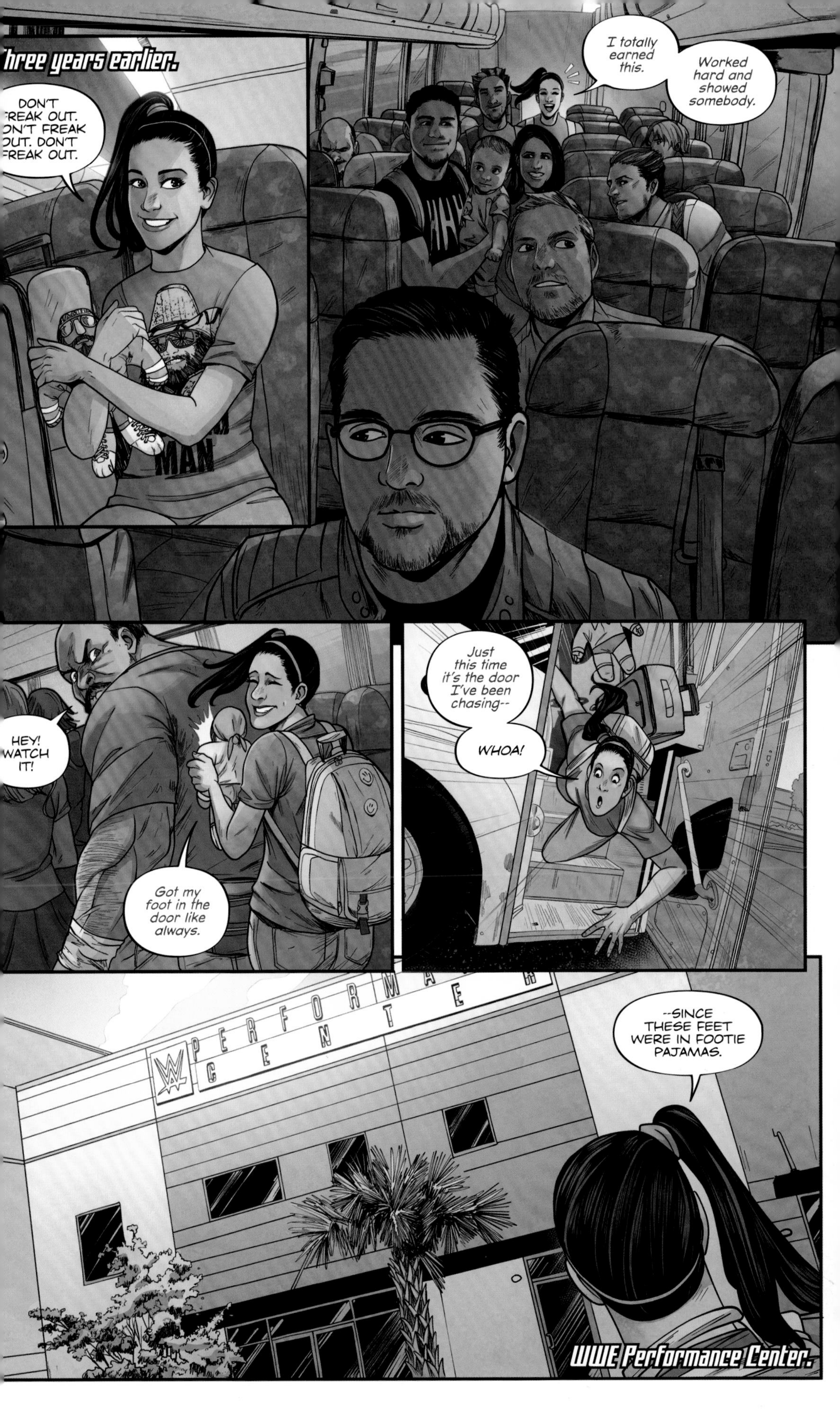
Three years earlier.
DON'T FREAK OUT. DON'T FREAK OUT. DON'T FREAK OUT.
I totally earned this.
Worked hard and showed somebody.
HEY! WATCH IT!
Got my foot in the door like always.
Just this time it's the door I've been chasing--
WHOA!
--SINCE THESE FEET WERE IN FOOTIE PAJAMAS.
PERFORMANCE CENTER
WWE Performance Center.

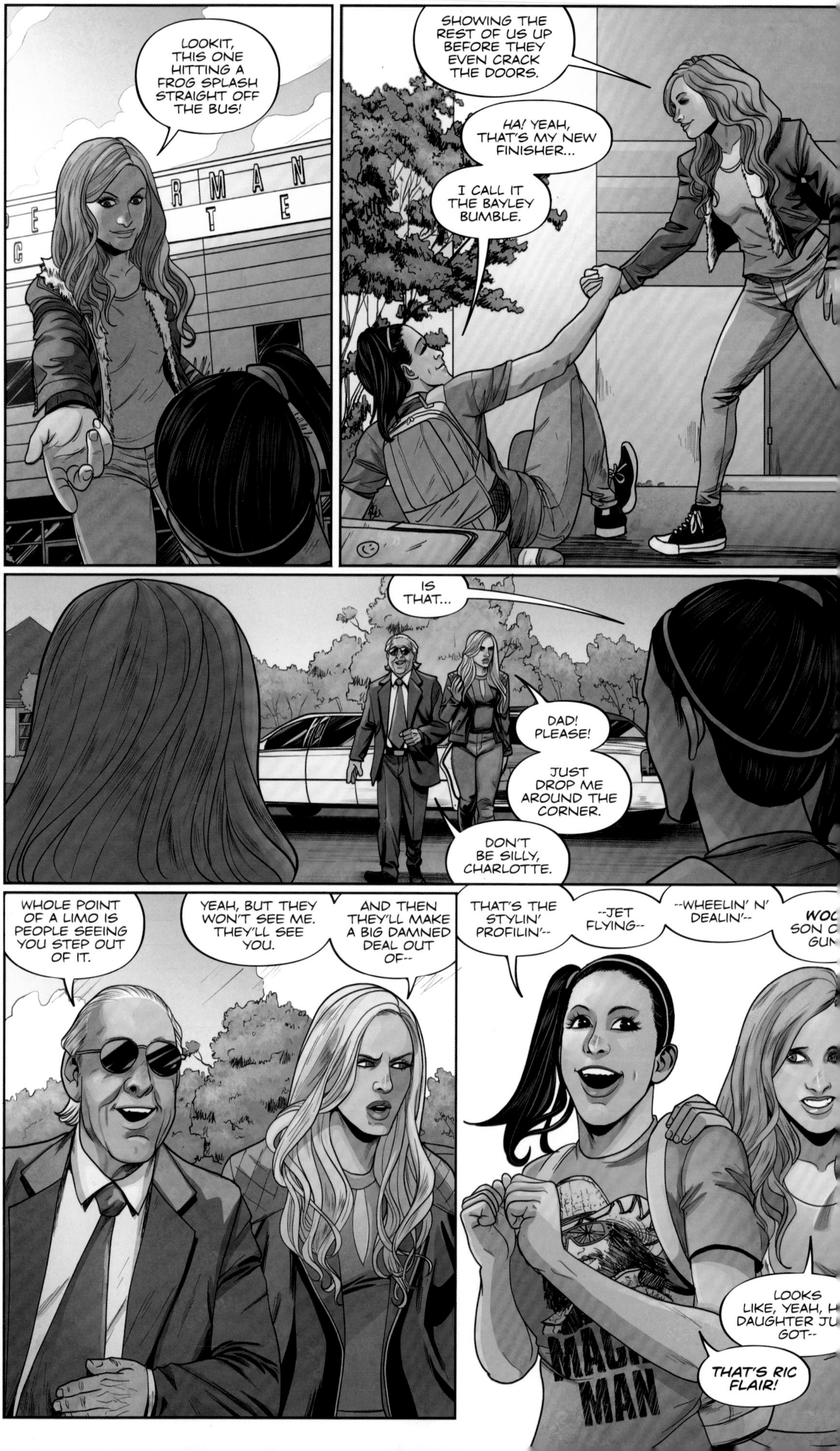
LOOKIT, THIS ONE HITTING A FROG SPLASH STRAIGHT OFF THE BUS!
SHOWING THE REST OF US UP BEFORE THEY EVEN CRACK THE DOORS.
HA! YEAH, THAT'S MY NEW FINISHER...
I CALL IT THE BAYLEY BUMBLE.
IS THAT...
DAD! PLEASE!
JUST DROP ME AROUND THE CORNER.
DON'T BE SILLY, CHARLOTTE.
WHOLE POINT OF A LIMO IS PEOPLE SEEING YOU STEP OUT OF IT.
YEAH, BUT THEY WON'T SEE ME. THEY'LL SEE YOU.
AND THEN THEY'LL MAKE A BIG DAMNED DEAL OUT OF--
THAT'S THE STYLIN' PROFILIN'--
--JET FLYING--
--WHEELIN' N' DEALIN'--
WOO SON O GUN
LOOKS LIKE, YEAH, H DAUGHTER JU GOT--
THAT'S RIC FLAIR!

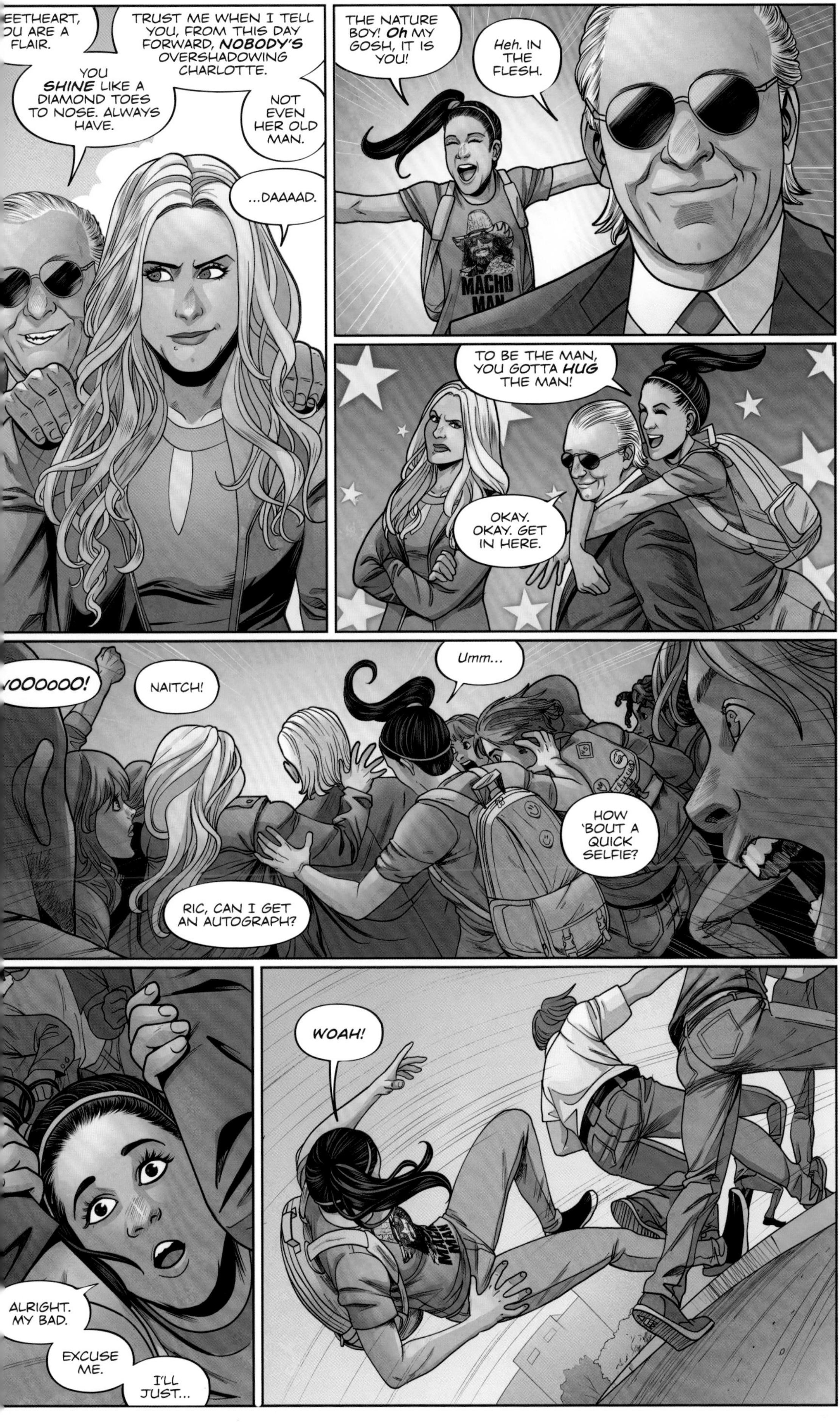
EETHEART, OU ARE A FLAIR.
YOU SHINE LIKE A DIAMOND TOES TO NOSE. ALWAYS HAVE.
TRUST ME WHEN I TELL YOU, FROM THIS DAY FORWARD, NOBODY'S OVERSHADOWING CHARLOTTE.
NOT EVEN HER OLD MAN.
...DAAAAD.
THE NATURE BOY! Oh MY GOSH, IT IS YOU!
Heh. IN THE FLESH.
MACHO MAN
TO BE THE MAN, YOU GOTTA HUG THE MAN!
OKAY. OKAY. GET IN HERE.
OOOOOO!
NAITCH!
Umm...
HOW 'BOUT A QUICK SELFIE?
RIC, CAN I GET AN AUTOGRAPH?
ALRIGHT. MY BAD.
EXCUSE ME.
I'LL JUST...
WOAH!

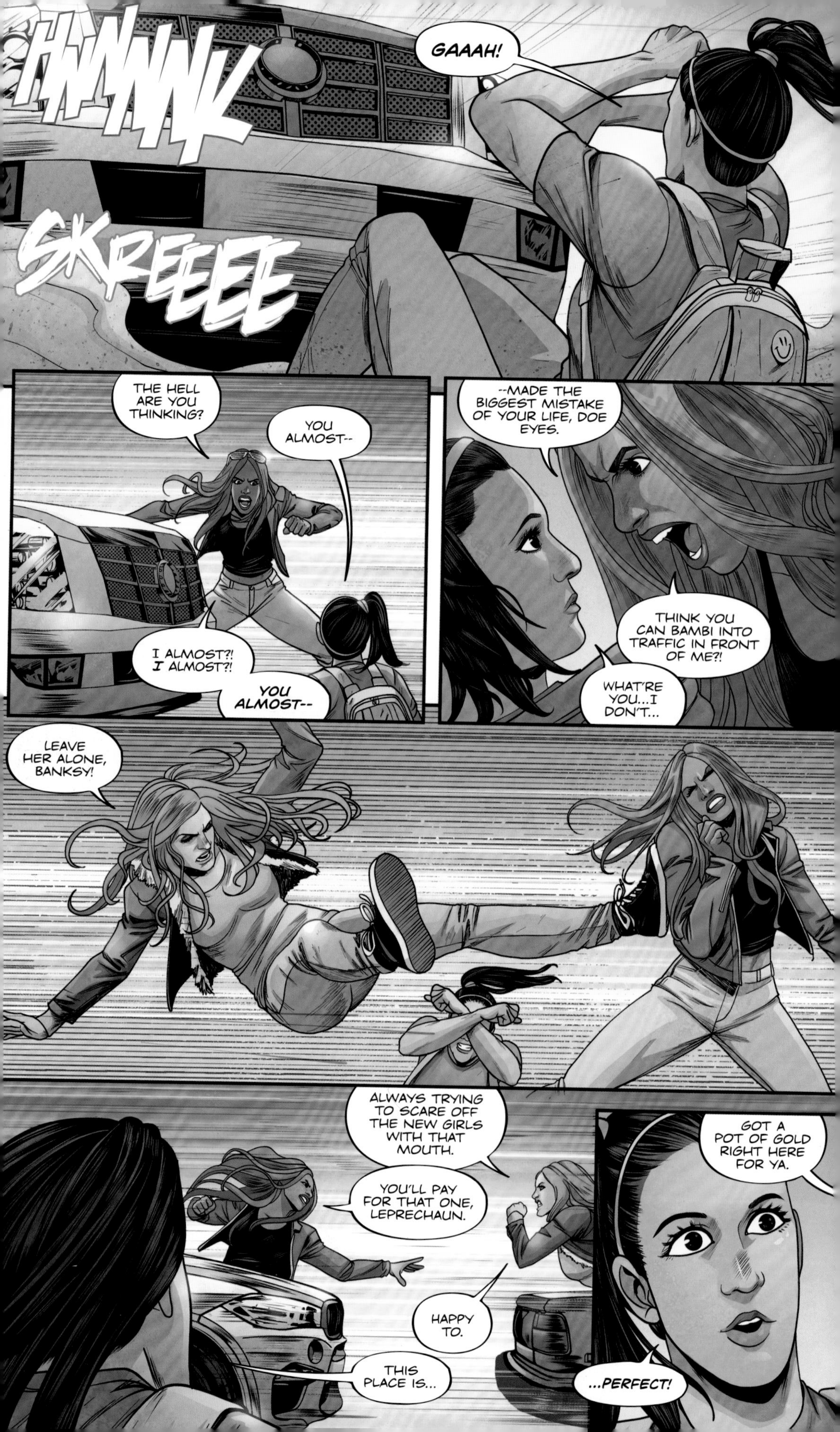
HWWANK
GAAAH!
SKREEEEE
THE HELL ARE YOU THINKING?
YOU ALMOST--
I ALMOST?! I ALMOST?!
YOU ALMOST--
--MADE THE BIGGEST MISTAKE OF YOUR LIFE, DOE EYES.
THINK YOU CAN BAMBI INTO TRAFFIC IN FRONT OF ME?!
WHAT'RE YOU...I DON'T...
LEAVE HER ALONE, BANKSY!
ALWAYS TRYING TO SCARE OFF THE NEW GIRLS WITH THAT MOUTH.
YOU'LL PAY FOR THAT ONE, LEPRECHAUN.
HAPPY TO.
THIS PLACE IS...
GOT A POT OF GOLD RIGHT HERE FOR YA.
...PERFECT!

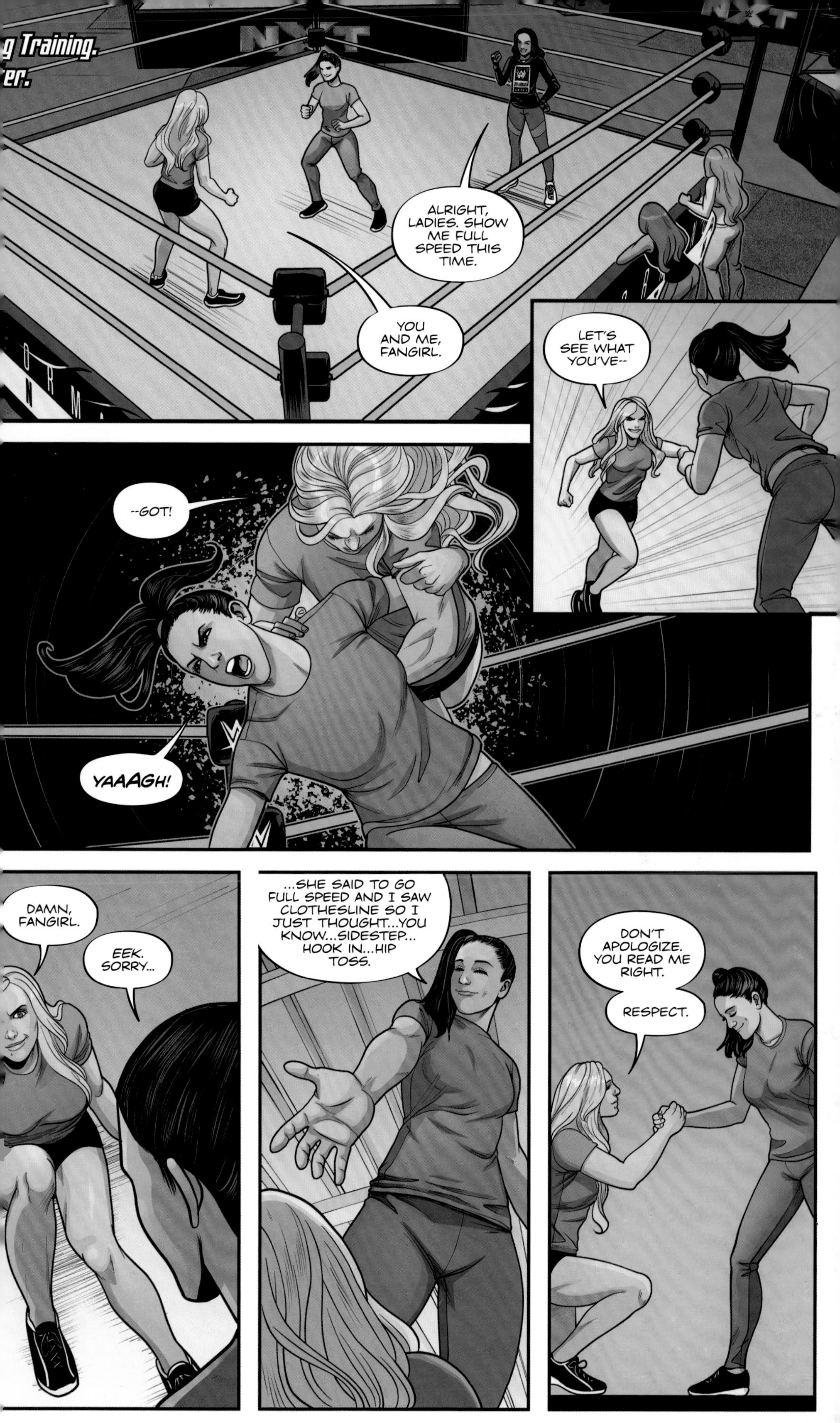
g Training.
er.
ALRIGHT, LADIES. SHOW ME FULL SPEED THIS TIME.
YOU AND ME, FANGIRL.
LET'S SEE WHAT YOU'VE--
--GOT!
YAAAGH!
DAMN, FANGIRL.
EEK. SORRY...
...SHE SAID TO GO FULL SPEED AND I SAW CLOTHESLINE SO I JUST THOUGHT...YOU KNOW...SIDESTEP... HOOK IN...HIP TOSS.
DON'T APOLOGIZE. YOU READ ME RIGHT.
RESPECT.

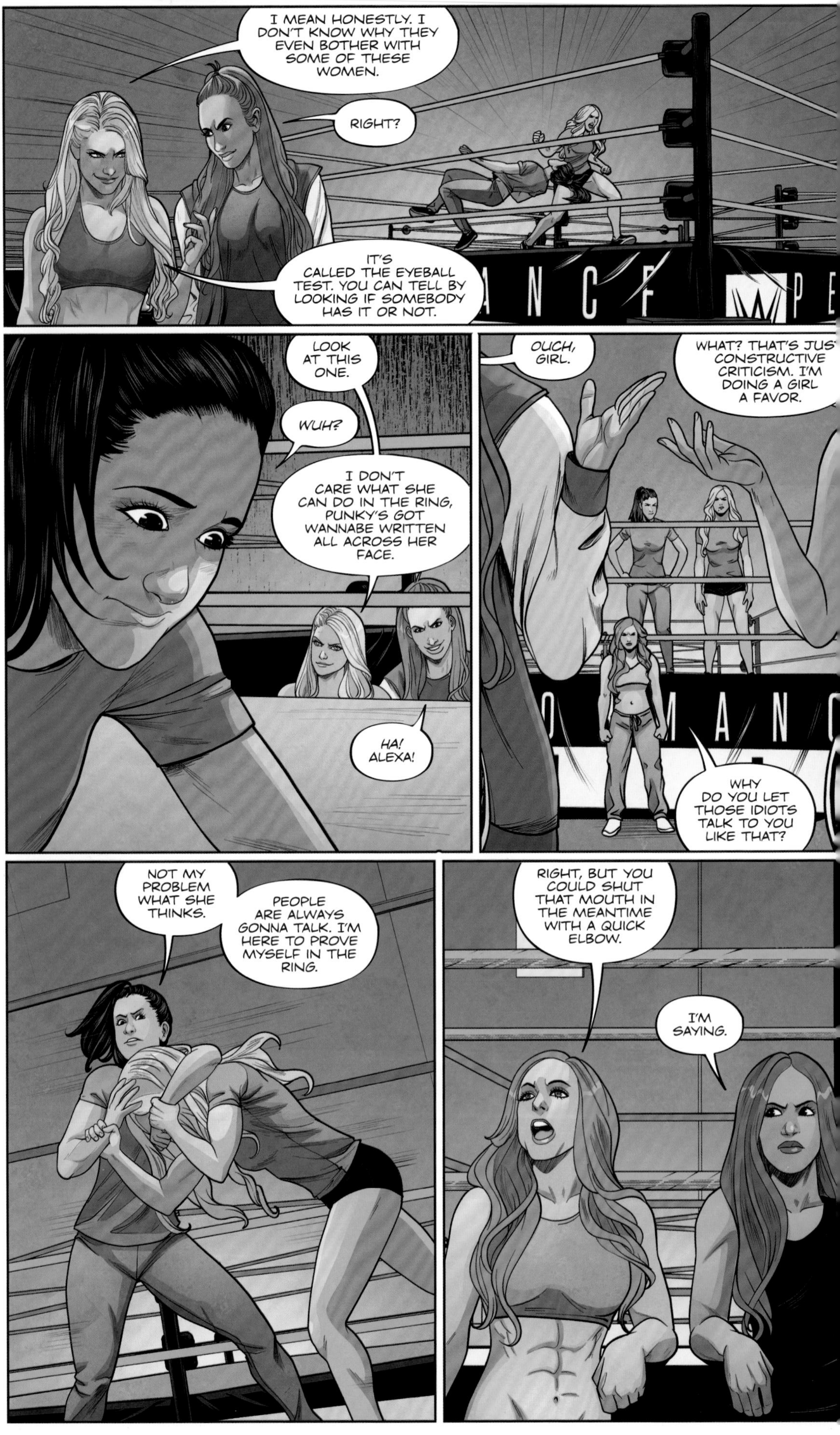
I MEAN HONESTLY. I DON'T KNOW WHY THEY EVEN BOTHER WITH SOME OF THESE WOMEN.
RIGHT?
IT'S CALLED THE EYEBALL TEST. YOU CAN TELL BY LOOKING IF SOMEBODY HAS IT OR NOT.
LOOK AT THIS ONE.
WUH?
I DON'T CARE WHAT SHE CAN DO IN THE RING, PUNKY'S GOT WANNABE WRITTEN ALL ACROSS HER FACE.
HA! ALEXA!
OUCH, GIRL.
WHAT? THAT'S JUST CONSTRUCTIVE CRITICISM. I'M DOING A GIRL A FAVOR.
WHY DO YOU LET THOSE IDIOTS TALK TO YOU LIKE THAT?
NOT MY PROBLEM WHAT SHE THINKS.
PEOPLE ARE ALWAYS GONNA TALK. I'M HERE TO PROVE MYSELF IN THE RING.
RIGHT, BUT YOU COULD SHUT THAT MOUTH IN THE MEANTIME WITH A QUICK ELBOW.
I'M SAYING.

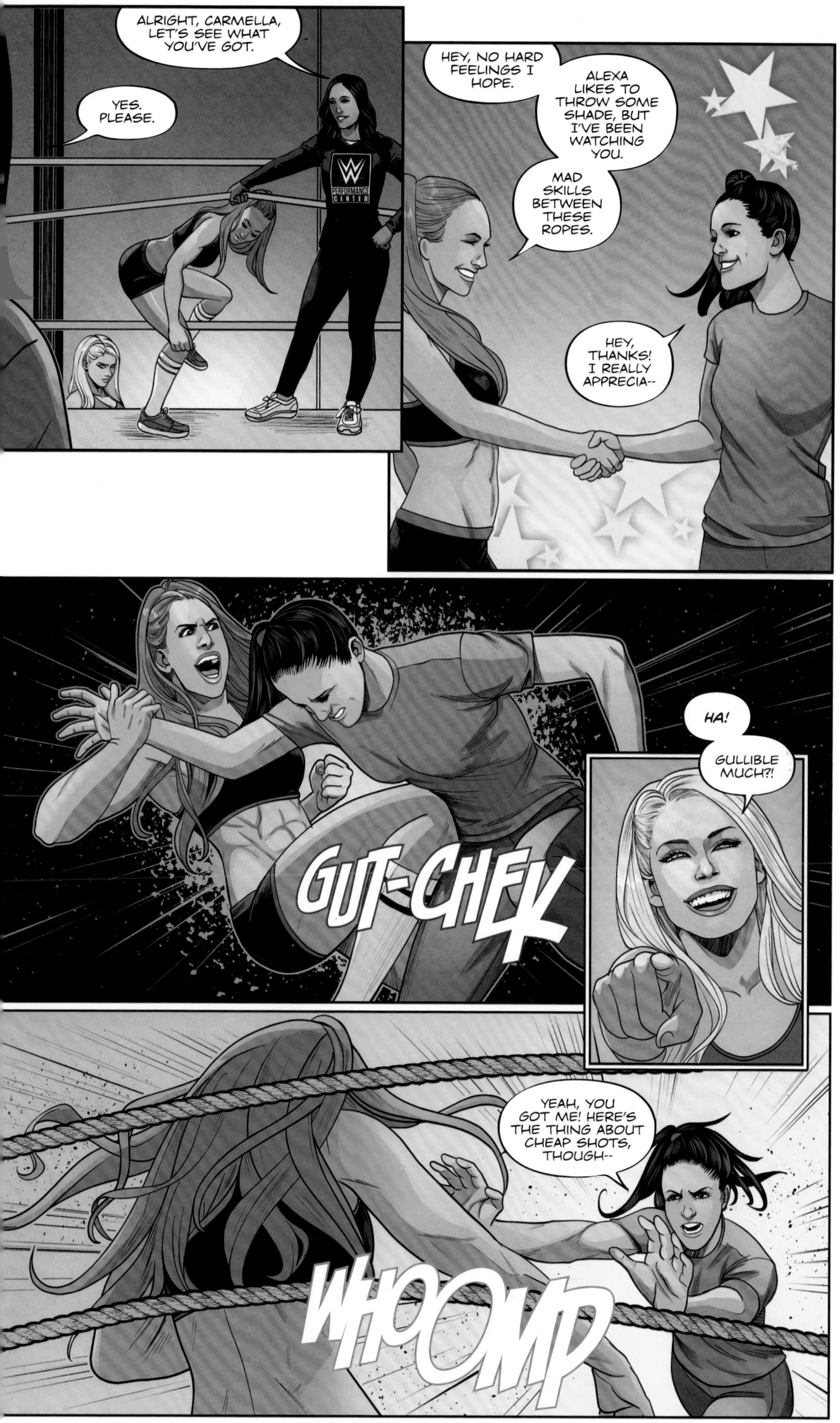
ALRIGHT, CARMELLA, LET'S SEE WHAT YOU'VE GOT.
YES. PLEASE.
PERFORMANCE CENTER
HEY, NO HARD FEELINGS I HOPE.
ALEXA LIKES TO THROW SOME SHADE, BUT I'VE BEEN WATCHING YOU.
MAD SKILLS BETWEEN THESE ROPES.
HEY, THANKS! I REALLY APPRECIA--
GUT-CHEK
HA!
GULLIBLE MUCH?!
YEAH, YOU GOT ME! HERE'S THE THING ABOUT CHEAP SHOTS, THOUGH--
WHOOMP

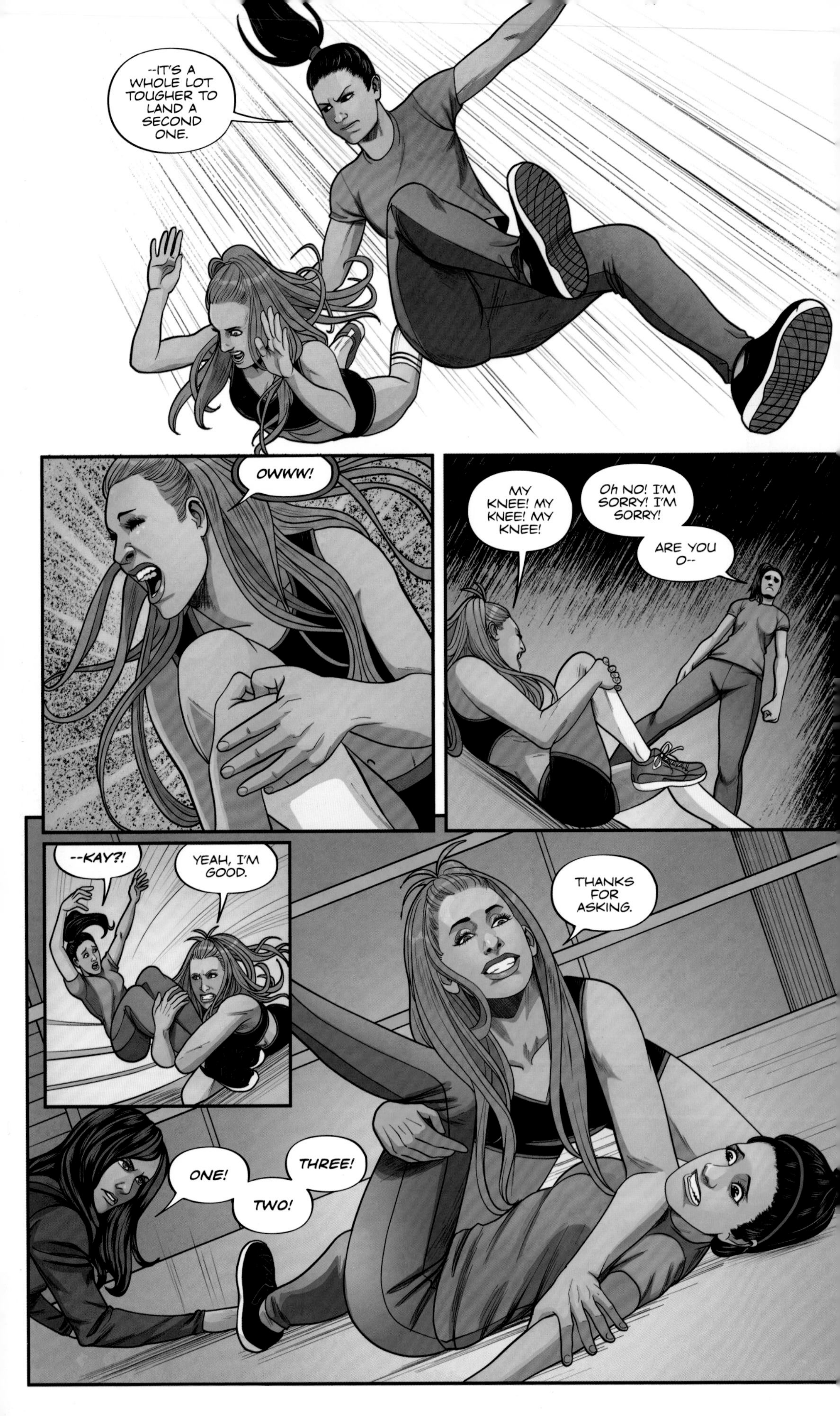
--IT'S A WHOLE LOT TOUGHER TO LAND A SECOND ONE.
OWWW!
MY KNEE! MY KNEE! MY KNEE!
Oh NO! I'M SORRY! I'M SORRY!
ARE YOU O--
--KAY?!
YEAH, I'M GOOD.
THANKS FOR ASKING.
ONE!
TWO!
THREE!

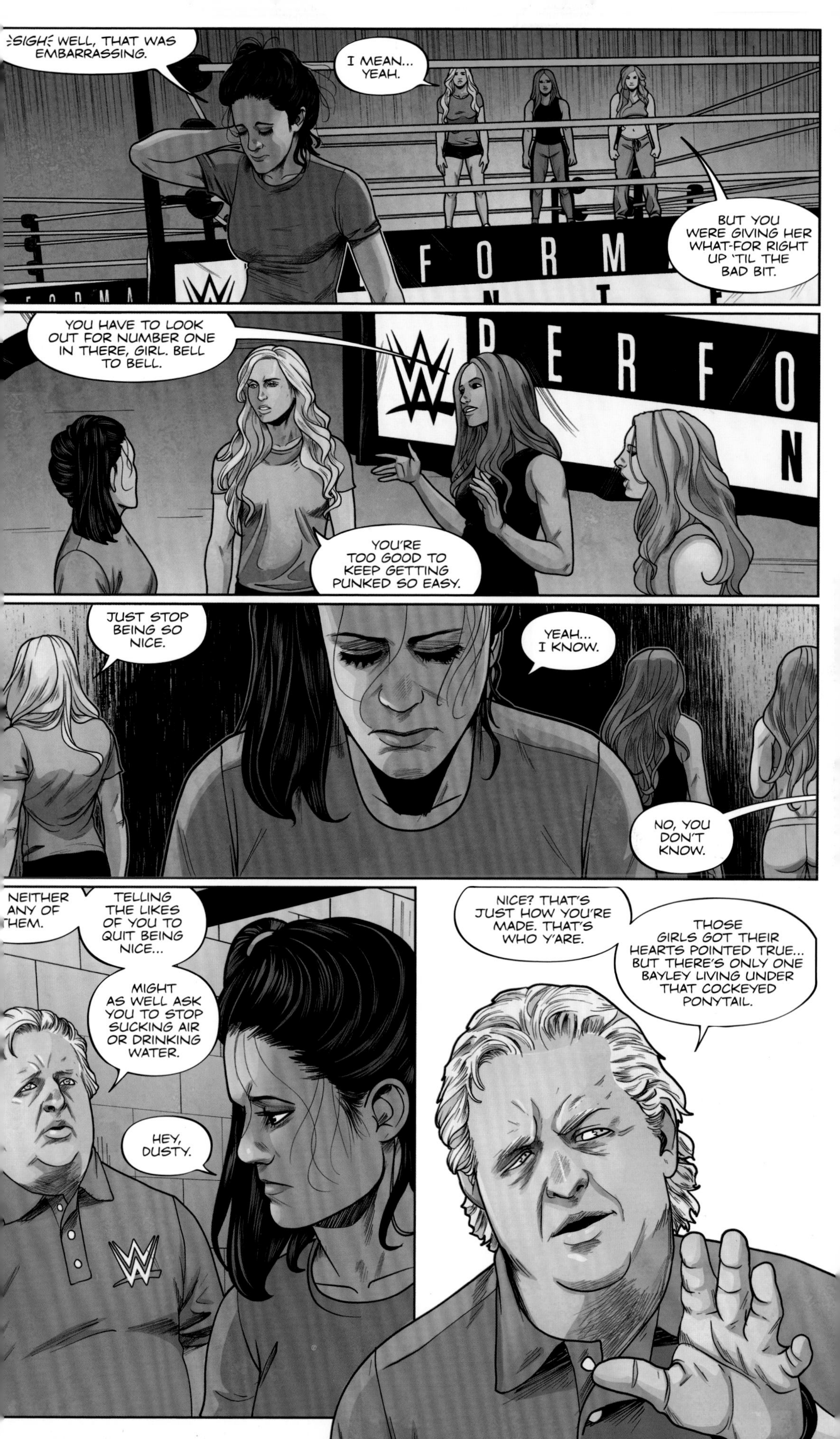
SIGH WELL, THAT WAS EMBARRASSING.
I MEAN... YEAH.
BUT YOU WERE GIVING HER WHAT-FOR RIGHT UP 'TIL THE BAD BIT.
YOU HAVE TO LOOK OUT FOR NUMBER ONE IN THERE, GIRL. BELL TO BELL.
YOU'RE TOO GOOD TO KEEP GETTING PUNKED SO EASY.
JUST STOP BEING SO NICE.
YEAH... I KNOW.
NO, YOU DON'T KNOW.
NEITHER ANY OF THEM.
TELLING THE LIKES OF YOU TO QUIT BEING NICE...
MIGHT AS WELL ASK YOU TO STOP SUCKING AIR OR DRINKING WATER.
HEY, DUSTY.
NICE? THAT'S JUST HOW YOU'RE MADE. THAT'S WHO Y'ARE.
THOSE GIRLS GOT THEIR HEARTS POINTED TRUE... BUT THERE'S ONLY ONE BAYLEY LIVING UNDER THAT COCKEYED PONYTAIL.

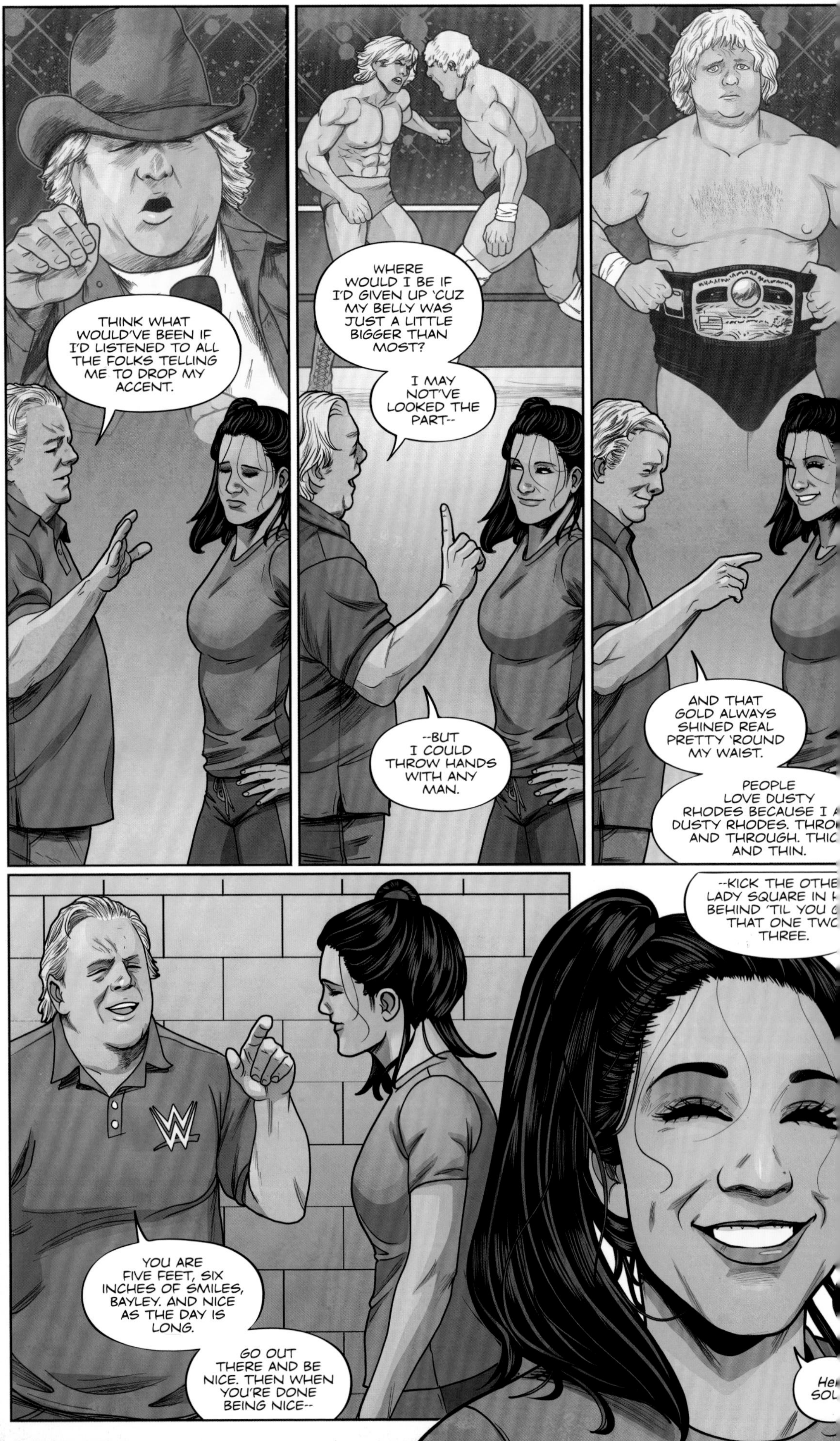
THINK WHAT WOULD'VE BEEN IF I'D LISTENED TO ALL THE FOLKS TELLING ME TO DROP MY ACCENT.
WHERE WOULD I BE IF I'D GIVEN UP 'CUZ MY BELLY WAS JUST A LITTLE BIGGER THAN MOST?
I MAY NOT'VE LOOKED THE PART--
--BUT I COULD THROW HANDS WITH ANY MAN.
AND THAT GOLD ALWAYS SHINED REAL PRETTY 'ROUND MY WAIST.
PEOPLE LOVE DUSTY RHODES BECAUSE I DUSTY RHODES. THRO AND THROUGH. THIC AND THIN.
YOU ARE FIVE FEET, SIX INCHES OF SMILES, BAYLEY. AND NICE AS THE DAY IS LONG.
GO OUT THERE AND BE NICE. THEN WHEN YOU'RE DONE BEING NICE--
--KICK THE OTHE LADY SQUARE IN H BEHIND 'TIL YOU THAT ONE TWO THREE.

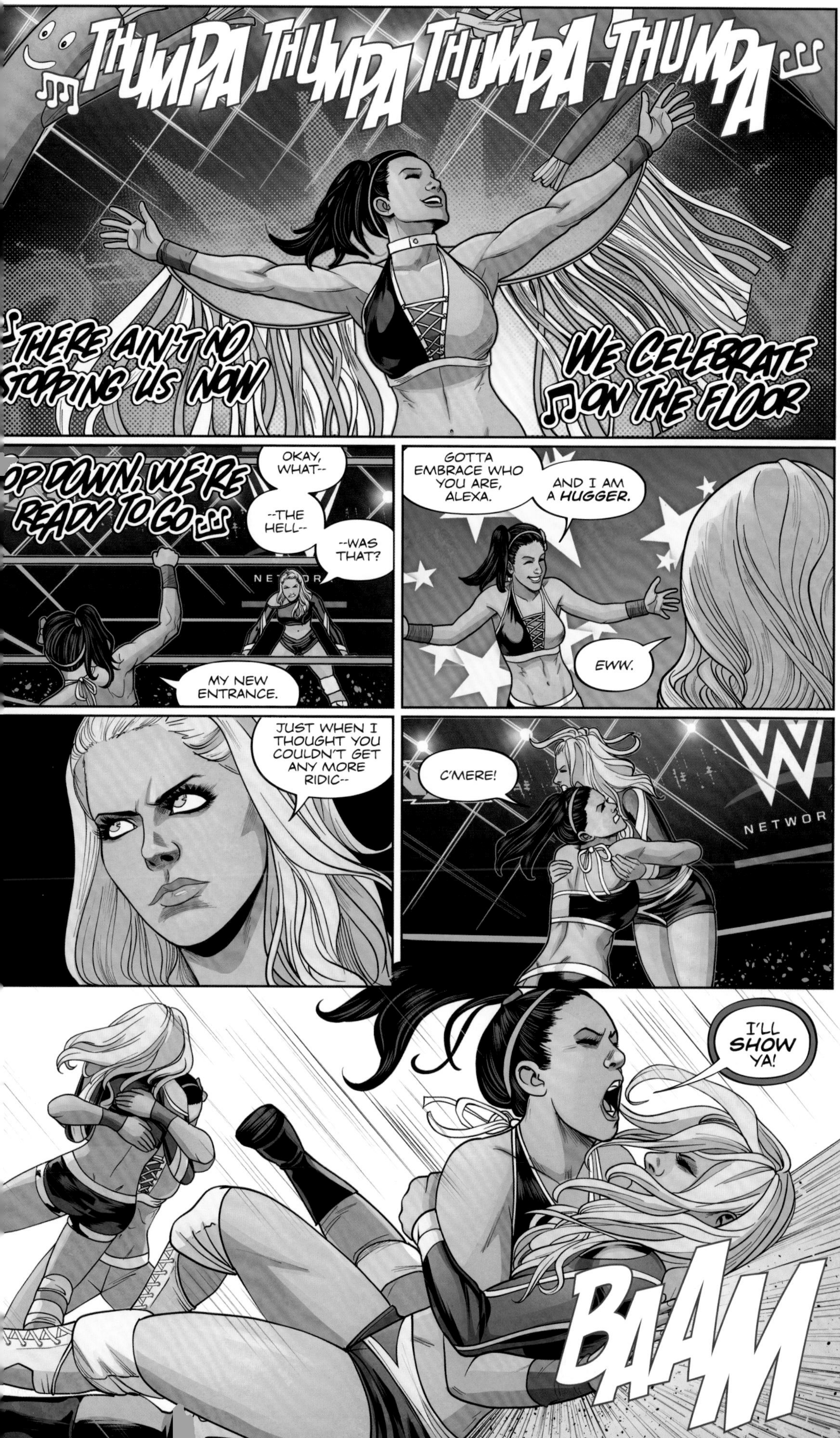
THUMPA THUMPA THUMPA THUMPA
THERE AIN'T NO STOPPING US NOW
WE CELEBRATE ON THE FLOOR
OP DOWN, WE'RE READY TO GO
OKAY, WHAT--
--THE HELL--
--WAS THAT?
NETWOR
MY NEW ENTRANCE.
GOTTA EMBRACE WHO YOU ARE, ALEXA.
AND I AM A HUGGER.
EWW.
JUST WHEN I THOUGHT YOU COULDN'T GET ANY MORE RIDIC--
C'MERE!
NETWOR
I'LL SHOW YA!
BAAM

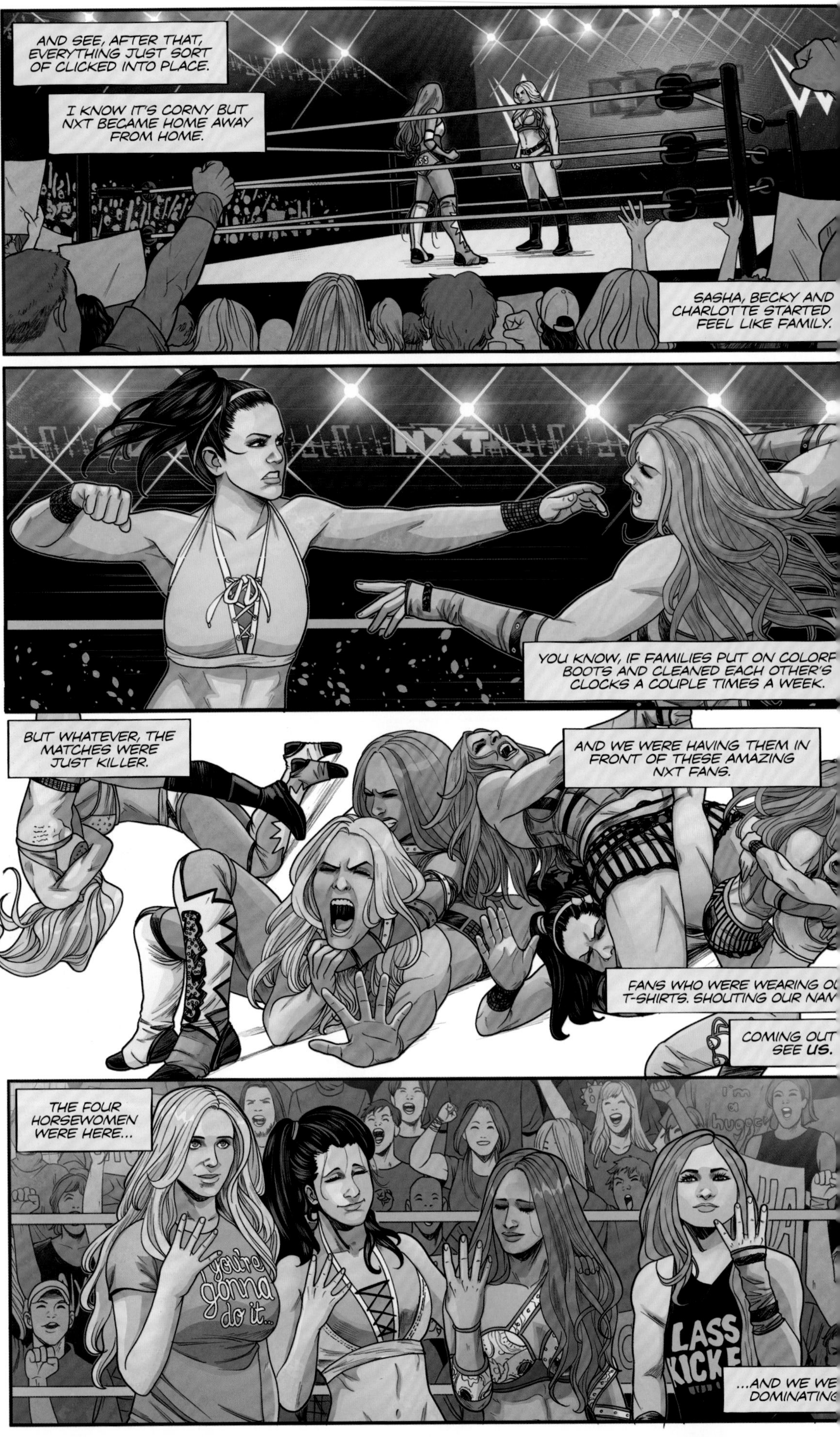
AND SEE, AFTER THAT, EVERYTHING JUST SORT OF CLICKED INTO PLACE.
I KNOW IT'S CORNY BUT NXT BECAME HOME AWAY FROM HOME.
SASHA, BECKY AND CHARLOTTE STARTED FEEL LIKE FAMILY.
NXT
YOU KNOW, IF FAMILIES PUT ON COLORF BOOTS AND CLEANED EACH OTHER'S CLOCKS A COUPLE TIMES A WEEK.
BUT WHATEVER, THE MATCHES WERE JUST KILLER.
AND WE WERE HAVING THEM IN FRONT OF THESE AMAZING NXT FANS.
FANS WHO WERE WEARING OU T-SHIRTS. SHOUTING OUR NAM
COMING OUT SEE US.
THE FOUR HORSEWOMEN WERE HERE...
you're gonna do it...
LASS KICKE
...AND WE WE DOMINATING

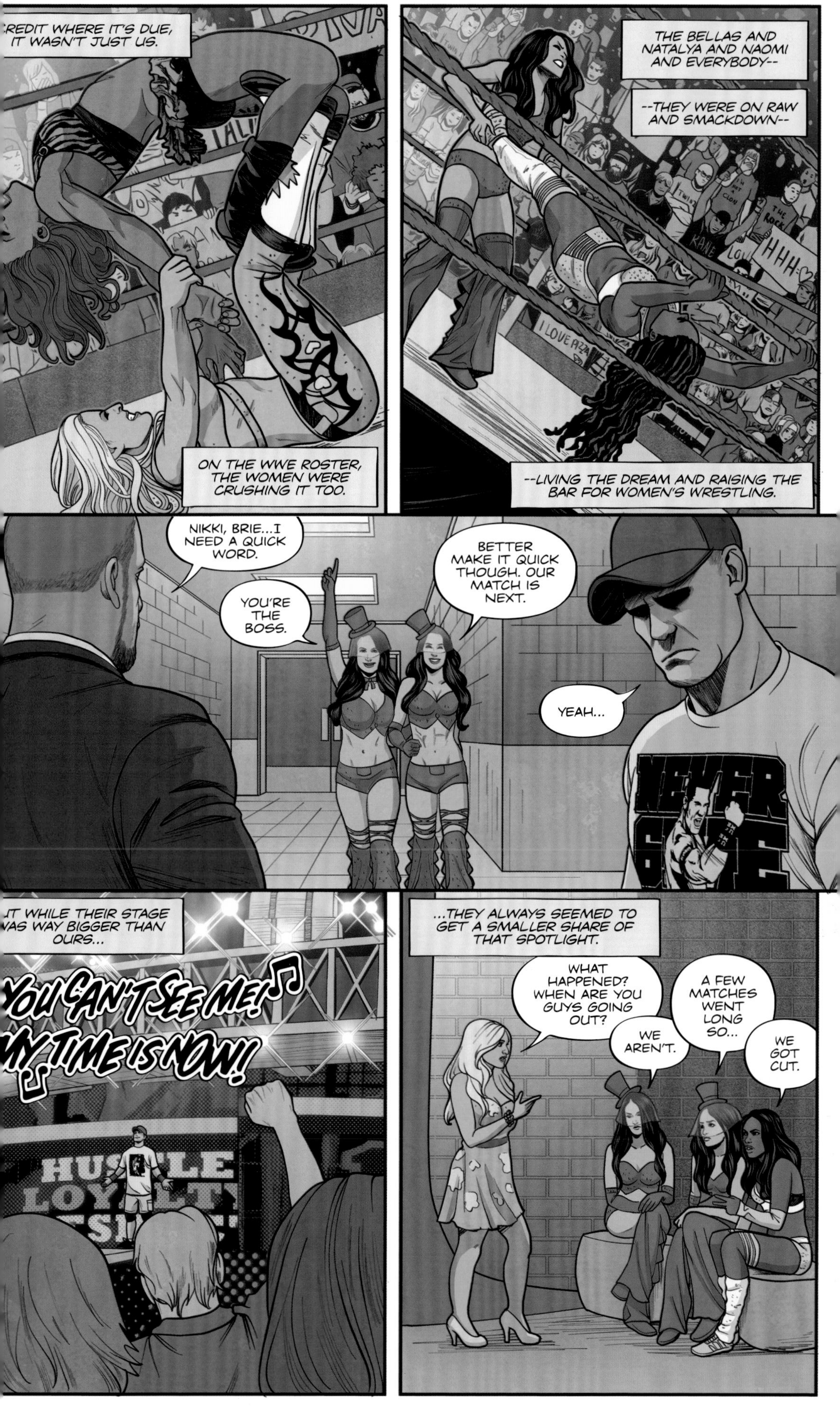
CREDIT WHERE IT'S DUE, IT WASN'T JUST US.
ON THE WWE ROSTER, THE WOMEN WERE CRUSHING IT TOO.
THE BELLAS AND NATALYA AND NAOMI AND EVERYBODY--
--THEY WERE ON RAW AND SMACKDOWN--
--LIVING THE DREAM AND RAISING THE BAR FOR WOMEN'S WRESTLING.
NIKKI, BRIE...I NEED A QUICK WORD.
YOU'RE THE BOSS.
BETTER MAKE IT QUICK THOUGH. OUR MATCH IS NEXT.
YEAH...
UT WHILE THEIR STAGE WAS WAY BIGGER THAN OURS...
YOU CAN'T SEE ME! MY TIME IS NOW!
...THEY ALWAYS SEEMED TO GET A SMALLER SHARE OF THAT SPOTLIGHT.
WHAT HAPPENED? WHEN ARE YOU GUYS GOING OUT?
WE AREN'T.
A FEW MATCHES WENT LONG SO...
WE GOT CUT.

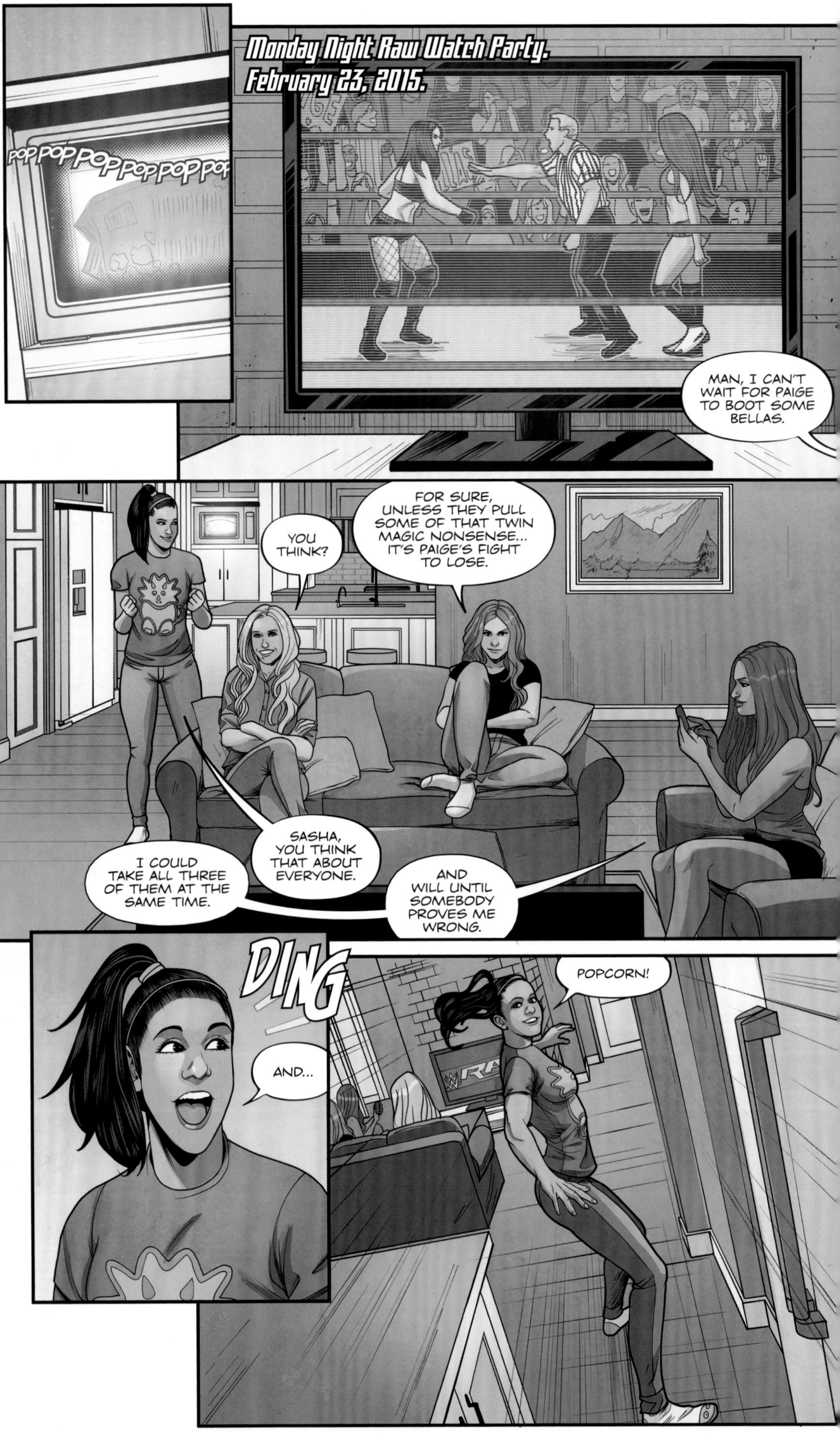
POP POP POP POP POP POP
Monday Night Raw Watch Party.
February 23, 2015.
MAN, I CAN'T WAIT FOR PAIGE TO BOOT SOME BELLAS.
YOU THINK?
FOR SURE, UNLESS THEY PULL SOME OF THAT TWIN MAGIC NONSENSE... IT'S PAIGE'S FIGHT TO LOSE.
I COULD TAKE ALL THREE OF THEM AT THE SAME TIME.
SASHA, YOU THINK THAT ABOUT EVERYONE.
AND WILL UNTIL SOMEBODY PROVES ME WRONG.
DING
AND...
POPCORN!

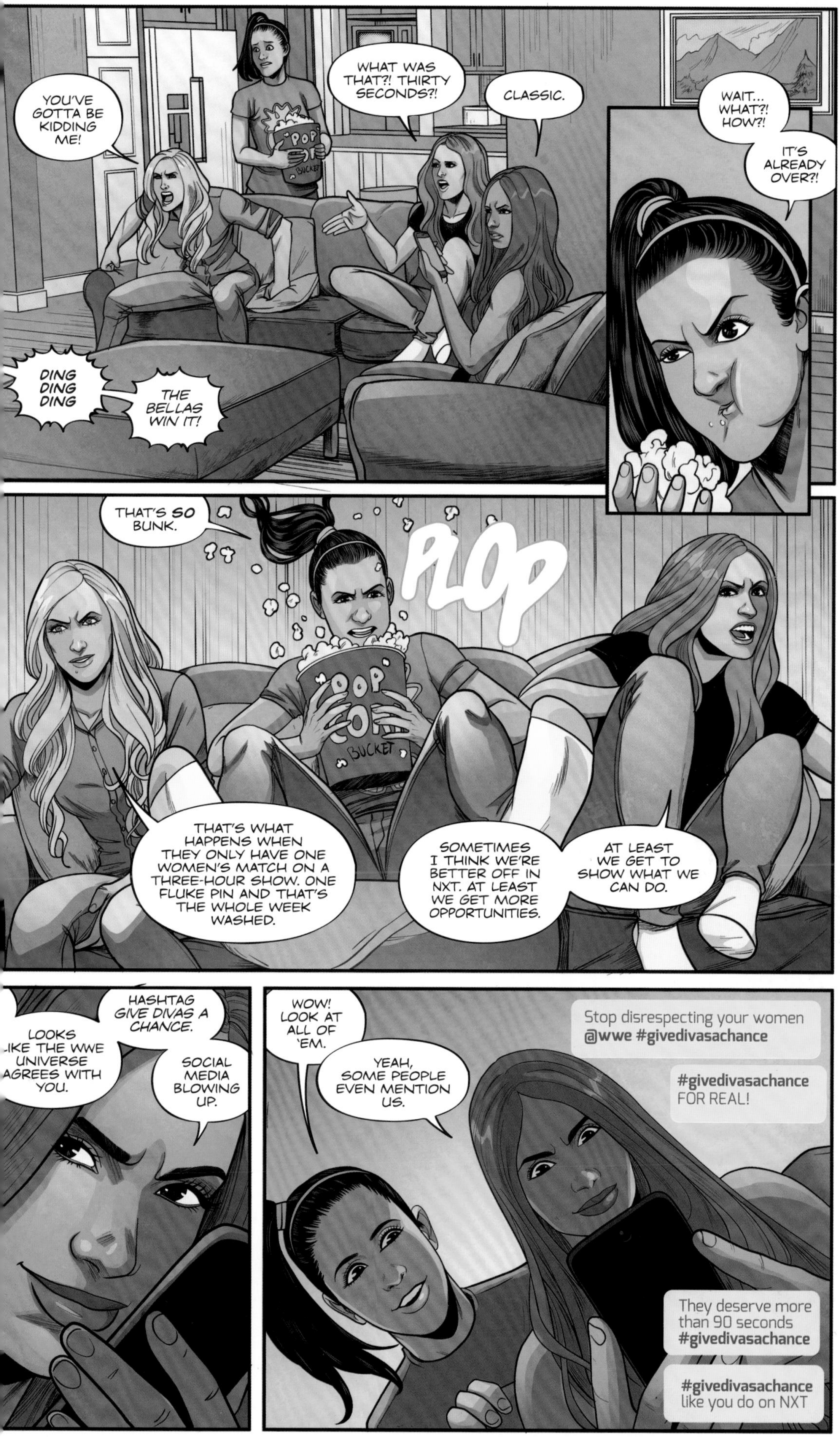
YOU'VE GOTTA BE KIDDING ME!
WHAT WAS THAT?! THIRTY SECONDS?!
CLASSIC.
DING DING DING
THE BELLAS WIN IT!
WAIT... WHAT?! HOW?!
IT'S ALREADY OVER?!
THAT'S SO BUNK.
PLOP
POP CORN BUCKET
THAT'S WHAT HAPPENS WHEN THEY ONLY HAVE ONE WOMEN'S MATCH ON A THREE-HOUR SHOW. ONE FLUKE PIN AND THAT'S THE WHOLE WEEK WASHED.
SOMETIMES I THINK WE'RE BETTER OFF IN NXT. AT LEAST WE GET MORE OPPORTUNITIES.
AT LEAST WE GET TO SHOW WHAT WE CAN DO.
LOOKS LIKE THE WWE UNIVERSE AGREES WITH YOU.
HASHTAG GIVE DIVAS A CHANCE.
SOCIAL MEDIA BLOWING UP.
WOW! LOOK AT ALL OF 'EM.
YEAH, SOME PEOPLE EVEN MENTION US.
Stop disrespecting your women @wwe #givedivasachance
#givedivasachance FOR REAL!
They deserve more than 90 seconds #givedivasachance
#givedivasachance like you do on NXT

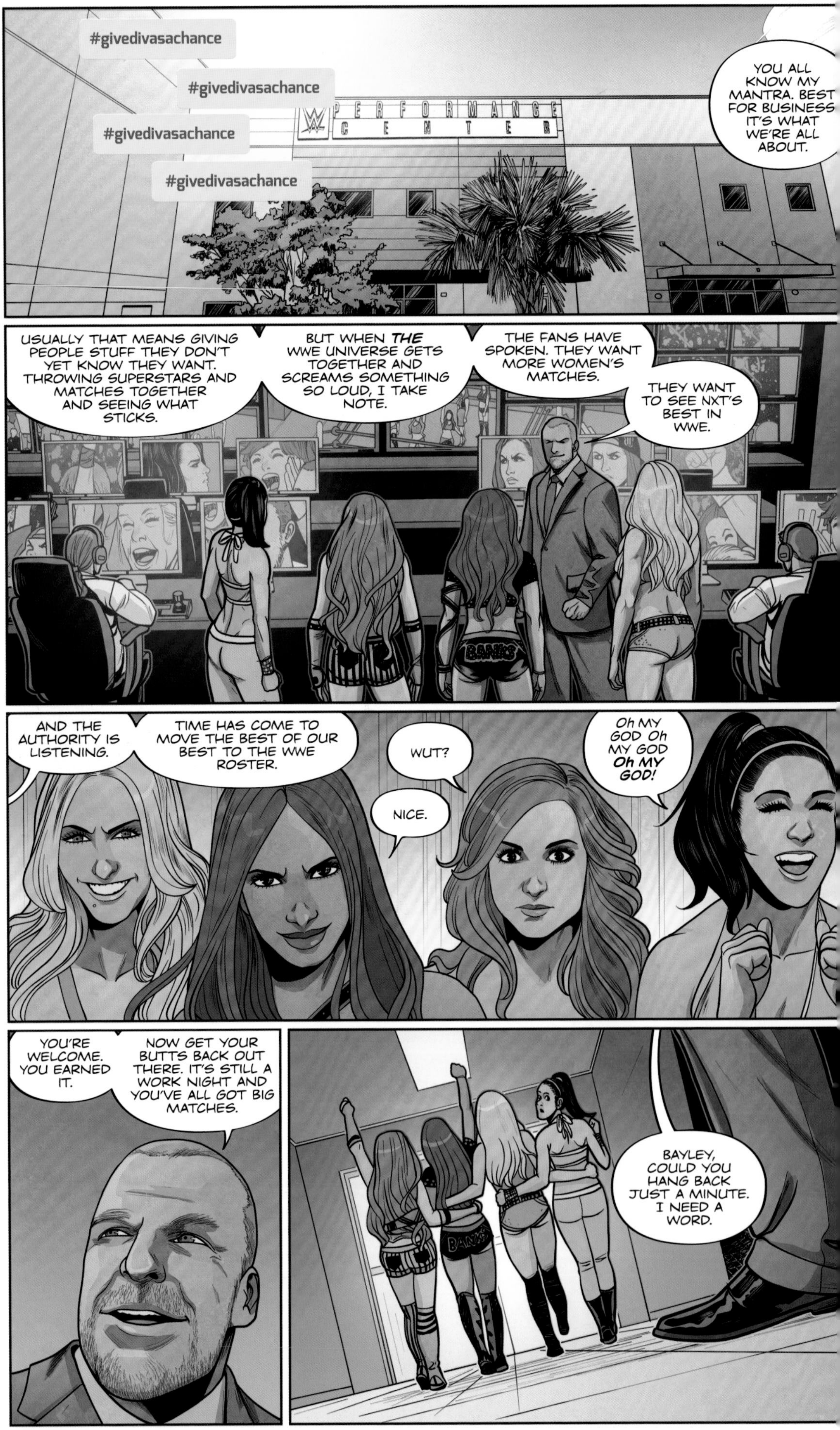

#givedivasachance
#givedivasachance
PERFORMANCE CENTER
#givedivasachance
#givedivasachance
YOU ALL KNOW MY MANTRA. BEST FOR BUSINESS IT'S WHAT WE'RE ALL ABOUT.
USUALLY THAT MEANS GIVING PEOPLE STUFF THEY DON'T YET KNOW THEY WANT. THROWING SUPERSTARS AND MATCHES TOGETHER AND SEEING WHAT STICKS.
BUT WHEN ***THE*** WWE UNIVERSE GETS TOGETHER AND SCREAMS SOMETHING SO LOUD, I TAKE NOTE.
THE FANS HAVE SPOKEN. THEY WANT MORE WOMEN'S MATCHES.
THEY WANT TO SEE NXT'S BEST IN WWE.
BANKS
AND THE AUTHORITY IS LISTENING.
TIME HAS COME TO MOVE THE BEST OF OUR BEST TO THE WWE ROSTER.
WUT?
NICE.
Oh MY GOD Oh MY GOD ***Oh MY GOD!***
YOU'RE WELCOME. YOU EARNED IT.
NOW GET YOUR BUTTS BACK OUT THERE. IT'S STILL A WORK NIGHT AND YOU'VE ALL GOT BIG MATCHES.
BANKS
BAYLEY, COULD YOU HANG BACK JUST A MINUTE. I NEED A WORD.

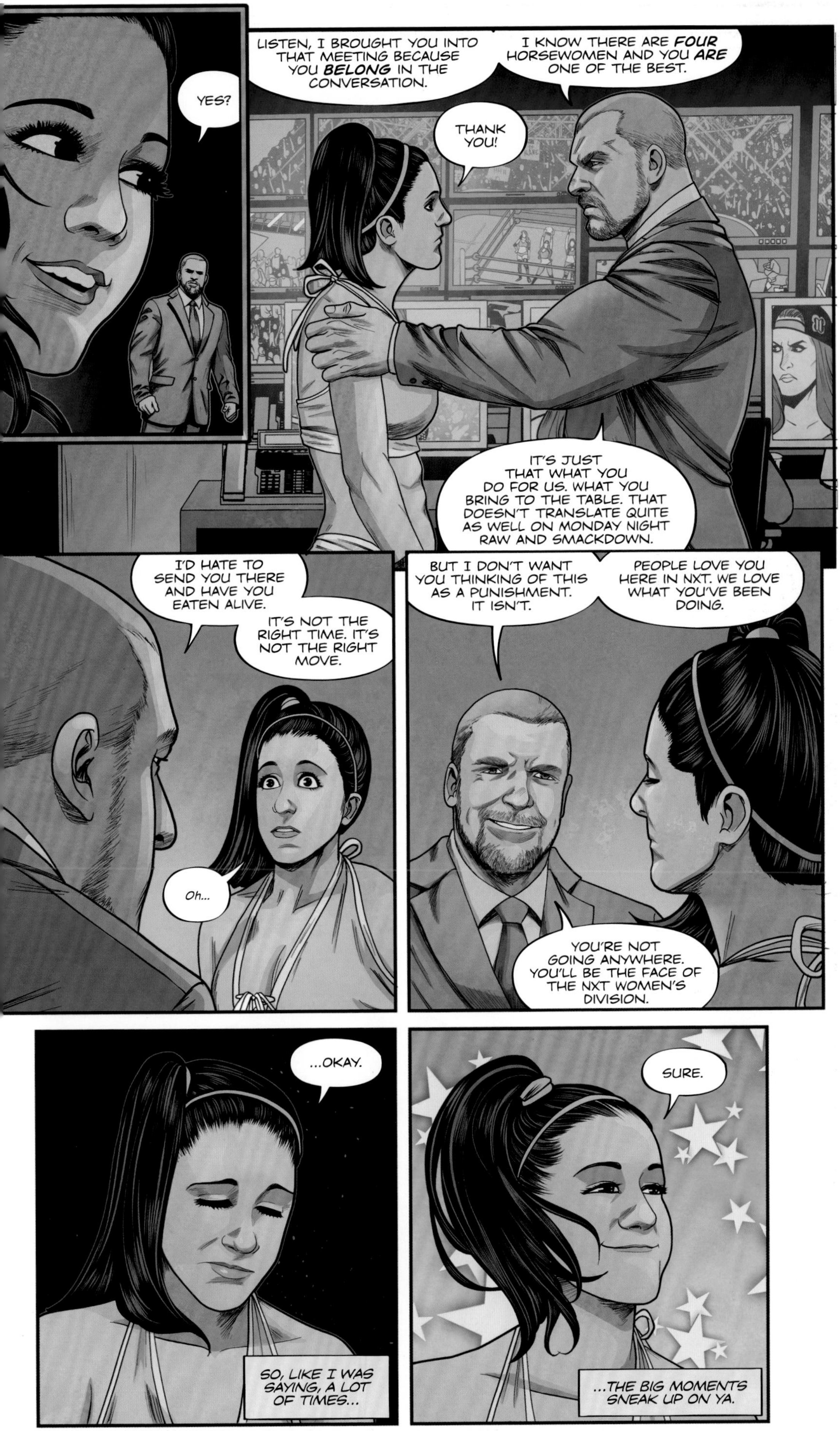
YES?
LISTEN, I BROUGHT YOU INTO THAT MEETING BECAUSE YOU BELONG IN THE CONVERSATION.
I KNOW THERE ARE FOUR HORSEWOMEN AND YOU ARE ONE OF THE BEST.
THANK YOU!
IT'S JUST THAT WHAT YOU DO FOR US. WHAT YOU BRING TO THE TABLE. THAT DOESN'T TRANSLATE QUITE AS WELL ON MONDAY NIGHT RAW AND SMACKDOWN.
I'D HATE TO SEND YOU THERE AND HAVE YOU EATEN ALIVE.
IT'S NOT THE RIGHT TIME. IT'S NOT THE RIGHT MOVE.
Oh...
BUT I DON'T WANT YOU THINKING OF THIS AS A PUNISHMENT. IT ISN'T.
PEOPLE LOVE YOU HERE IN NXT. WE LOVE WHAT YOU'VE BEEN DOING.
YOU'RE NOT GOING ANYWHERE. YOU'LL BE THE FACE OF THE NXT WOMEN'S DIVISION.
...OKAY.
SO, LIKE I WAS SAYING, A LOT OF TIMES...
SURE.
...THE BIG MOMENTS SNEAK UP ON YA.

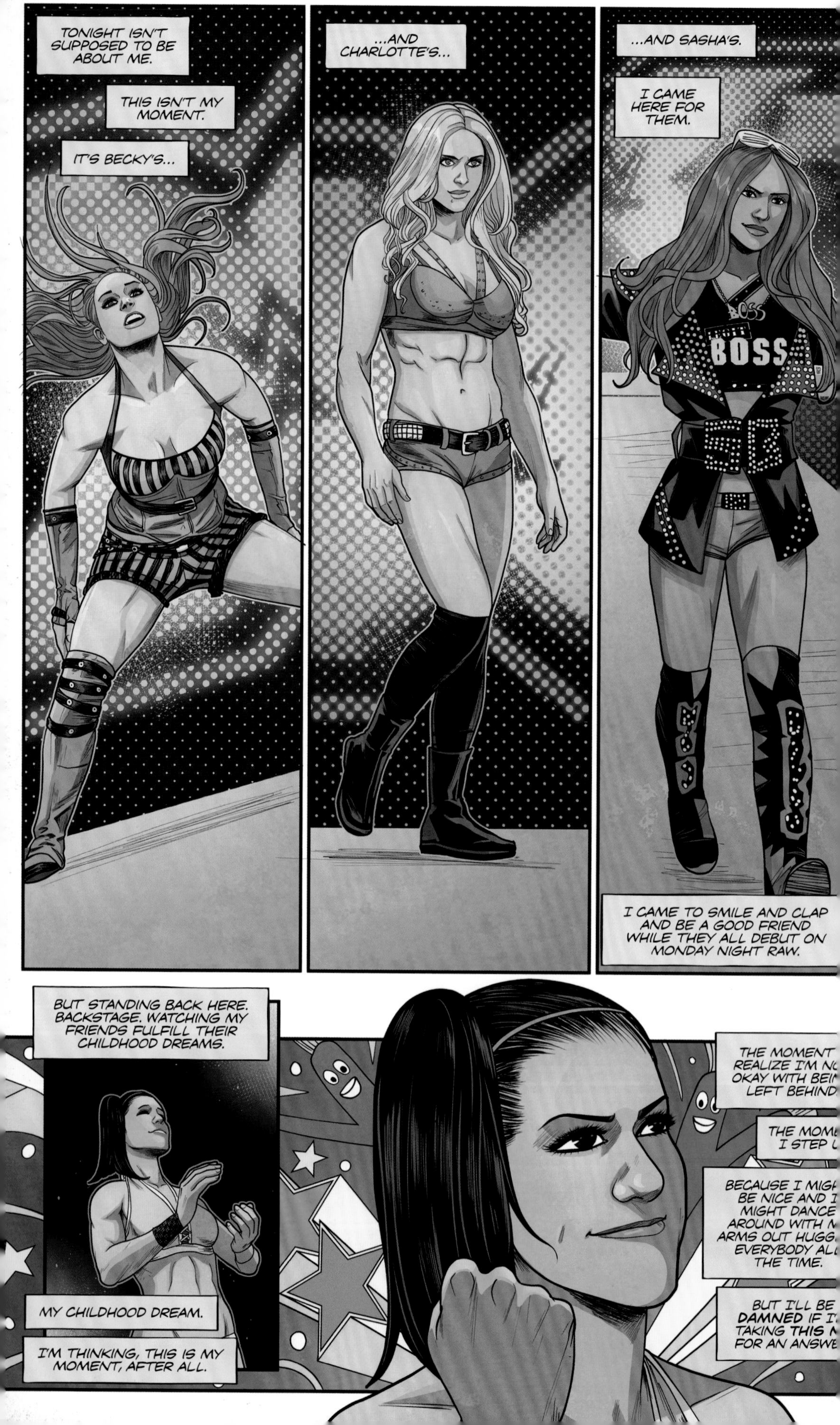
TONIGHT ISN'T SUPPOSED TO BE ABOUT ME.
THIS ISN'T MY MOMENT.
IT'S BECKY'S...
...AND CHARLOTTE'S...
...AND SASHA'S.
I CAME HERE FOR THEM.
BOSS
I CAME TO SMILE AND CLAP AND BE A GOOD FRIEND WHILE THEY ALL DEBUT ON MONDAY NIGHT RAW.
BUT STANDING BACK HERE. BACKSTAGE. WATCHING MY FRIENDS FULFILL THEIR CHILDHOOD DREAMS.
MY CHILDHOOD DREAM.
I'M THINKING, THIS IS MY MOMENT, AFTER ALL.
THE MOMENT
REALIZE I'M N
OKAY WITH BEI
LEFT BEHIND
THE MOM
I STEP
BECAUSE I MIG
BE NICE AND I
MIGHT DANCE
AROUND WITH
ARMS OUT HUGG
EVERYBODY AL
THE TIME.
BUT I'LL BE
DAMNED IF I
TAKING THIS
FOR AN ANSWE

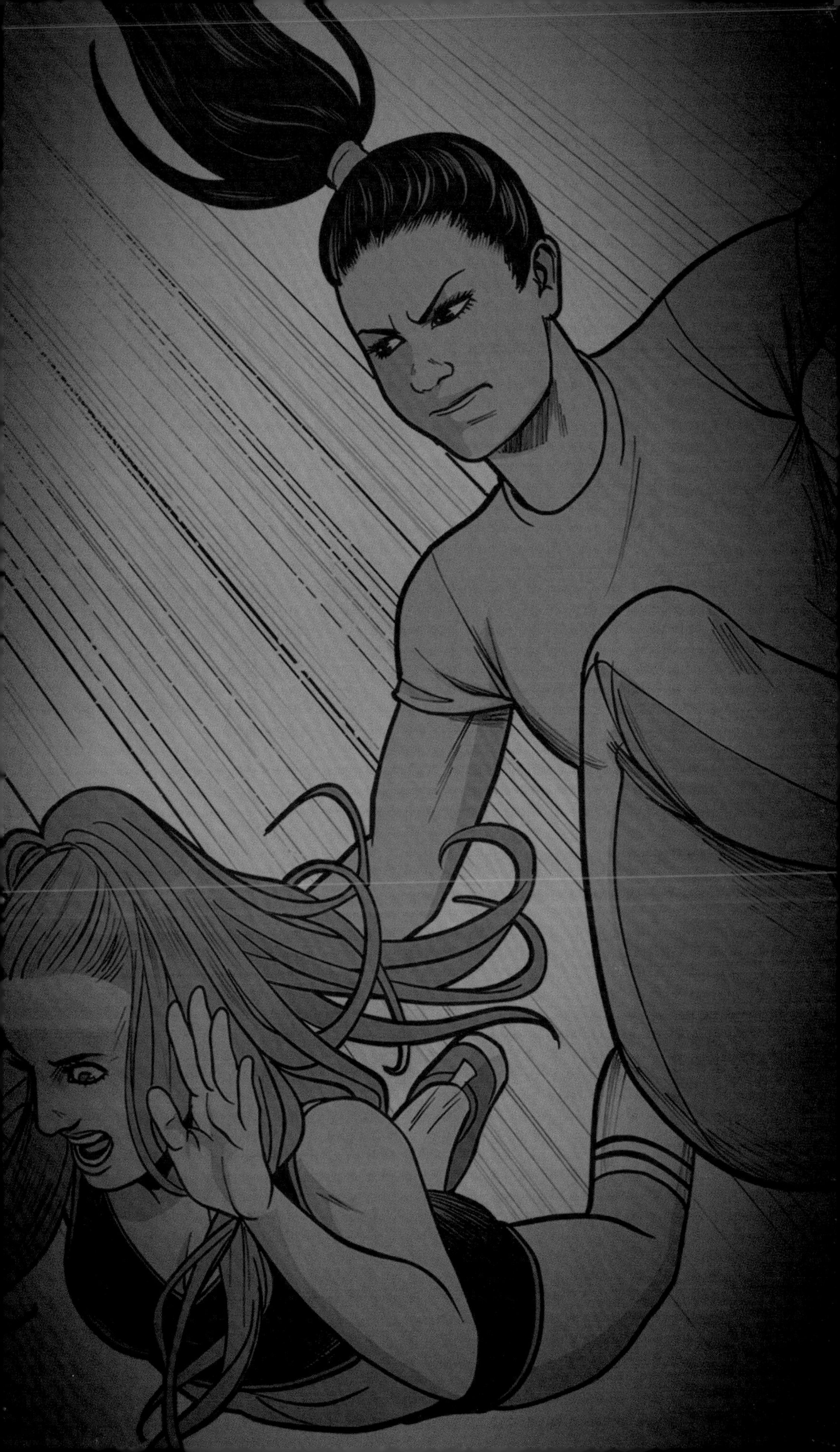

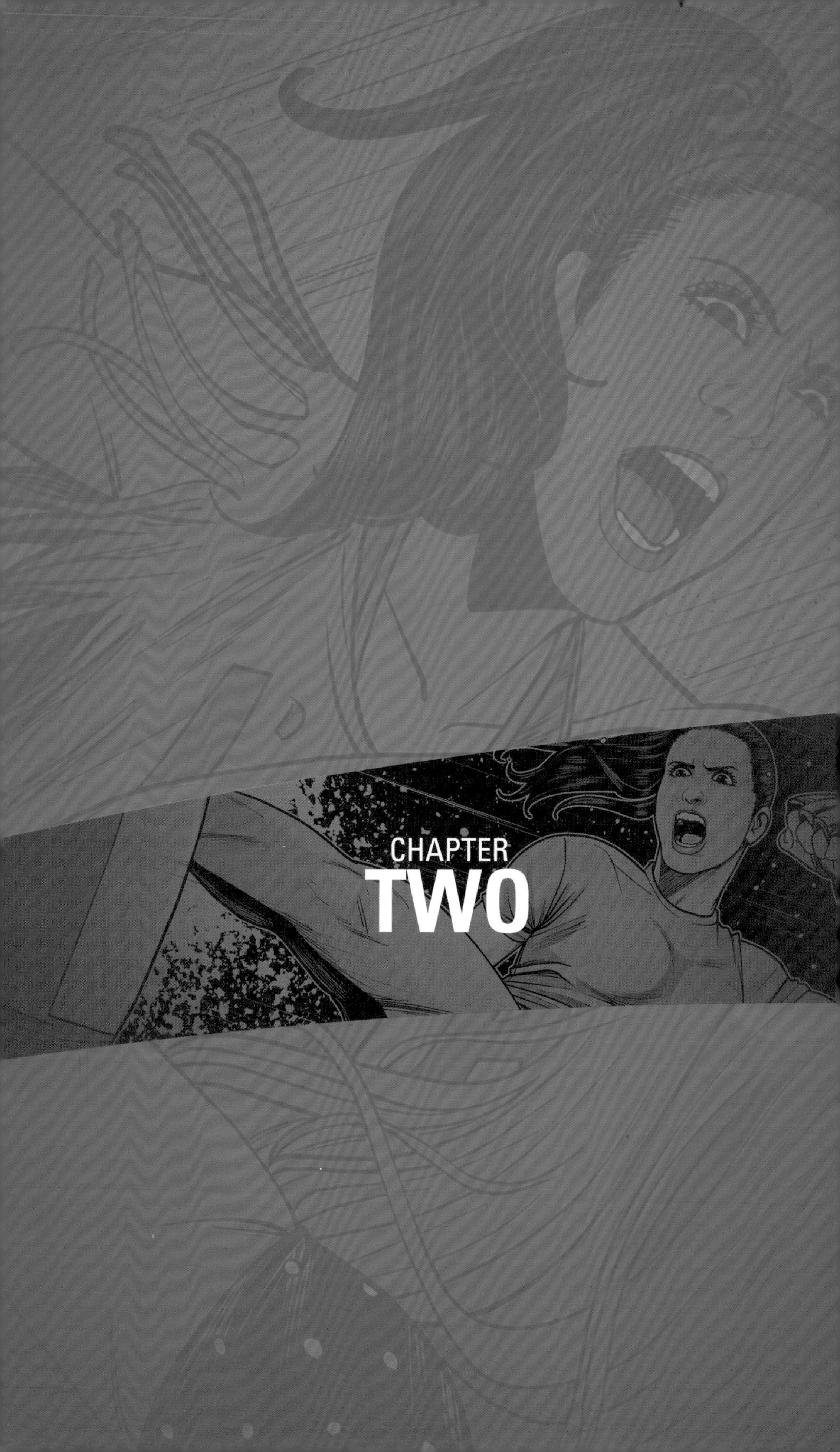
CHAPTER
TWO

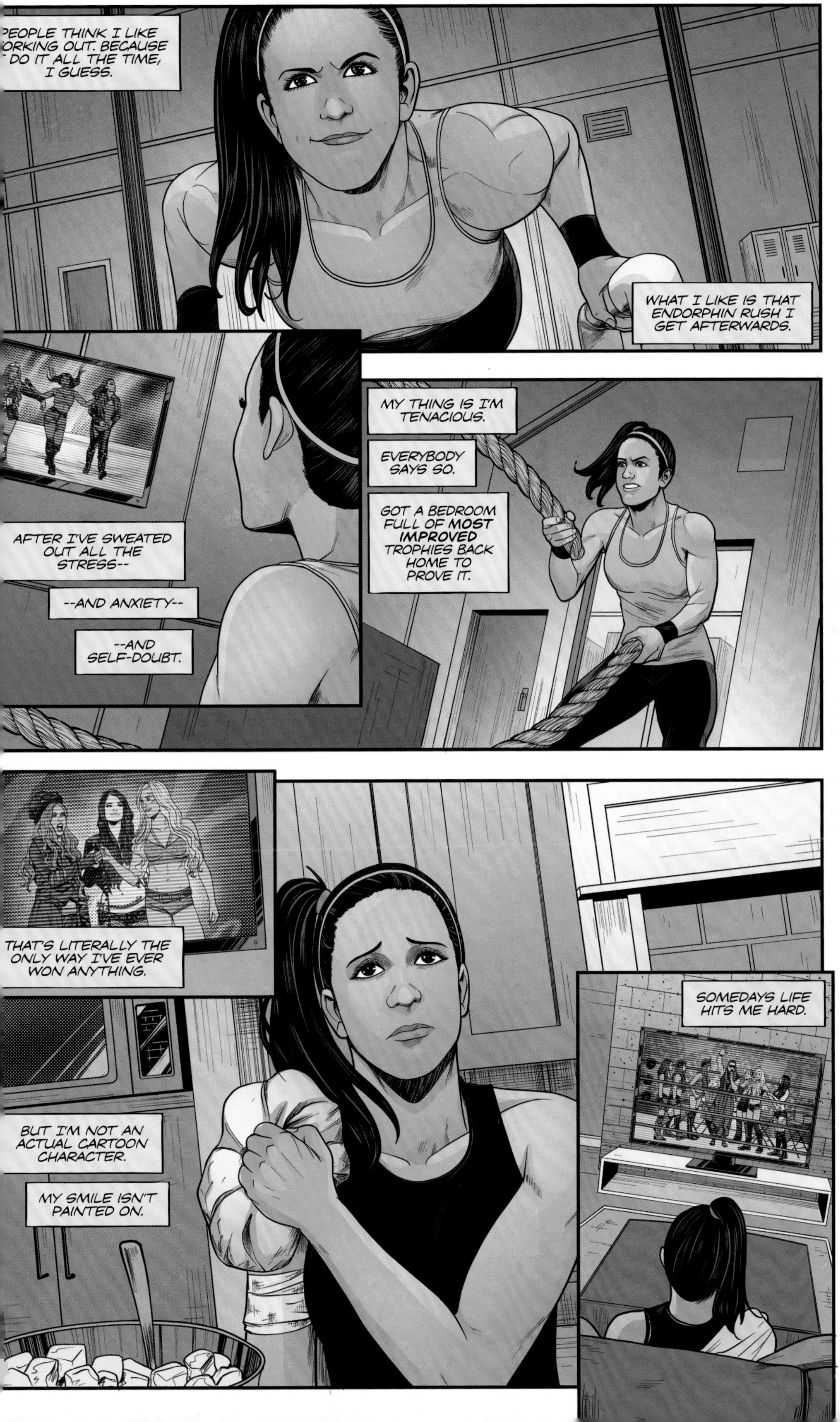
PEOPLE THINK I LIKE
ORKING OUT. BECAUSE
I DO IT ALL THE TIME,
I GUESS.
WHAT I LIKE IS THAT ENDORPHIN RUSH I GET AFTERWARDS.
AFTER I'VE SWEATED OUT ALL THE STRESS--
--AND ANXIETY--
--AND SELF-DOUBT.
MY THING IS I'M TENACIOUS.
EVERYBODY SAYS SO.
GOT A BEDROOM FULL OF **MOST IMPROVED** TROPHIES BACK HOME TO PROVE IT.
THAT'S LITERALLY THE ONLY WAY I'VE EVER WON ANYTHING.
BUT I'M NOT AN ACTUAL CARTOON CHARACTER.
MY SMILE ISN'T PAINTED ON.
SOMEDAYS LIFE HITS ME HARD.

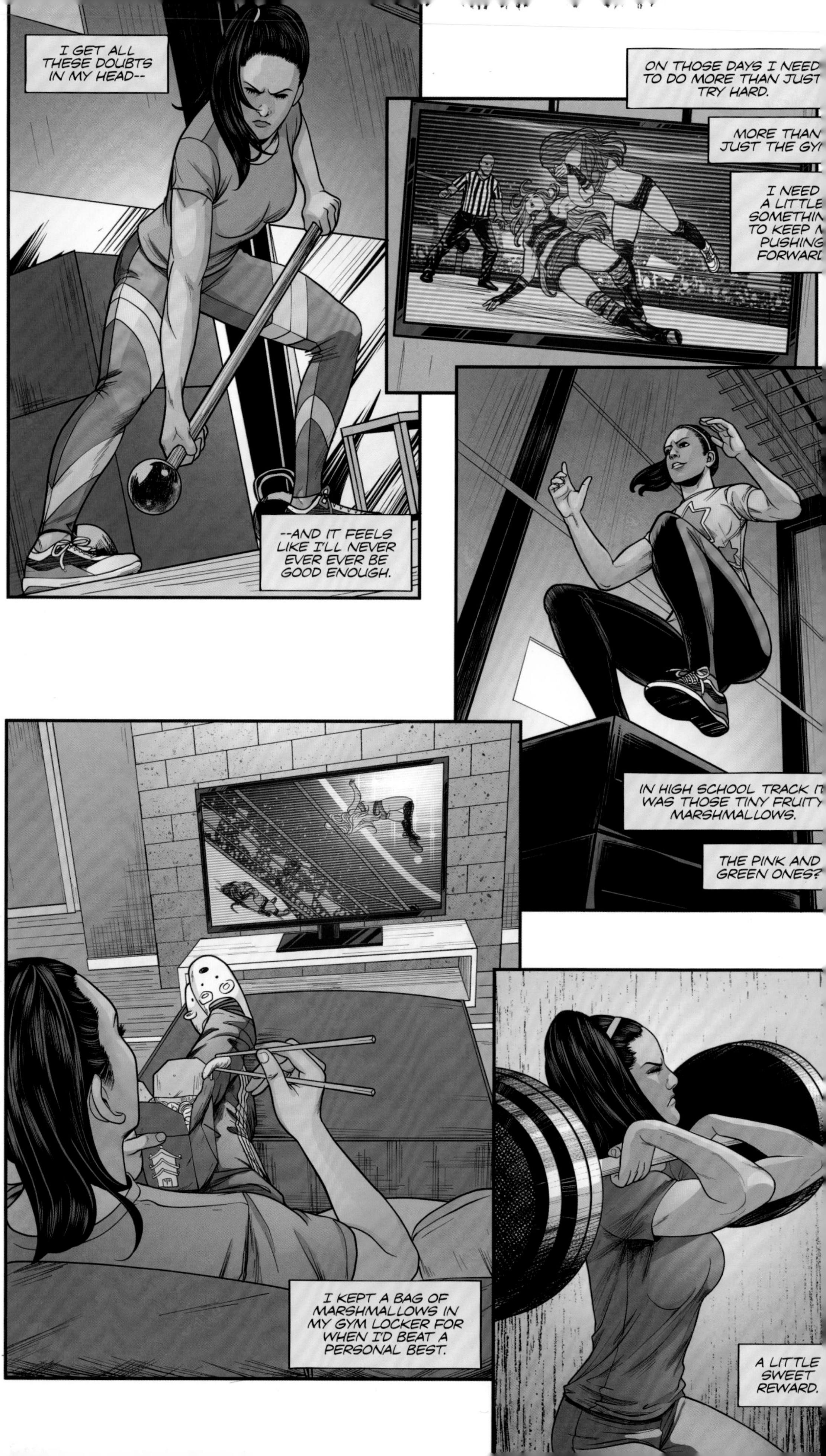
I GET ALL THESE DOUBTS IN MY HEAD--
--AND IT FEELS LIKE I'LL NEVER EVER EVER BE GOOD ENOUGH.
ON THOSE DAYS I NEED TO DO MORE THAN JUST TRY HARD.
MORE THAN JUST THE GY
I NEED A LITTLE SOMETHIN TO KEEP M PUSHING FORWARD
IN HIGH SCHOOL TRACK IT WAS THOSE TINY FRUITY MARSHMALLOWS.
THE PINK AND GREEN ONES?
I KEPT A BAG OF MARSHMALLOWS IN MY GYM LOCKER FOR WHEN I'D BEAT A PERSONAL BEST.
A LITTLE SWEET REWARD.

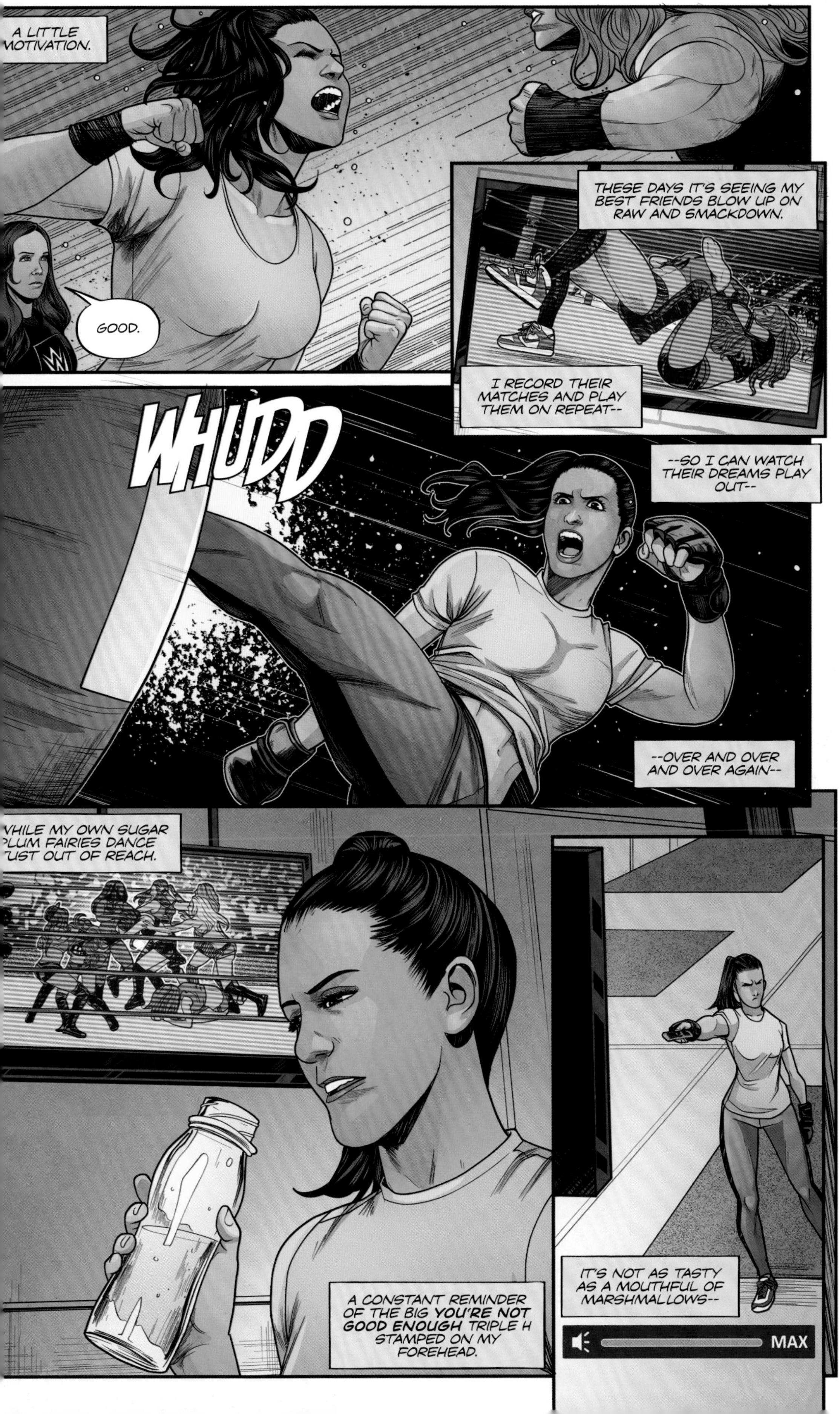
A LITTLE MOTIVATION.
GOOD.
THESE DAYS IT'S SEEING MY BEST FRIENDS BLOW UP ON RAW AND SMACKDOWN.
I RECORD THEIR MATCHES AND PLAY THEM ON REPEAT--
WHUDD
--SO I CAN WATCH THEIR DREAMS PLAY OUT--
--OVER AND OVER AND OVER AGAIN--
WHILE MY OWN SUGAR PLUM FAIRIES DANCE JUST OUT OF REACH.
A CONSTANT REMINDER OF THE BIG **YOU'RE NOT GOOD ENOUGH** TRIPLE H STAMPED ON MY FOREHEAD.
IT'S NOT AS TASTY AS A MOUTHFUL OF MARSHMALLOWS--
MAX

--BUT IT'S WORKING.

I'M BETTE NOW. WA BETTER

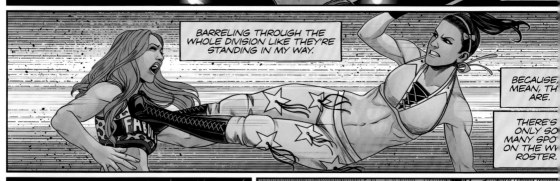

BARRELING THROUGH THE WHOLE DIVISION LIKE THEY'RE STANDING IN MY WAY.

BECAUSE MEAN, TH ARE.

THERE'S ONLY SO MANY SPO ON THE W ROSTER.

AND HUNTER STRAIGHT UP TOLD ME I'M NOT GETTING ONE.

I CAN EITHER WAIT FOR HIM TO CHANGE HIS MIND--

--OR I CAN KEEP GRABBING Ws--

--PILE THESE GIRLS SKY HIGH

--AND GET THER ON MY OWN.

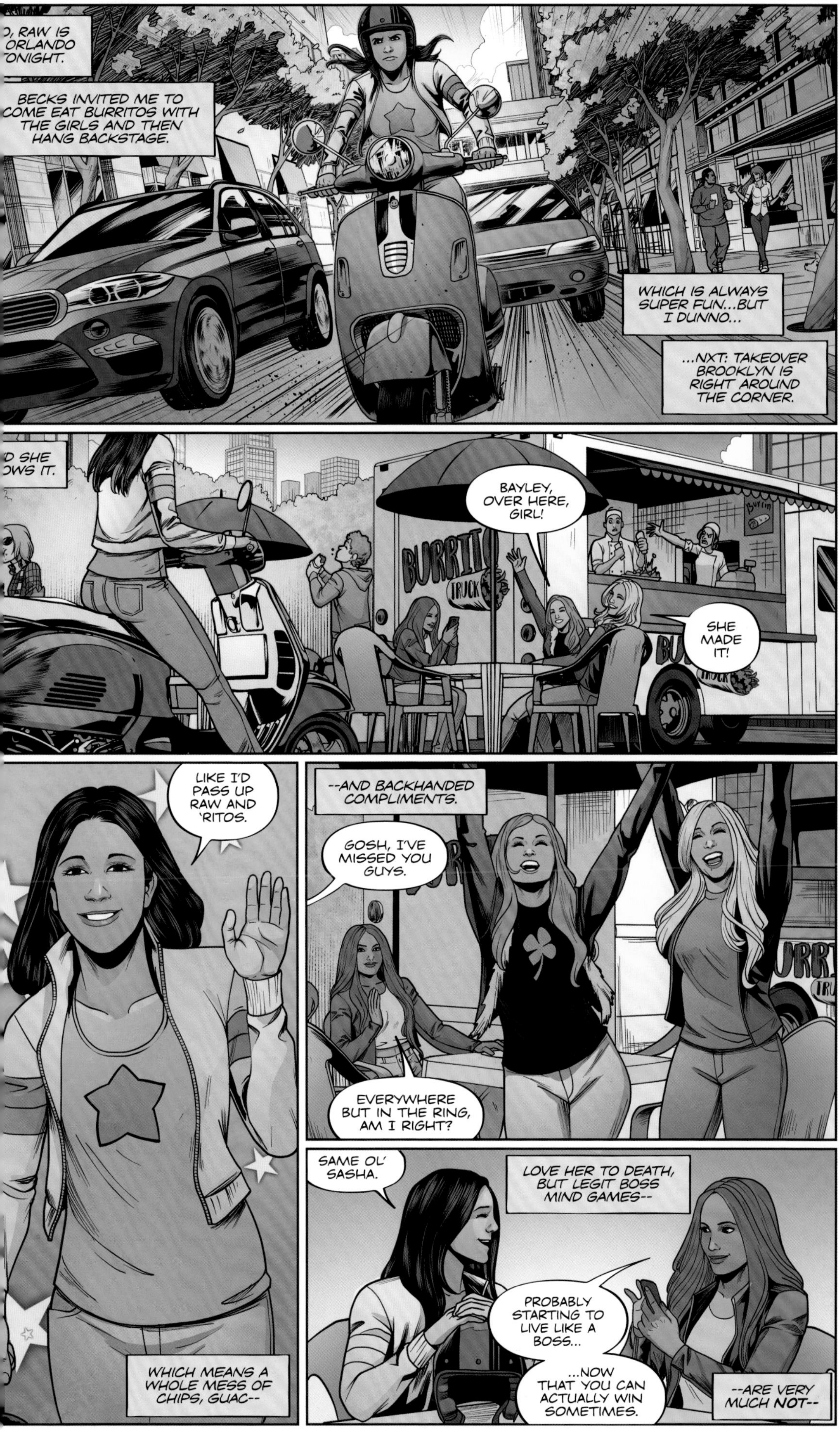
O, RAW IS ORLANDO TONIGHT.
BECKS INVITED ME TO COME EAT BURRITOS WITH THE GIRLS AND THEN HANG BACKSTAGE.
WHICH IS ALWAYS SUPER FUN...BUT I DUNNO...
...NXT: TAKEOVER BROOKLYN IS RIGHT AROUND THE CORNER.
D SHE OWS IT.
BAYLEY, OVER HERE, GIRL!
BURRITO TRUCK
SHE MADE IT!
LIKE I'D PASS UP RAW AND 'RITOS.
WHICH MEANS A WHOLE MESS OF CHIPS, GUAC--
--AND BACKHANDED COMPLIMENTS.
GOSH, I'VE MISSED YOU GUYS.
EVERYWHERE BUT IN THE RING, AM I RIGHT?
SAME OL' SASHA.
LOVE HER TO DEATH, BUT LEGIT BOSS MIND GAMES--
PROBABLY STARTING TO LIVE LIKE A BOSS...
...NOW THAT YOU CAN ACTUALLY WIN SOMETIMES.
--ARE VERY MUCH NOT--

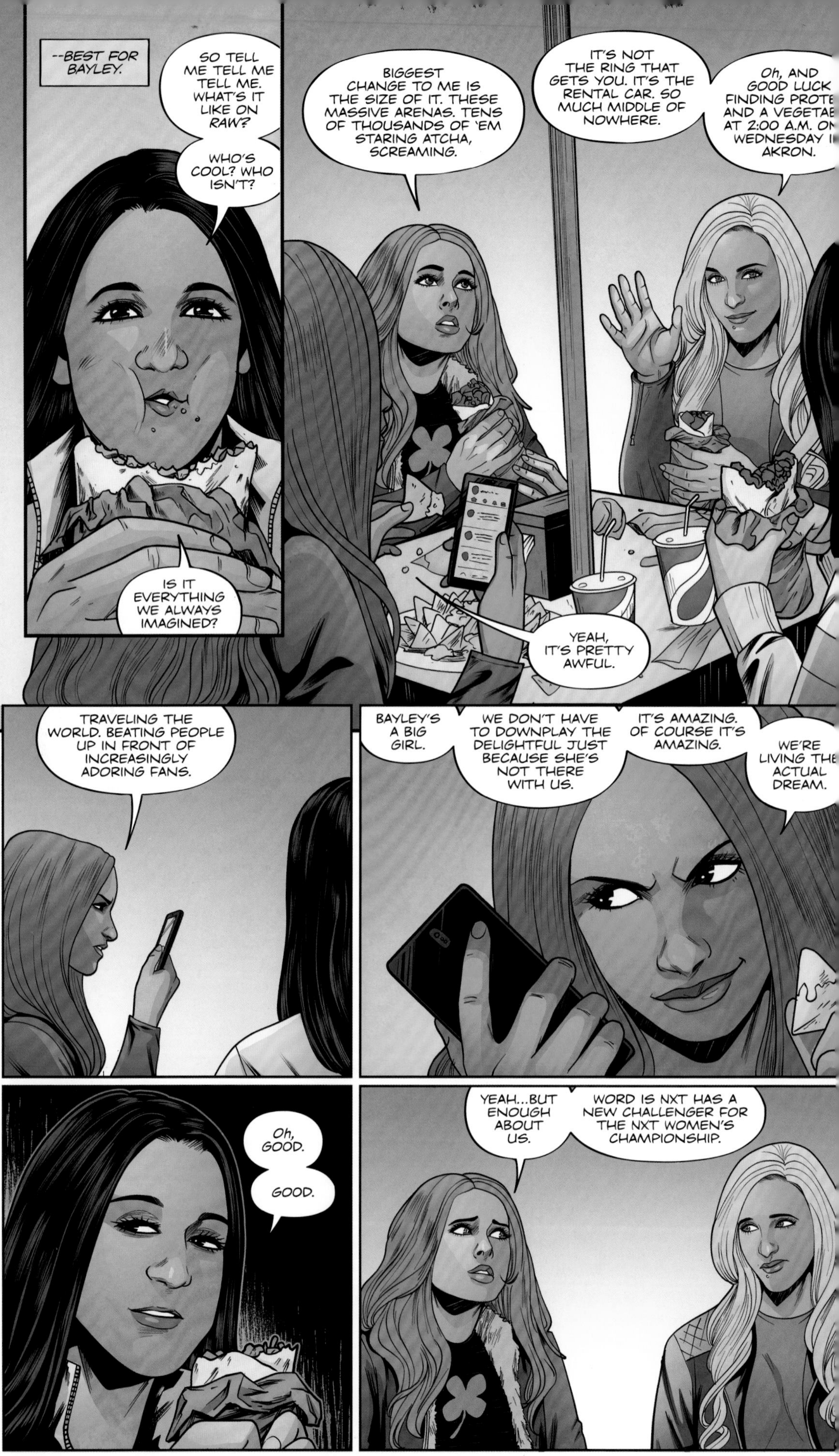
--BEST FOR BAYLEY.
SO TELL ME TELL ME TELL ME. WHAT'S IT LIKE ON *RAW?*
WHO'S COOL? WHO ISN'T?
IS IT EVERYTHING WE ALWAYS IMAGINED?
BIGGEST CHANGE TO ME IS THE SIZE OF IT. THESE MASSIVE ARENAS. TENS OF THOUSANDS OF 'EM STARING ATCHA, SCREAMING.
IT'S NOT THE RING THAT GETS YOU. IT'S THE RENTAL CAR. SO MUCH MIDDLE OF NOWHERE.
Oh, AND GOOD LUCK FINDING PROTE AND A VEGETAB AT 2:00 A.M. ON WEDNESDAY I AKRON.
YEAH, IT'S PRETTY AWFUL.
TRAVELING THE WORLD. BEATING PEOPLE UP IN FRONT OF INCREASINGLY ADORING FANS.
BAYLEY'S A BIG GIRL.
WE DON'T HAVE TO DOWNPLAY THE DELIGHTFUL JUST BECAUSE SHE'S NOT THERE WITH US.
IT'S AMAZING. OF COURSE IT'S AMAZING.
WE'RE LIVING THE ACTUAL DREAM.
Oh, GOOD.
GOOD.
YEAH...BUT ENOUGH ABOUT US.
WORD IS NXT HAS A NEW CHALLENGER FOR THE NXT WOMEN'S CHAMPIONSHIP.

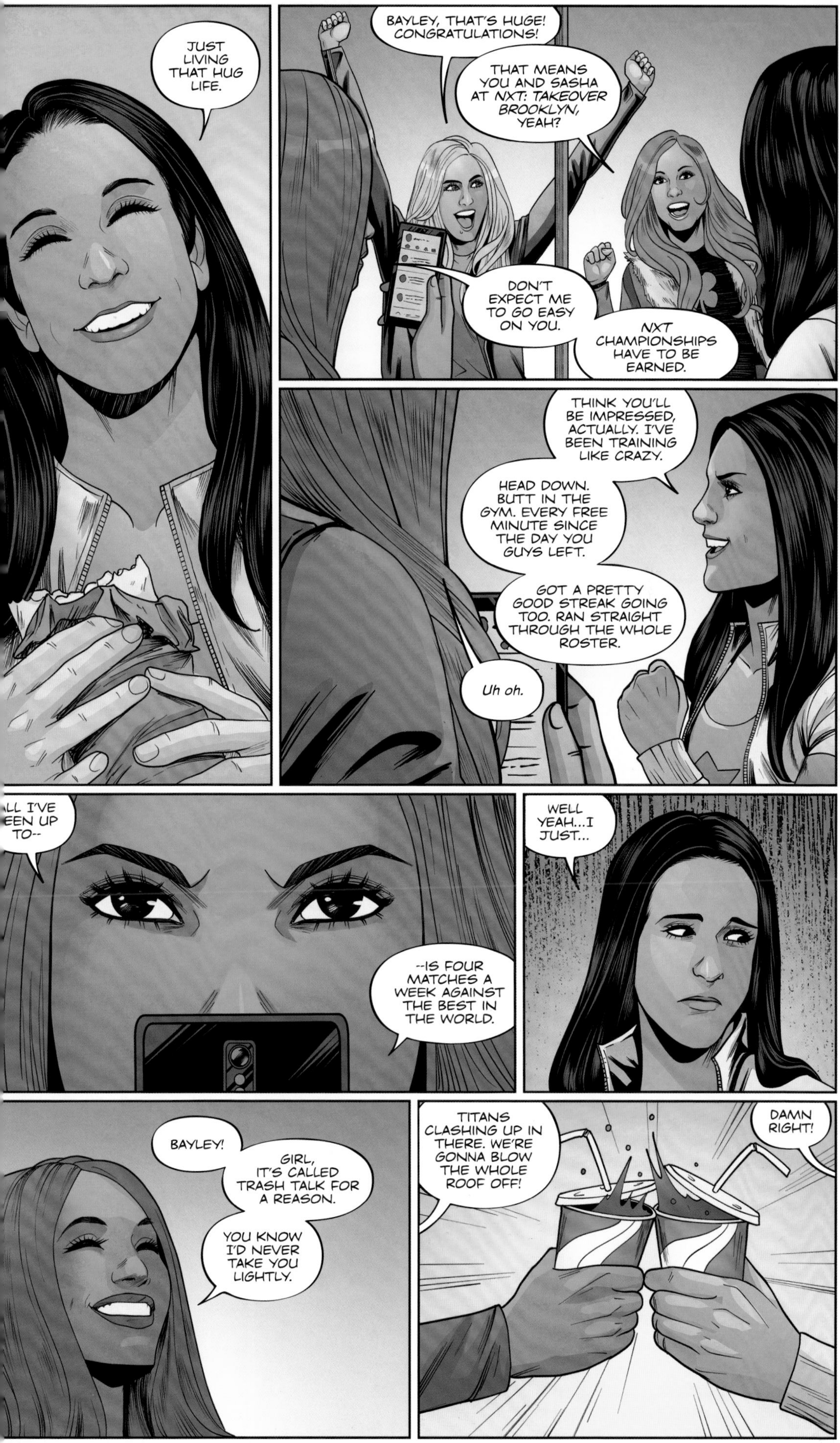
JUST LIVING THAT HUG LIFE.
BAYLEY, THAT'S HUGE! CONGRATULATIONS!
THAT MEANS YOU AND SASHA AT NXT: TAKEOVER BROOKLYN, YEAH?
DON'T EXPECT ME TO GO EASY ON YOU.
NXT CHAMPIONSHIPS HAVE TO BE EARNED.
THINK YOU'LL BE IMPRESSED, ACTUALLY. I'VE BEEN TRAINING LIKE CRAZY.
HEAD DOWN. BUTT IN THE GYM. EVERY FREE MINUTE SINCE THE DAY YOU GUYS LEFT.
GOT A PRETTY GOOD STREAK GOING TOO. RAN STRAIGHT THROUGH THE WHOLE ROSTER.
Uh oh.
LL I'VE EEN UP TO--
--IS FOUR MATCHES A WEEK AGAINST THE BEST IN THE WORLD.
WELL YEAH...I JUST...
BAYLEY!
GIRL, IT'S CALLED TRASH TALK FOR A REASON.
YOU KNOW I'D NEVER TAKE YOU LIGHTLY.
TITANS CLASHING UP IN THERE. WE'RE GONNA BLOW THE WHOLE ROOF OFF!
DAMN RIGHT!

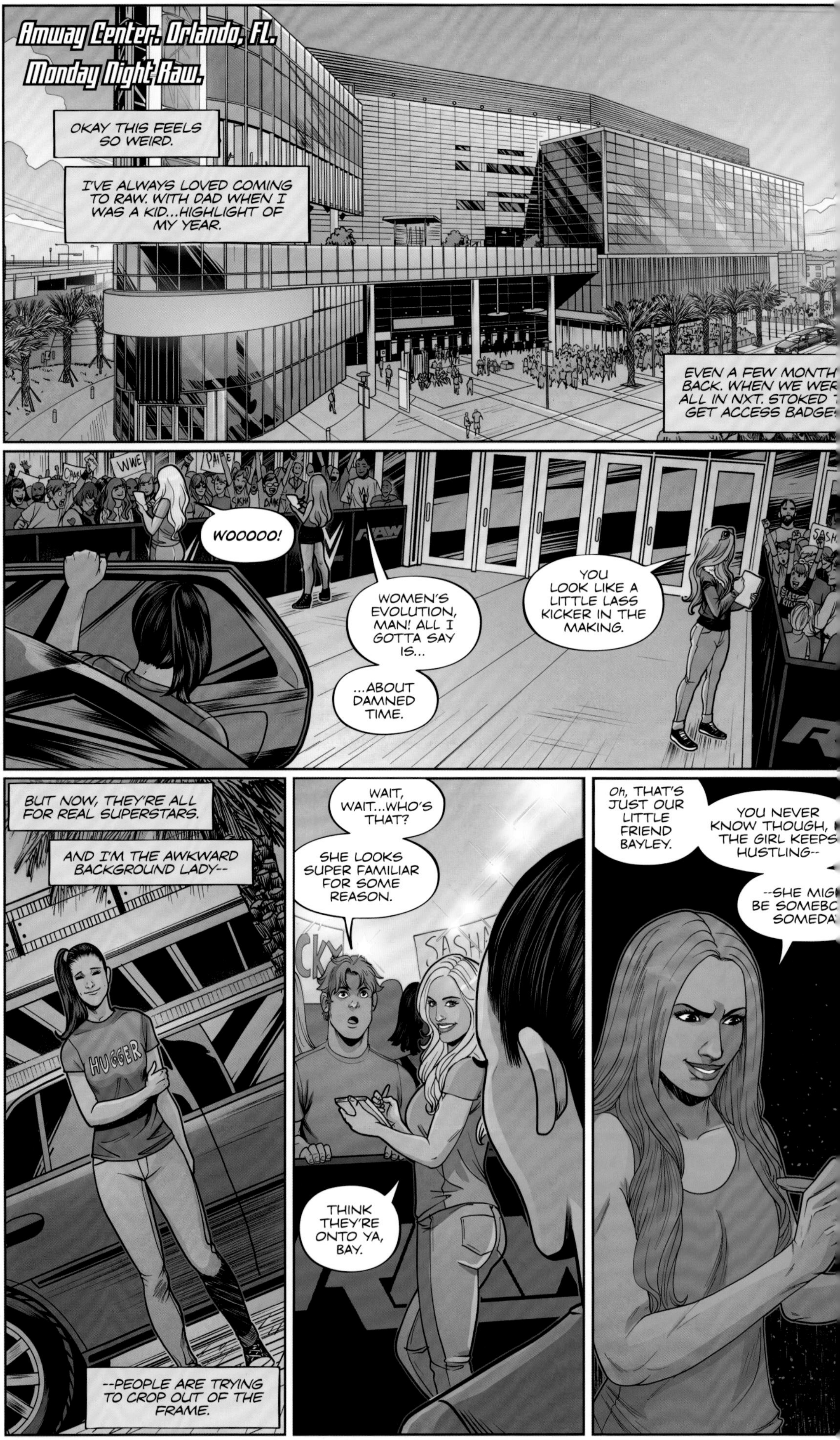
Amway Center. Orlando, FL.
Monday Night Raw.
OKAY THIS FEELS SO WEIRD.
I'VE ALWAYS LOVED COMING TO RAW. WITH DAD WHEN I WAS A KID...HIGHLIGHT OF MY YEAR.
EVEN A FEW MONTH BACK. WHEN WE WER ALL IN NXT. STOKED GET ACCESS BADGE
WOOOOO!
WOMEN'S EVOLUTION, MAN! ALL I GOTTA SAY IS...
...ABOUT DAMNED TIME.
YOU LOOK LIKE A LITTLE LASS KICKER IN THE MAKING.
BUT NOW, THEY'RE ALL FOR REAL SUPERSTARS.
AND I'M THE AWKWARD BACKGROUND LADY--
--PEOPLE ARE TRYING TO CROP OUT OF THE FRAME.
WAIT, WAIT...WHO'S THAT?
SHE LOOKS SUPER FAMILIAR FOR SOME REASON.
THINK THEY'RE ONTO YA, BAY.
Oh, THAT'S JUST OUR LITTLE FRIEND BAYLEY.
YOU NEVER KNOW THOUGH, THE GIRL KEEPS HUSTLING--
--SHE MIG BE SOMEBO SOMEDA

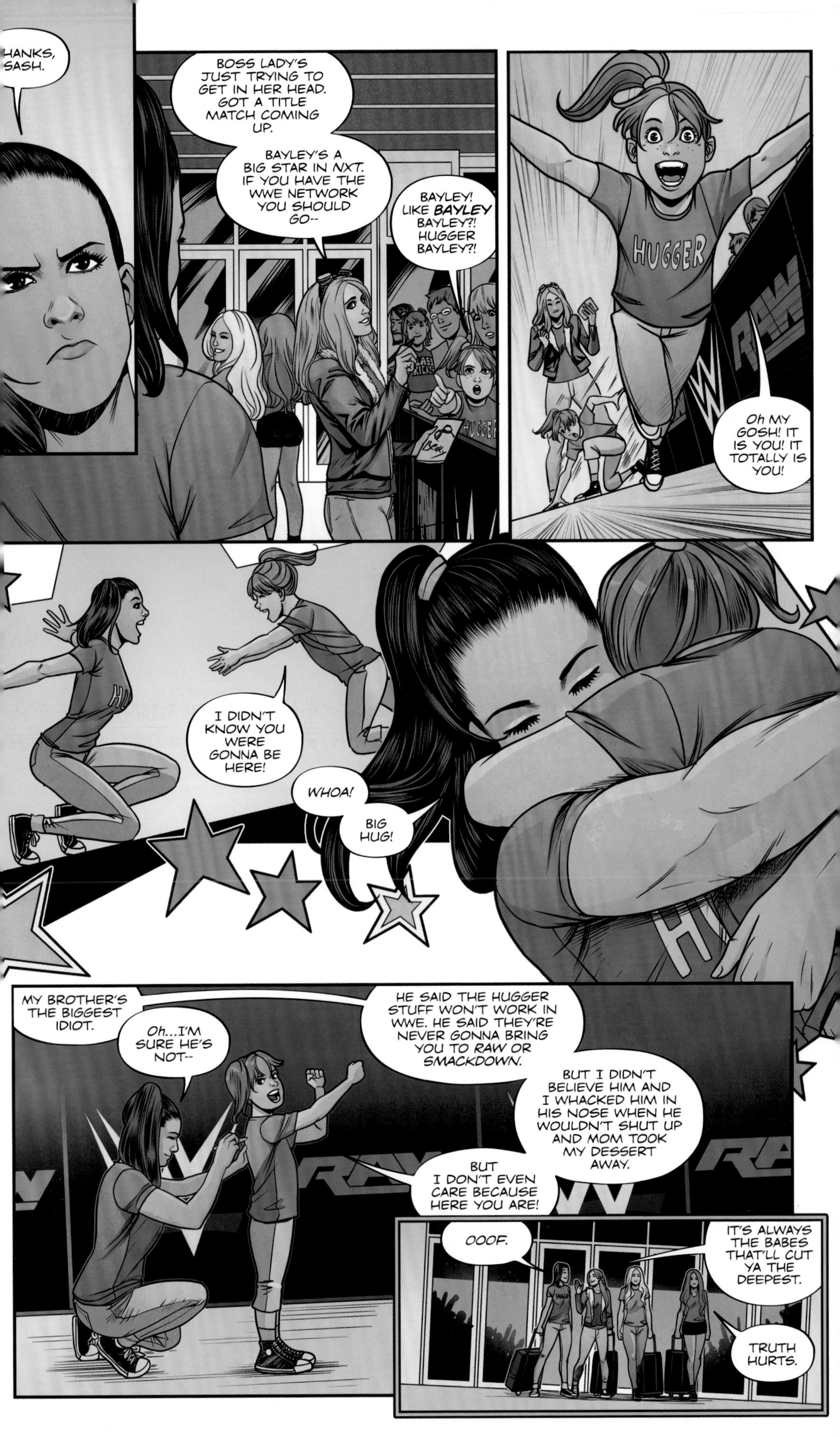
HANKS, SASH.
BOSS LADY'S JUST TRYING TO GET IN HER HEAD. GOT A TITLE MATCH COMING UP.
BAYLEY'S A BIG STAR IN NXT. IF YOU HAVE THE WWE NETWORK YOU SHOULD GO--
BAYLEY! LIKE **BAYLEY** BAYLEY?! HUGGER BAYLEY?!
HUGGER
HUGGER
Oh MY GOSH! IT IS YOU! IT TOTALLY IS YOU!
I DIDN'T KNOW YOU WERE GONNA BE HERE!
WHOA!
BIG HUG!
MY BROTHER'S THE BIGGEST IDIOT.
Oh...I'M SURE HE'S NOT--
HE SAID THE HUGGER STUFF WON'T WORK IN WWE. HE SAID THEY'RE NEVER GONNA BRING YOU TO *RAW* OR *SMACKDOWN*.
BUT I DIDN'T BELIEVE HIM AND I WHACKED HIM IN HIS NOSE WHEN HE WOULDN'T SHUT UP AND MOM TOOK MY DESSERT AWAY.
BUT I DON'T EVEN CARE BECAUSE HERE YOU ARE!
OOOF.
IT'S ALWAYS THE BABES THAT'LL CUT YA THE DEEPEST.
TRUTH HURTS.

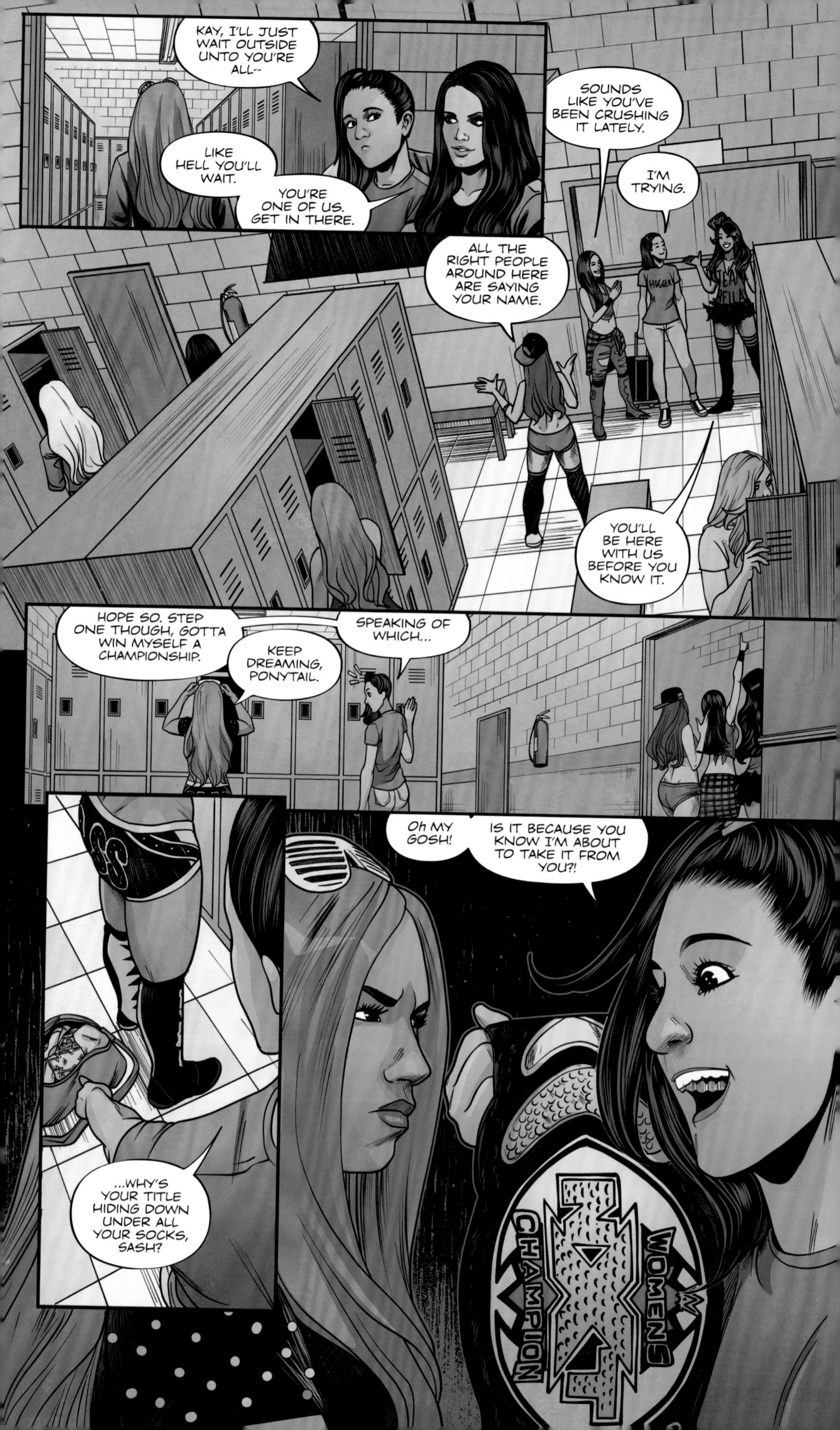

KAY, I'LL JUST WAIT OUTSIDE UNTO YOU'RE ALL--
LIKE HELL YOU'LL WAIT.
YOU'RE ONE OF US. GET IN THERE.
SOUNDS LIKE YOU'VE BEEN CRUSHING IT LATELY.
I'M TRYING.
ALL THE RIGHT PEOPLE AROUND HERE ARE SAYING YOUR NAME.
YOU'LL BE HERE WITH US BEFORE YOU KNOW IT.
HOPE SO. STEP ONE THOUGH, GOTTA WIN MYSELF A CHAMPIONSHIP.
KEEP DREAMING, PONYTAIL.
SPEAKING OF WHICH...
...WHY'S YOUR TITLE HIDING DOWN UNDER ALL YOUR SOCKS, SASH?
Oh MY GOSH!
IS IT BECAUSE YOU KNOW I'M ABOUT TO TAKE IT FROM YOU?!
WOMENS
CHAMPION

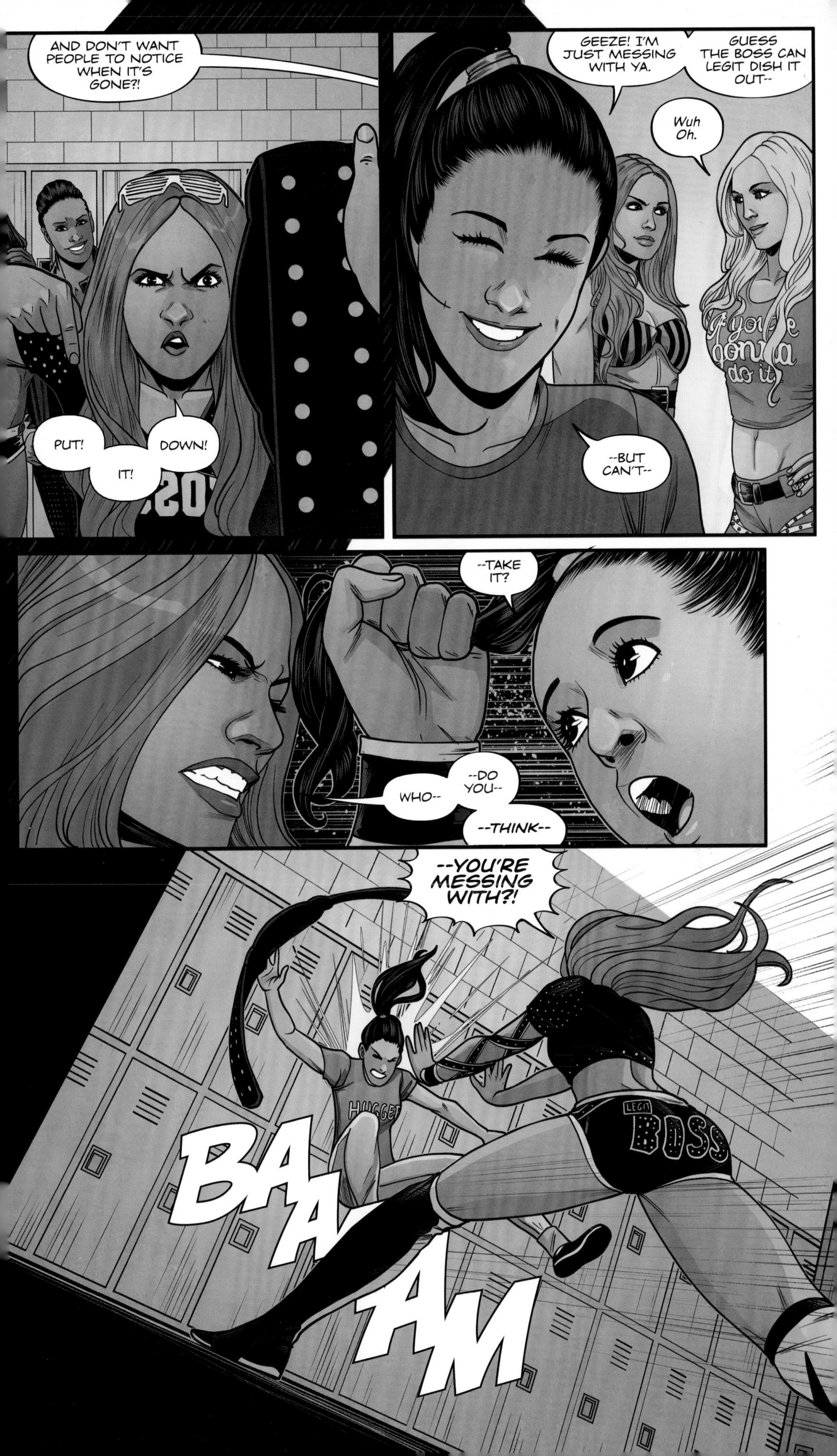
AND DON'T WANT PEOPLE TO NOTICE WHEN IT'S GONE?!
PUT!
IT!
DOWN!
GEEZE! I'M JUST MESSING WITH YA.
GUESS THE BOSS CAN LEGIT DISH IT OUT--
Wuh Oh.
--BUT CAN'T--
--TAKE IT?
WHO--
--DO YOU--
--THINK--
--YOU'RE MESSING WITH?!
BAAAM

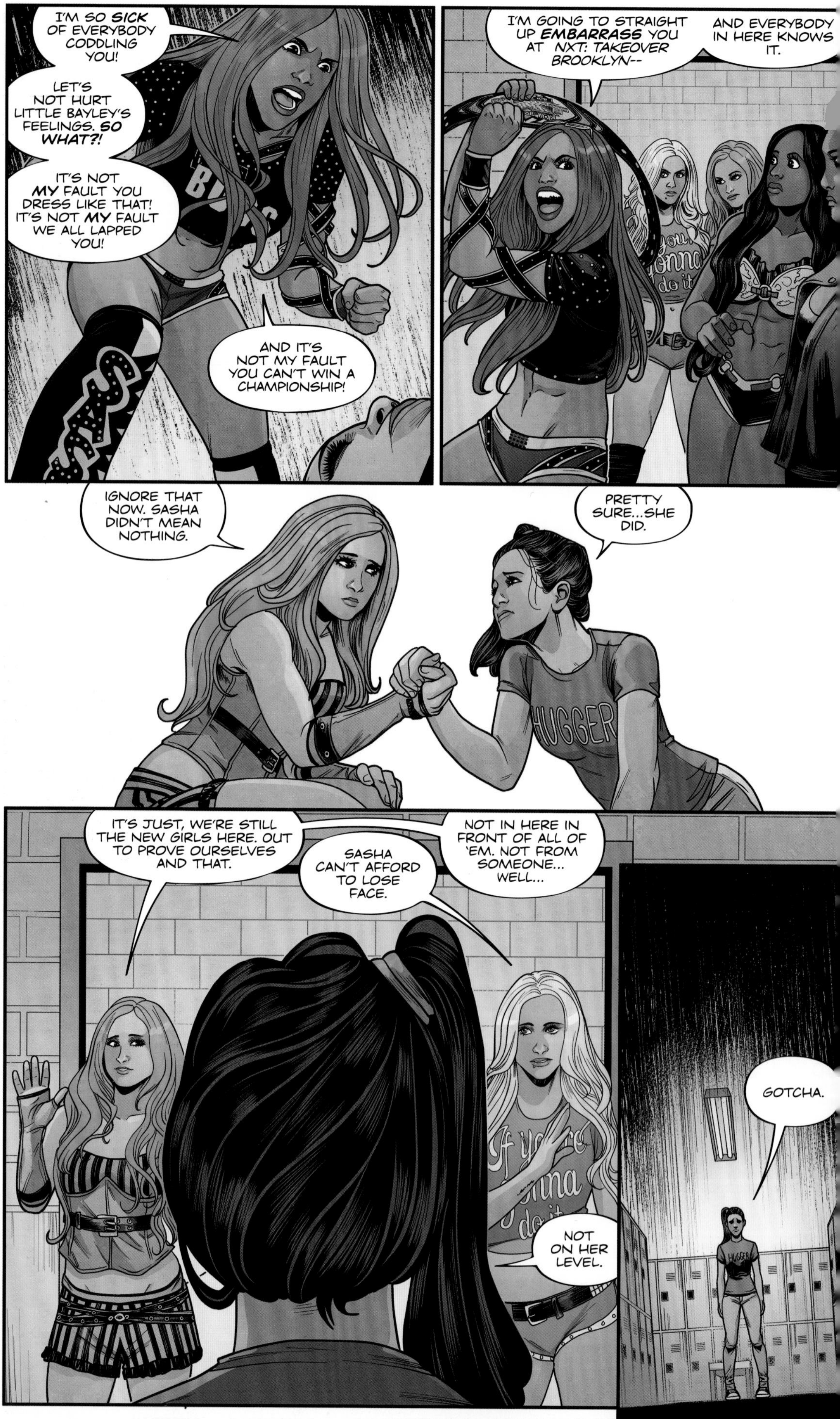
I'M SO SICK OF EVERYBODY CODDLING YOU!
LET'S NOT HURT LITTLE BAYLEY'S FEELINGS. SO WHAT?!
IT'S NOT MY FAULT YOU DRESS LIKE THAT! IT'S NOT MY FAULT WE ALL LAPPED YOU!
AND IT'S NOT MY FAULT YOU CAN'T WIN A CHAMPIONSHIP!
I'M GOING TO STRAIGHT UP EMBARRASS YOU AT NXT: TAKEOVER BROOKLYN--
AND EVERYBODY IN HERE KNOWS IT.
IGNORE THAT NOW. SASHA DIDN'T MEAN NOTHING.
PRETTY SURE...SHE DID.
HUGGER
IT'S JUST, WE'RE STILL THE NEW GIRLS HERE. OUT TO PROVE OURSELVES AND THAT.
SASHA CAN'T AFFORD TO LOSE FACE.
NOT IN HERE IN FRONT OF ALL OF 'EM. NOT FROM SOMEONE... WELL...
NOT ON HER LEVEL.
GOTCHA.

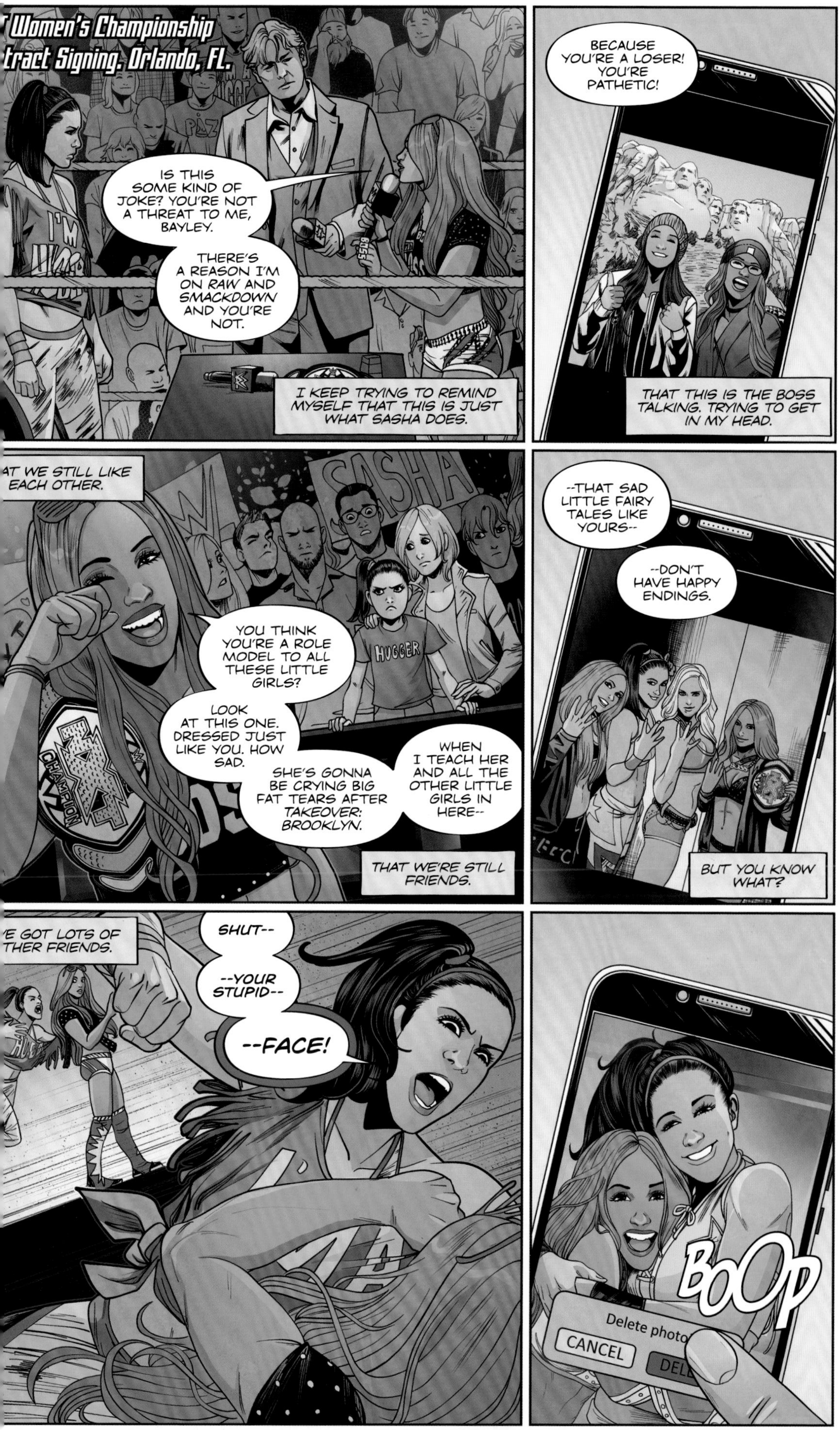
T Women's Championship
tract Signing. Orlando, FL.
IS THIS SOME KIND OF JOKE? YOU'RE NOT A THREAT TO ME, BAYLEY.
THERE'S A REASON I'M ON RAW AND SMACKDOWN AND YOU'RE NOT.
I KEEP TRYING TO REMIND MYSELF THAT THIS IS JUST WHAT SASHA DOES.
BECAUSE YOU'RE A LOSER! YOU'RE PATHETIC!
THAT THIS IS THE BOSS TALKING. TRYING TO GET IN MY HEAD.
AT WE STILL LIKE EACH OTHER.
YOU THINK YOU'RE A ROLE MODEL TO ALL THESE LITTLE GIRLS?
LOOK AT THIS ONE. DRESSED JUST LIKE YOU. HOW SAD.
SHE'S GONNA BE CRYING BIG FAT TEARS AFTER TAKEOVER: BROOKLYN.
WHEN I TEACH HER AND ALL THE OTHER LITTLE GIRLS IN HERE--
THAT WE'RE STILL FRIENDS.
--THAT SAD LITTLE FAIRY TALES LIKE YOURS--
--DON'T HAVE HAPPY ENDINGS.
BUT YOU KNOW WHAT?
'E GOT LOTS OF THER FRIENDS.
SHUT--
--YOUR STUPID--
--FACE!
BOOP
Delete photo
CANCEL
DEL

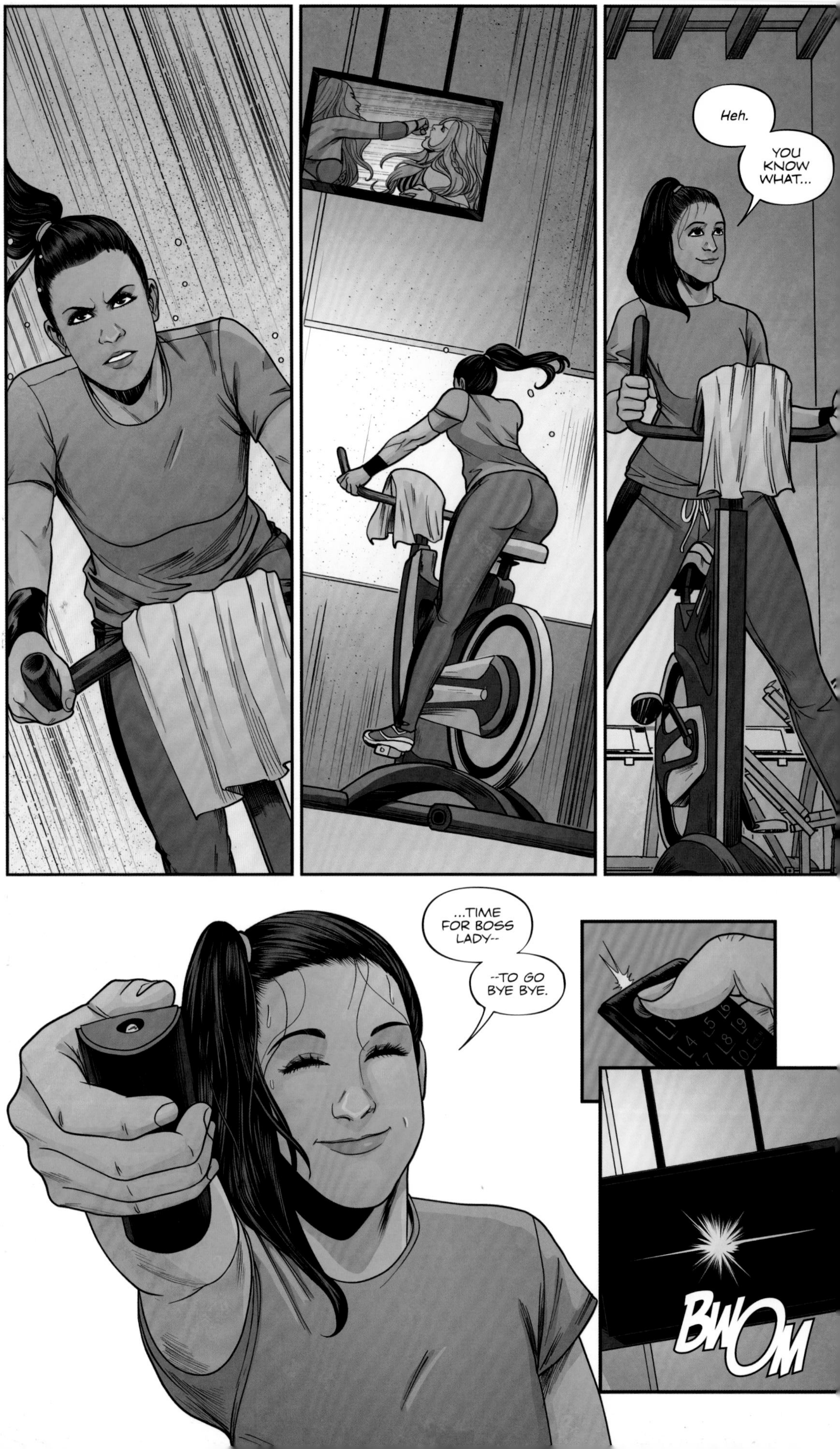
Heh.
YOU KNOW WHAT...
...TIME FOR BOSS LADY--
--TO GO BYE BYE.
BWOM

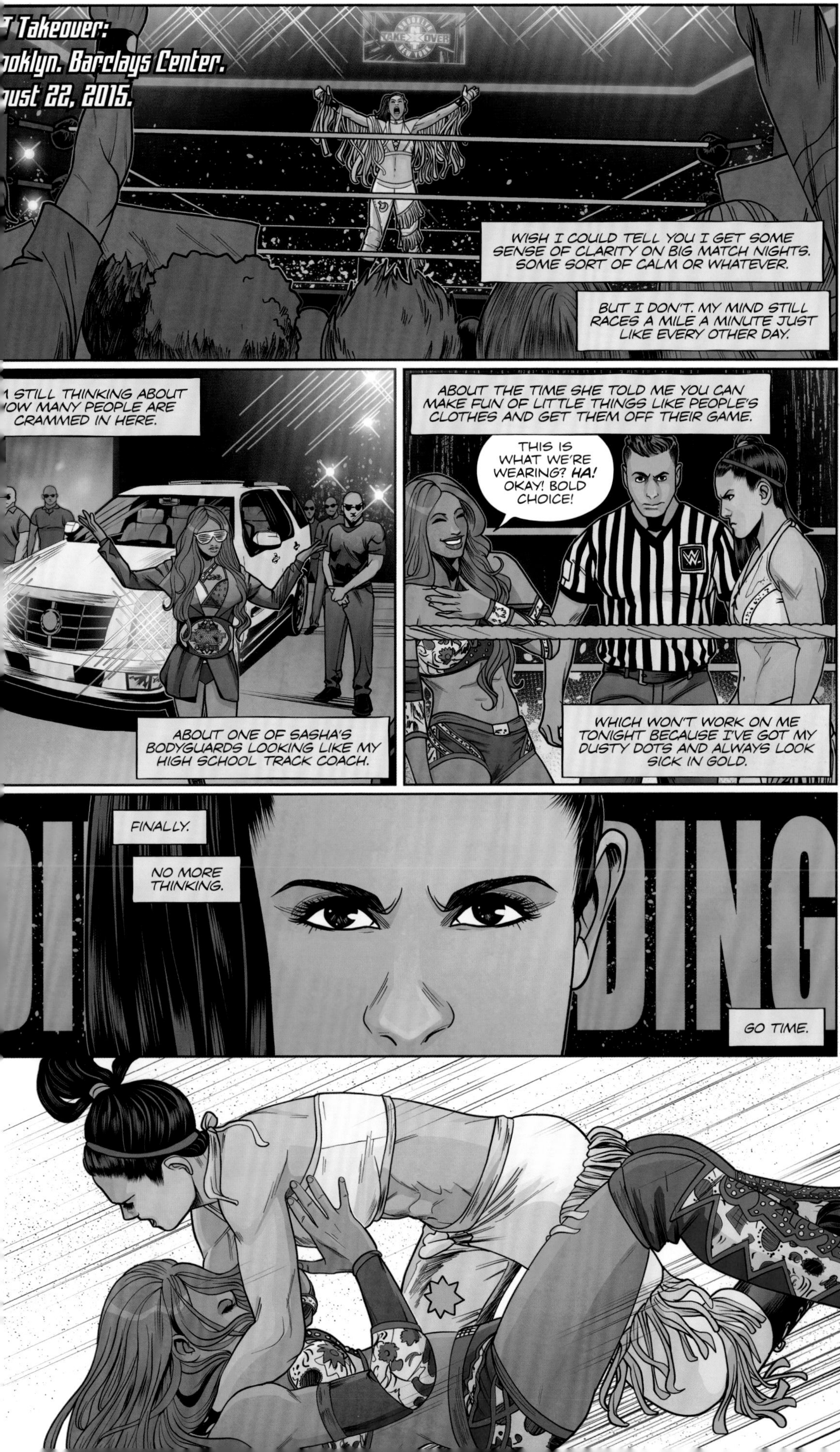
T Takeover:
ooklyn. Barclays Center.
ust 22, 2015.
WISH I COULD TELL YOU I GET SOME SENSE OF CLARITY ON BIG MATCH NIGHTS. SOME SORT OF CALM OR WHATEVER.
BUT I DON'T. MY MIND STILL RACES A MILE A MINUTE JUST LIKE EVERY OTHER DAY.
M STILL THINKING ABOUT OW MANY PEOPLE ARE CRAMMED IN HERE.
ABOUT ONE OF SASHA'S BODYGUARDS LOOKING LIKE MY HIGH SCHOOL TRACK COACH.
ABOUT THE TIME SHE TOLD ME YOU CAN MAKE FUN OF LITTLE THINGS LIKE PEOPLE'S CLOTHES AND GET THEM OFF THEIR GAME.
THIS IS WHAT WE'RE WEARING? HA! OKAY! BOLD CHOICE!
WHICH WON'T WORK ON ME TONIGHT BECAUSE I'VE GOT MY DUSTY DOTS AND ALWAYS LOOK SICK IN GOLD.
DI
FINALLY.
NO MORE THINKING.
DING
GO TIME.

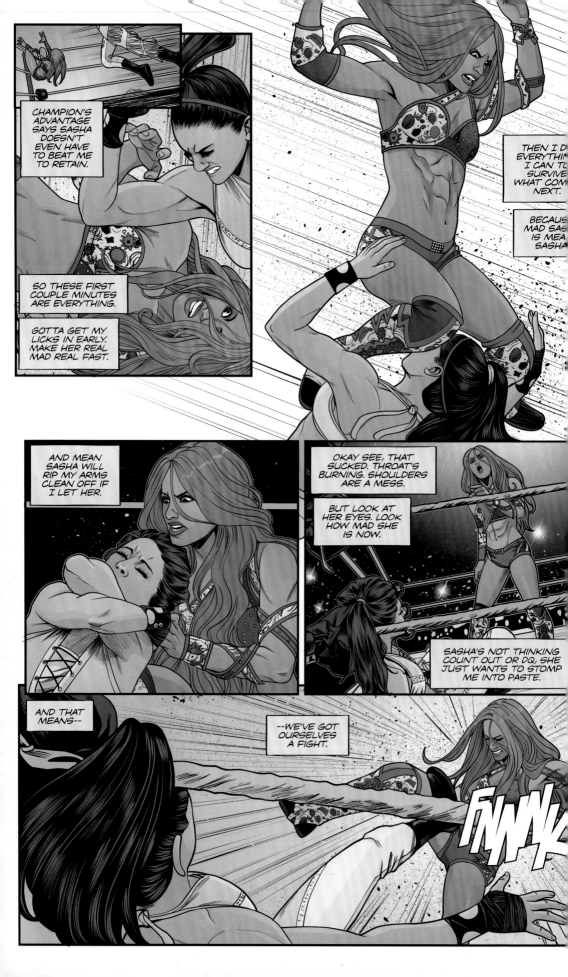

CHAMPION'S ADVANTAGE SAYS SASHA DOESN'T EVEN HAVE TO BEAT ME TO RETAIN.

SO THESE FIRST COUPLE MINUTES ARE EVERYTHING.

GOTTA GET MY LICKS IN EARLY. MAKE HER REAL MAD REAL FAST.

THEN I D EVERYTHI I CAN T SURVIVE WHAT COM NEXT.

BECAUS MAD SAS IS MEA SASHA

AND MEAN SASHA WILL RIP MY ARMS CLEAN OFF IF I LET HER.

OKAY SEE, THAT SUCKED. THROAT'S BURNING. SHOULDERS ARE A MESS.

BUT LOOK AT HER EYES. LOOK HOW MAD SHE IS NOW.

SASHA'S NOT THINKING COUNT OUT OR DQ, SHE JUST WANTS TO STOMP ME INTO PASTE.

AND THAT MEANS--

--WE'VE GOT OURSELVES A FIGHT.

FNNNK

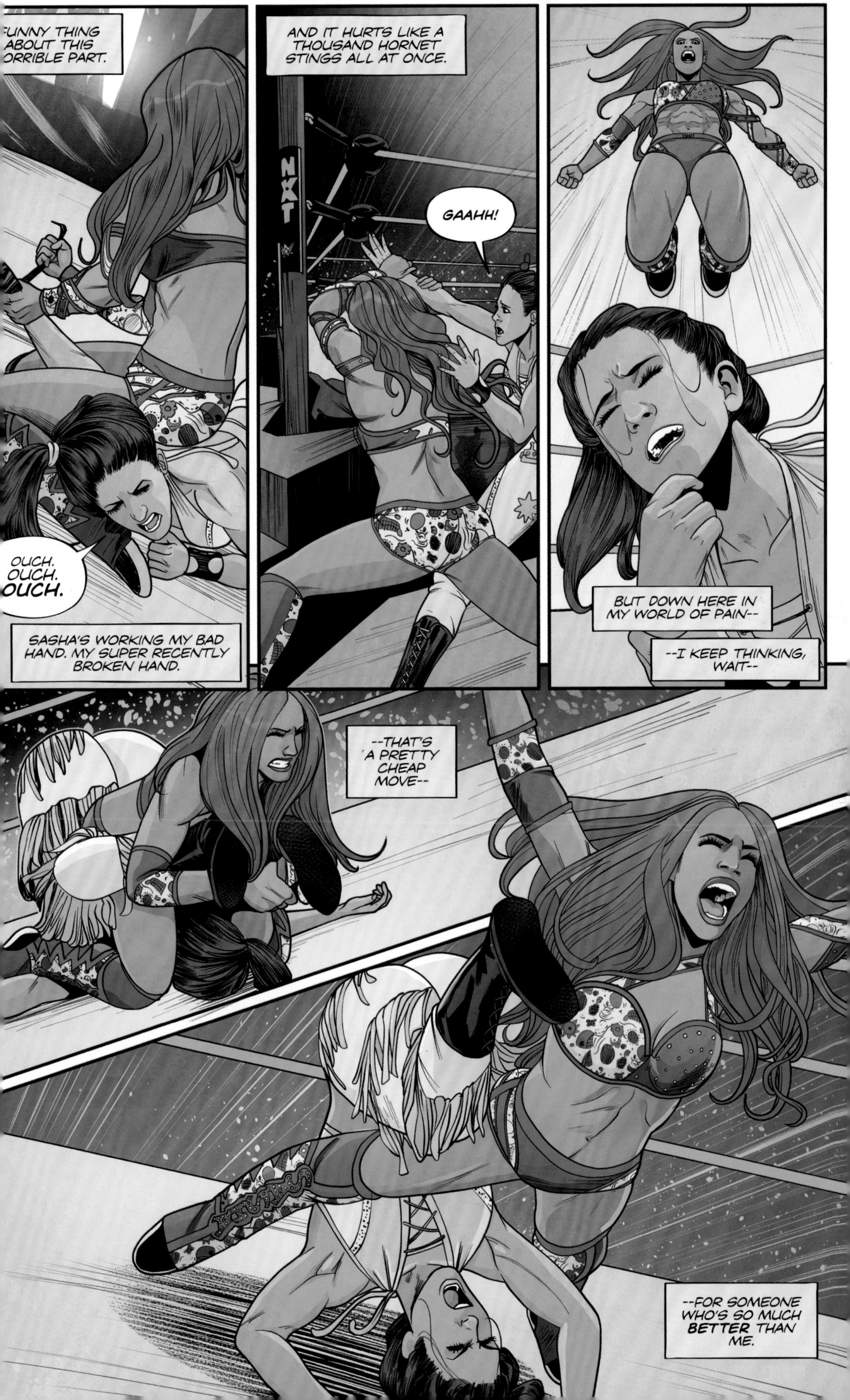

FUNNY THING ABOUT THIS ORRIBLE PART.
OUCH. OUCH. OUCH.
SASHA'S WORKING MY BAD HAND. MY SUPER RECENTLY BROKEN HAND.
AND IT HURTS LIKE A THOUSAND HORNET STINGS ALL AT ONCE.
GAAHH!
BUT DOWN HERE IN MY WORLD OF PAIN--
--I KEEP THINKING, WAIT--
--THAT'S A PRETTY CHEAP MOVE--
--FOR SOMEONE WHO'S SO MUCH BETTER THAN ME.

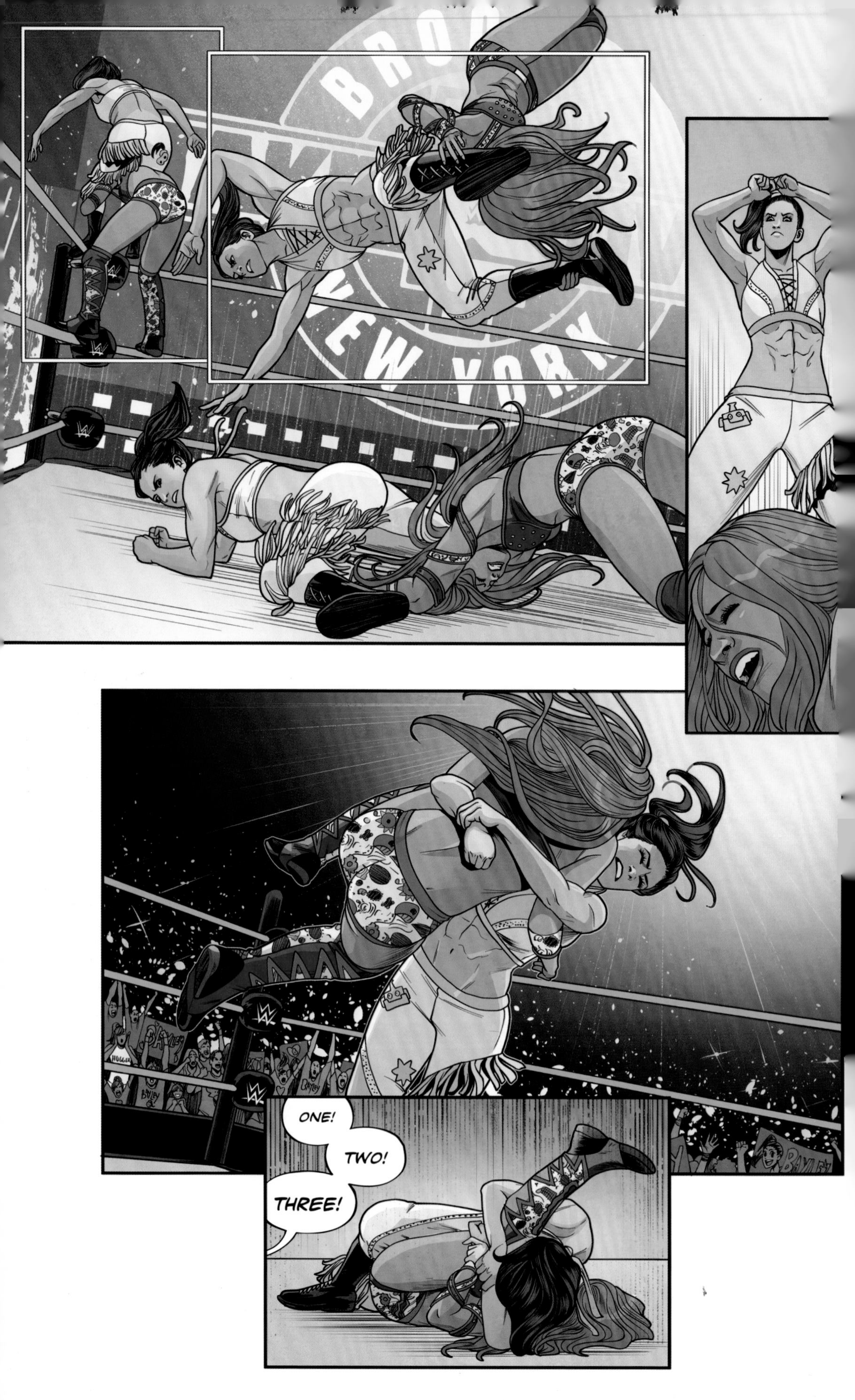
ONE!
TWO!
THREE!

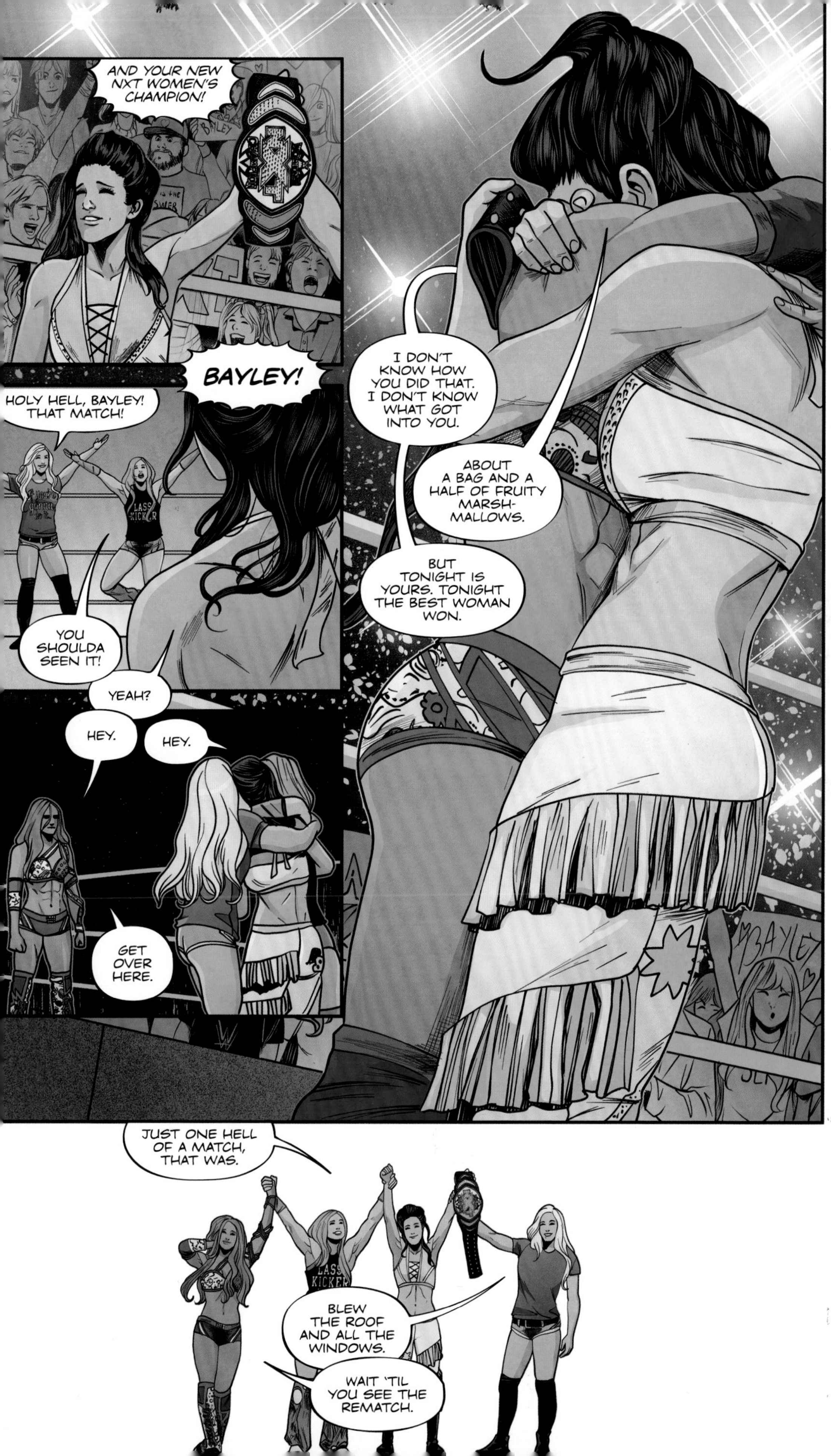
AND YOUR NEW NXT WOMEN'S CHAMPION!
BAYLEY!
HOLY HELL, BAYLEY! THAT MATCH!
YOU SHOULDA SEEN IT!
YEAH?
HEY.
HEY.
GET OVER HERE.
I DON'T KNOW HOW YOU DID THAT. I DON'T KNOW WHAT GOT INTO YOU.
ABOUT A BAG AND A HALF OF FRUITY MARSH-MALLOWS.
BUT TONIGHT IS YOURS. TONIGHT THE BEST WOMAN WON.
JUST ONE HELL OF A MATCH, THAT WAS.
BLEW THE ROOF AND ALL THE WINDOWS.
WAIT 'TIL YOU SEE THE REMATCH.

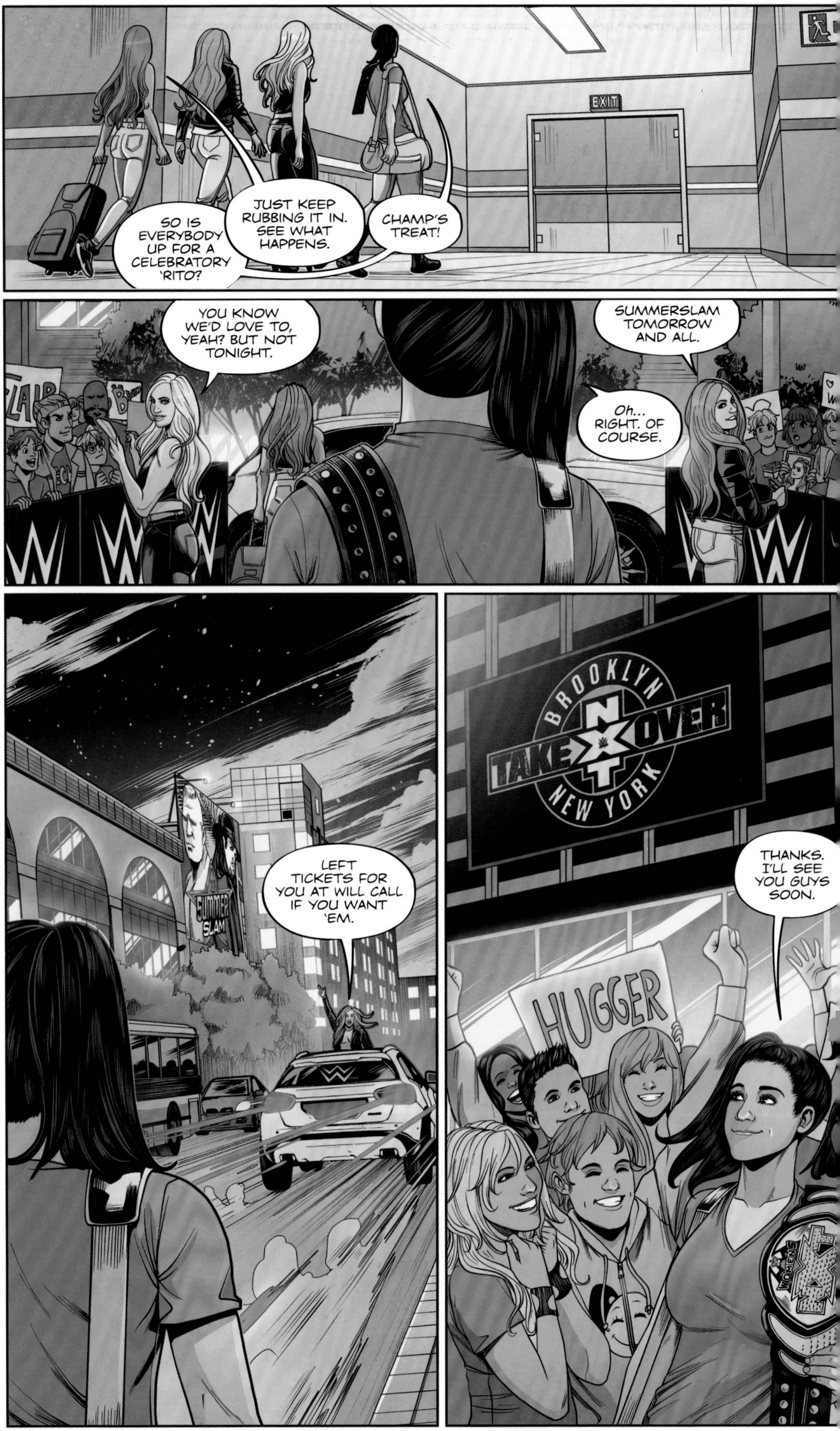
EXIT
SO IS EVERYBODY UP FOR A CELEBRATORY 'RITO?
JUST KEEP RUBBING IT IN. SEE WHAT HAPPENS.
CHAMP'S TREAT!
YOU KNOW WE'D LOVE TO, YEAH? BUT NOT TONIGHT.
SUMMERSLAM TOMORROW AND ALL.
Oh... RIGHT. OF COURSE.
LEFT TICKETS FOR YOU AT WILL CALL IF YOU WANT 'EM.
SUMMERSLAM
BROOKLYN
TAKEOVER
NEW YORK
THANKS. I'LL SEE YOU GUYS SOON.
HUGGER

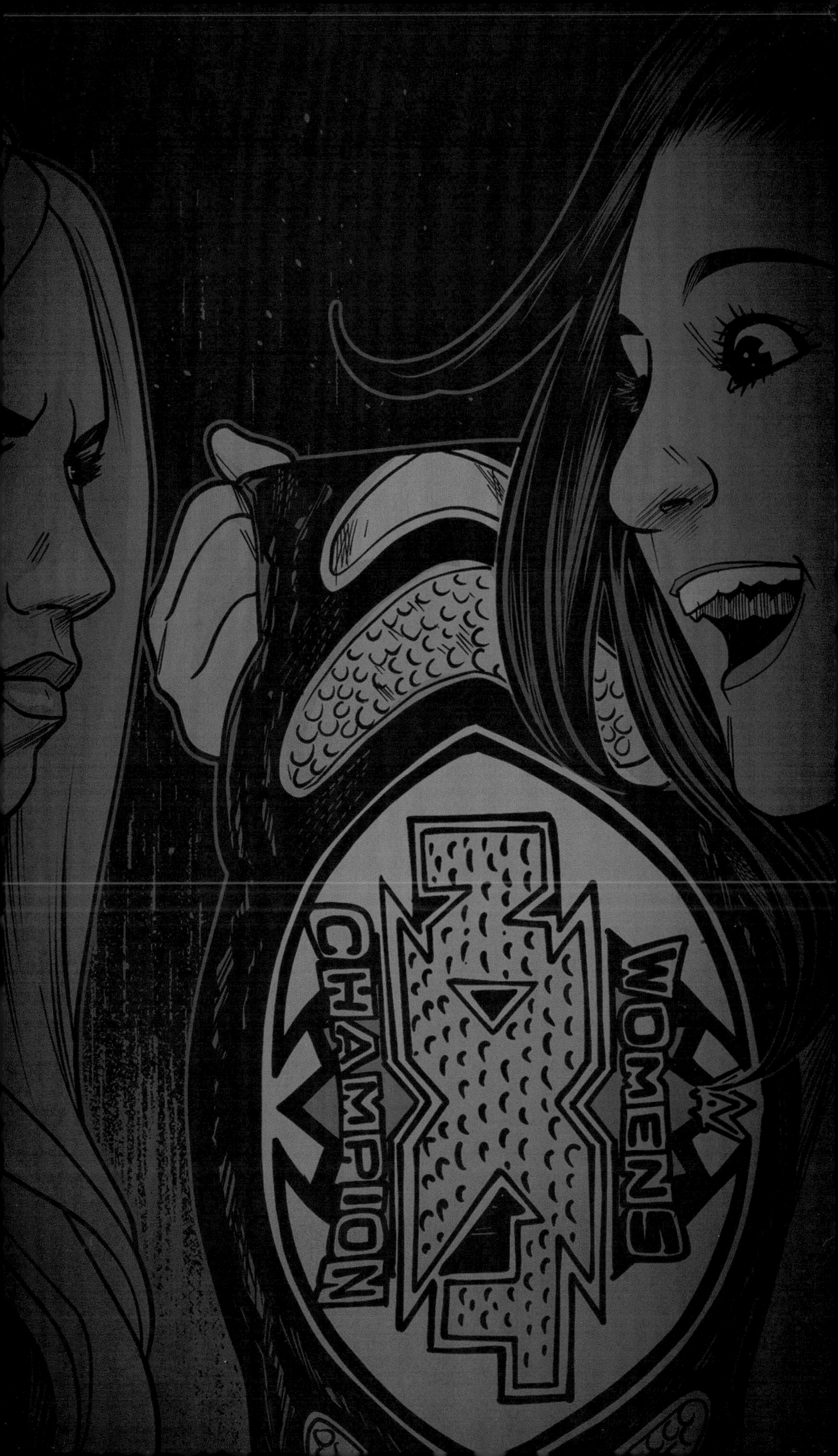
WOMENS
CHAMPION

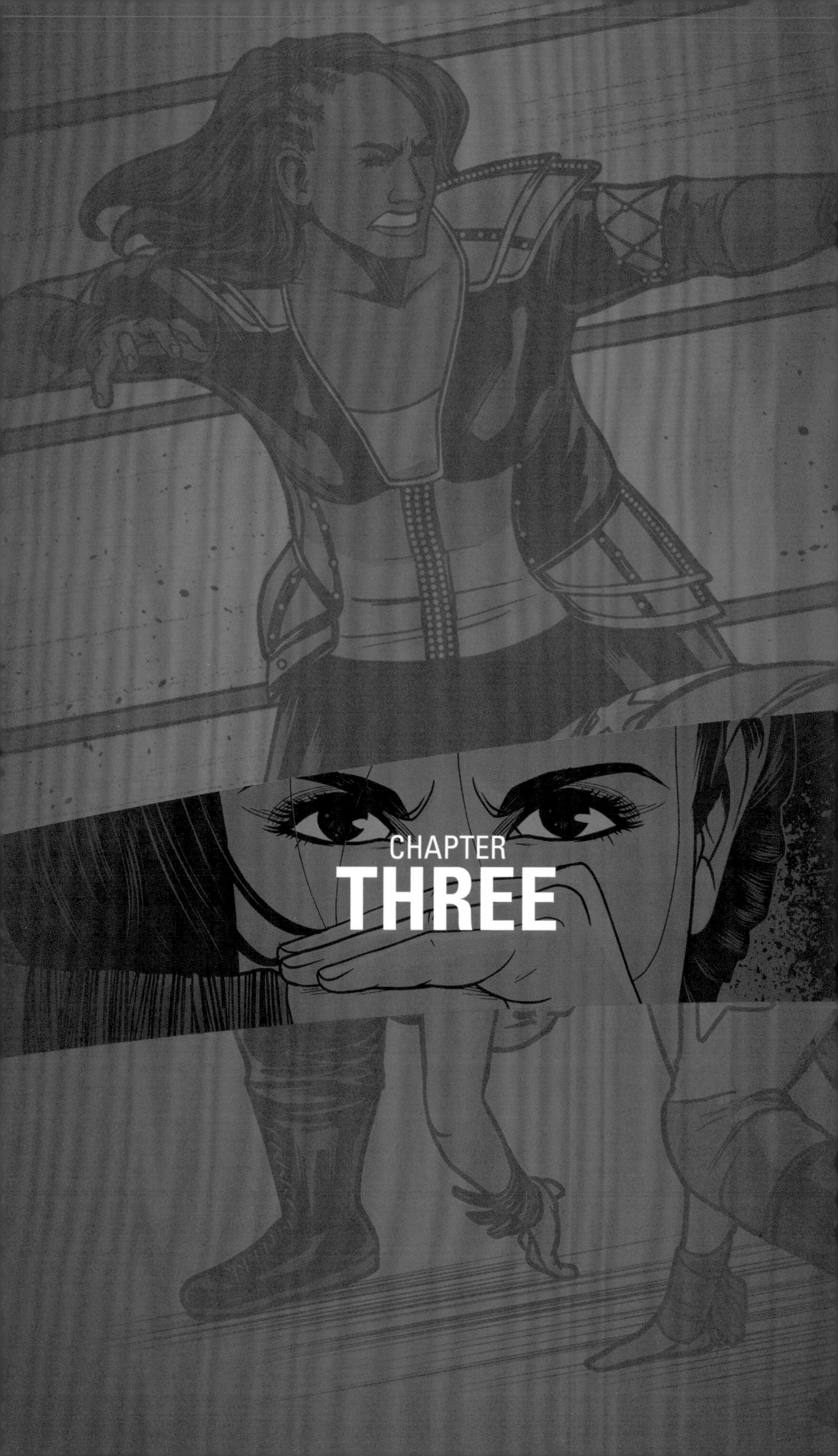
CHAPTER
THREE

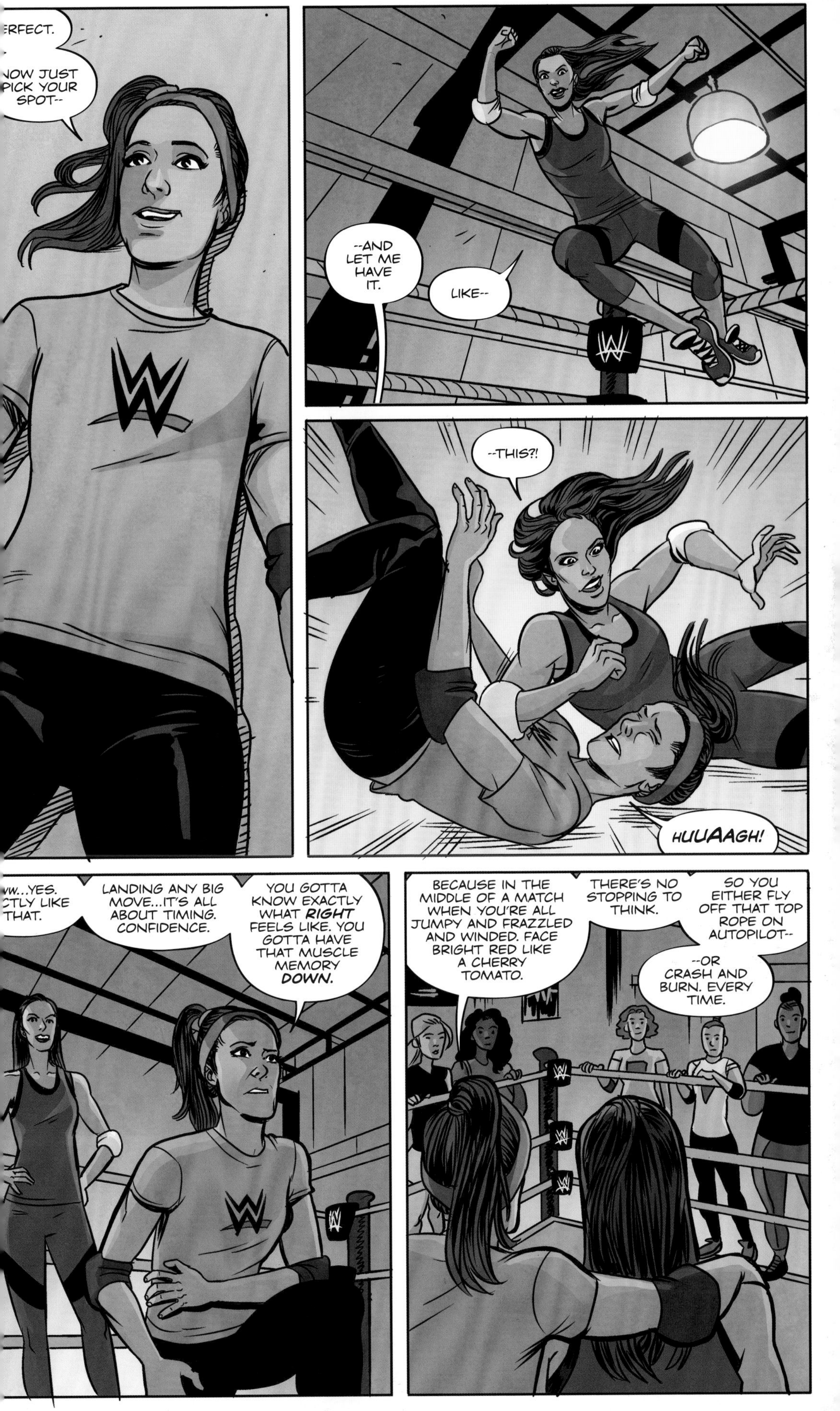

ERFECT.
NOW JUST PICK YOUR SPOT--
--AND LET ME HAVE IT.
LIKE--
--THIS?!
HUUAAGH!
WW...YES. CTLY LIKE THAT.
LANDING ANY BIG MOVE...IT'S ALL ABOUT TIMING. CONFIDENCE.
YOU GOTTA KNOW EXACTLY WHAT RIGHT FEELS LIKE. YOU GOTTA HAVE THAT MUSCLE MEMORY DOWN.
BECAUSE IN THE MIDDLE OF A MATCH WHEN YOU'RE ALL JUMPY AND FRAZZLED AND WINDED. FACE BRIGHT RED LIKE A CHERRY TOMATO.
THERE'S NO STOPPING TO THINK.
SO YOU EITHER FLY OFF THAT TOP ROPE ON AUTOPILOT--
--OR CRASH AND BURN. EVERY TIME.

KLAP KLAP KLAP

EYES AND EARS OPEN, LADIES. YOUR CHAMP SPEAKS THE TRUTH.

BAYLEY GOT TO WHERE SHE'S STANDING BY SHEER FORCE OF WILL.

SCRATCHING AND CLAWING UP A LADDER THAT DIDN'T EXPECT MUCH FROM HER.

THEN BEAT THE TITLE OFF OF SASHA BANKS. A *LEGIT BOSS.* A *WWE SUPERSTAR.*

BUT I'D ARGUE SHE ACTUALLY *WON IT* RIGHT THERE IN THAT TRAINING RING AND ACROSS THE HALL IN THE GYM.

WE'RE VERY PROUD OF WHAT *NXT* HAS BECOME AND OF THE FANBASE WE'VE BUILT.

BUT WE ALSO UNDERSTAND WWE SUPERSTARDOM REMAINS THE ULTIMATE GOAL. AND SHOOTING FOR THAT MEANS IMPROVING EVERY DAY.

BAYLEY THERE IS A SHINING EXAMPLE OF THAT PROCESS.

THANKS, BOSS.

NOW IT HER JOB NXT WOM CHAMPION HELP LIFT REST C YOU U

TRIPLE H ALWA SAYS WHAT H MEANS.

BUT SOMETIMES YOU HAVE TO LISTEN PRETTY CLOSE.

FOLLOW HER LEAD AND I HAVE NO DOUBT YOU'LL ALL SHINE JUST AS BRIGHT.

MAYBE EVEN BRIGHTER.

THE ONLY THING HE LIKES ABOUT ME CARRYING THIS TITLE--

--IS THAT SOMEBODY ELSE IS GONNA HAVE STEP UP AND TAKE I FROM ME.

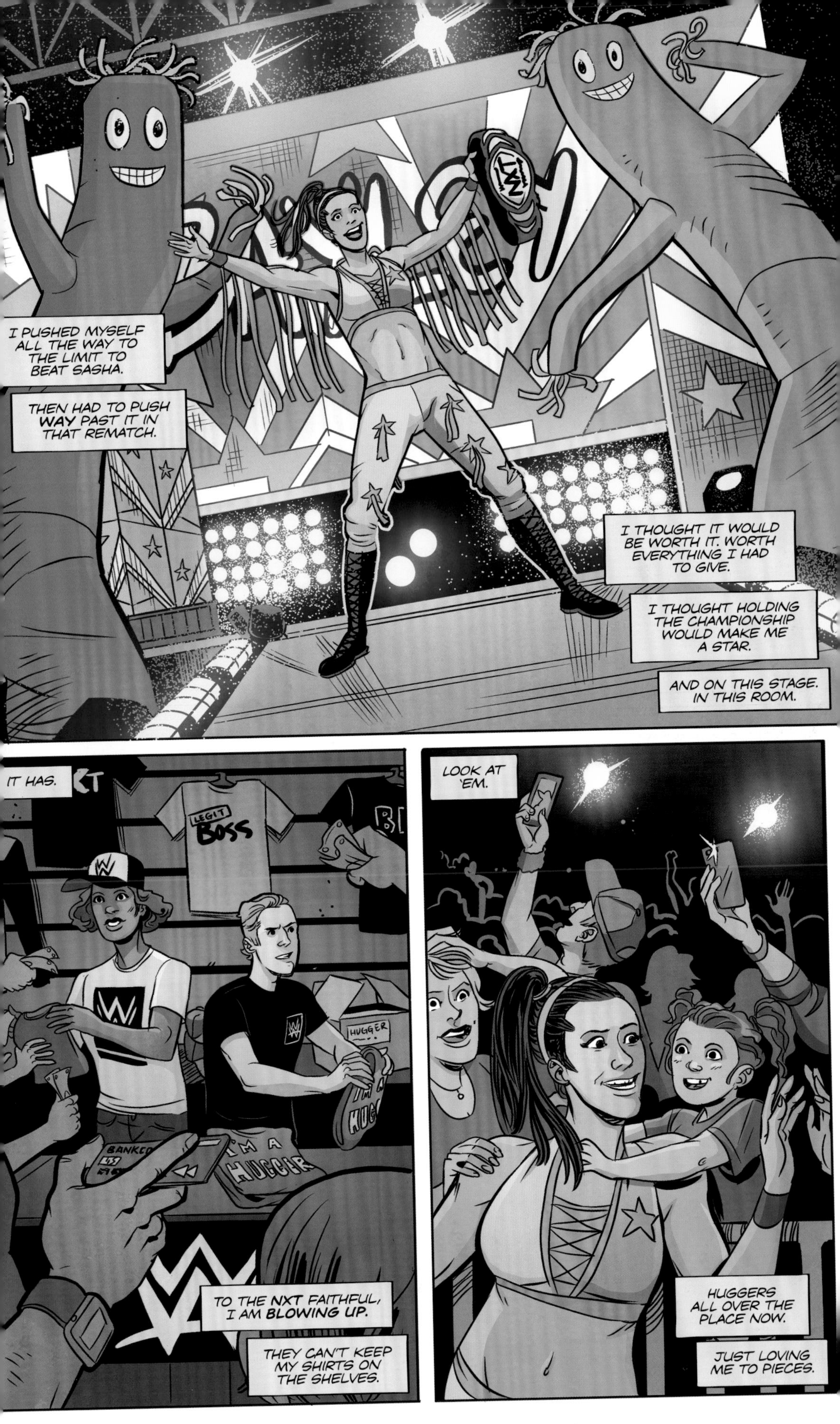
I PUSHED MYSELF ALL THE WAY TO THE LIMIT TO BEAT SASHA.
THEN HAD TO PUSH **WAY** PAST IT IN THAT REMATCH.
I THOUGHT IT WOULD BE WORTH IT. WORTH EVERYTHING I HAD TO GIVE.
I THOUGHT HOLDING THE CHAMPIONSHIP WOULD MAKE ME A STAR.
AND ON THIS STAGE. IN THIS ROOM.
IT HAS.
LEGIT BOSS
HUGGER
I'M A HUGGER
TO THE **NXT** FAITHFUL, I AM **BLOWING UP**.
THEY CAN'T KEEP MY SHIRTS ON THE SHELVES.
LOOK AT 'EM.
HUGGERS ALL OVER THE PLACE NOW.
JUST LOVING ME TO PIECES.

BUT TO THE MAN IN CHARGE--

--WELL, YOU HEARD HIM.

I'M THE LITTLE BAYLEY THAT COULD.

THE SURPRISINGL[Y] GOOD--

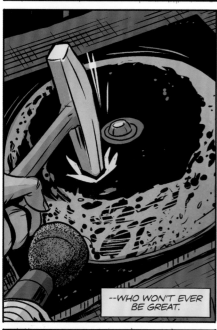

--WHO WON'T EVER BE GREAT.

WHICH PUTS MY CEILING RIGHT ABOUT...

...HERE[.]

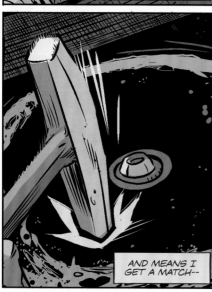

AND MEANS I GET A MATCH--

--EVERY SINGLE NIGHT.

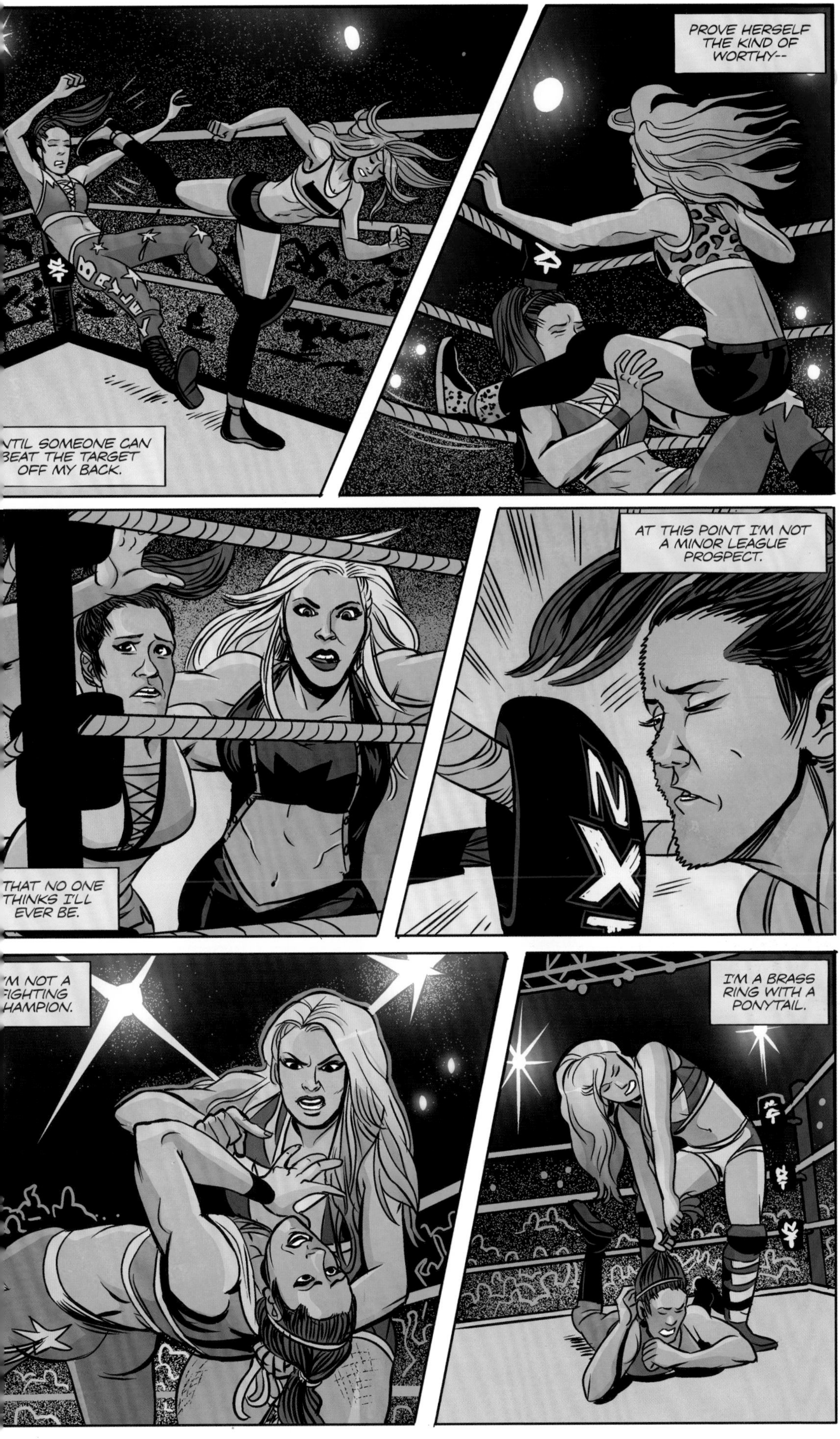
NTIL SOMEONE CAN
BEAT THE TARGET
OFF MY BACK.
PROVE HERSELF
THE KIND OF
WORTHY--
THAT NO ONE
THINKS I'LL
EVER BE.
AT THIS POINT I'M NOT
A MINOR LEAGUE
PROSPECT.
'M NOT A
FIGHTING
HAMPION.
I'M A BRASS
RING WITH A
PONYTAIL.

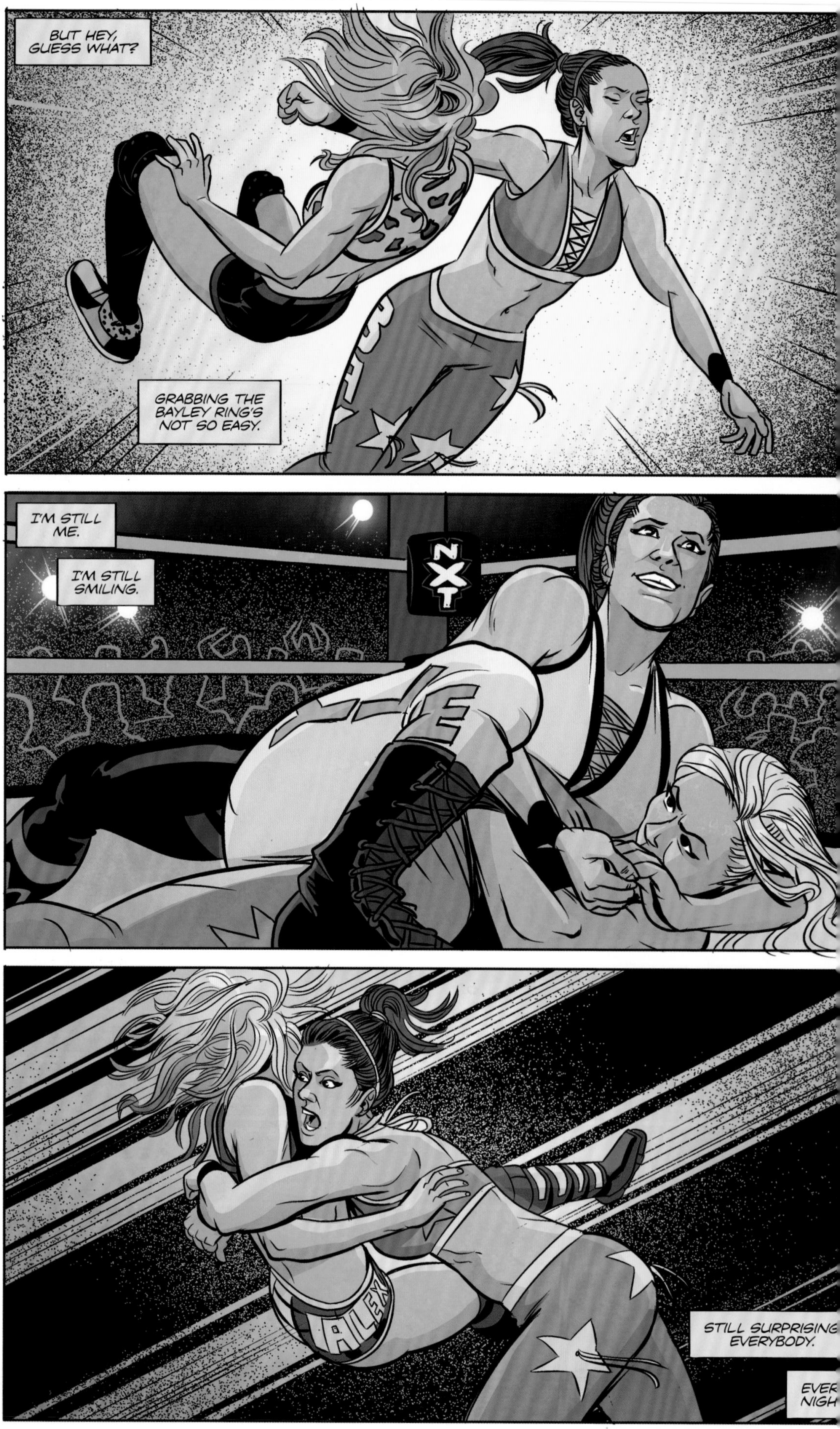
BUT HEY, GUESS WHAT?
GRABBING THE BAYLEY RING'S NOT SO EASY.
NXT
I'M STILL ME.
I'M STILL SMILING.
ALEX
STILL SURPRISING EVERYBODY.

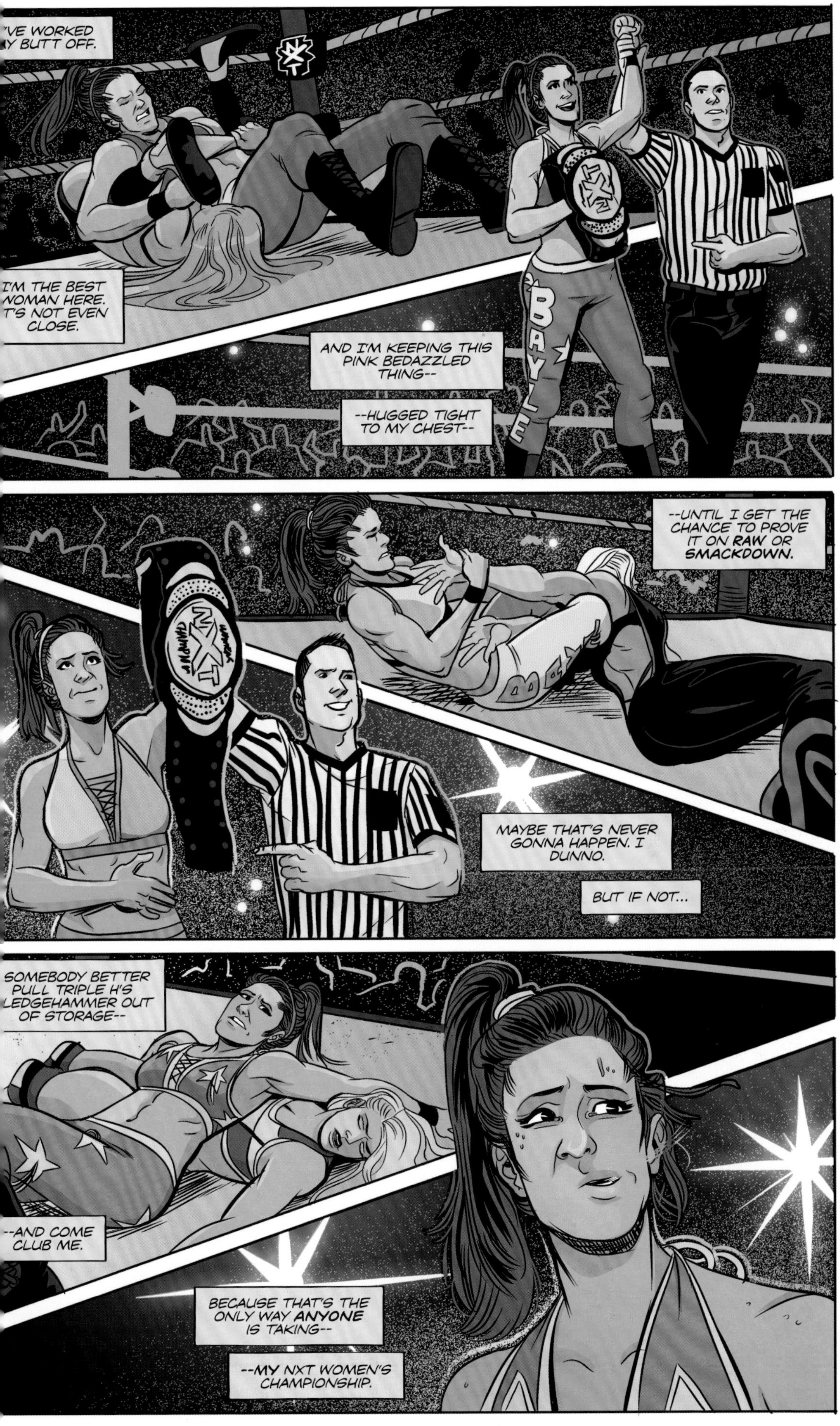

'VE WORKED
Y BUTT OFF.
I'M THE BEST
WOMAN HERE.
T'S NOT EVEN
CLOSE.
AND I'M KEEPING THIS
PINK BEDAZZLED
THING--
--HUGGED TIGHT
TO MY CHEST--
--UNTIL I GET THE
CHANCE TO PROVE
IT ON RAW OR
SMACKDOWN.
MAYBE THAT'S NEVER
GONNA HAPPEN. I
DUNNO.
BUT IF NOT...
SOMEBODY BETTER
PULL TRIPLE H'S
LEDGEHAMMER OUT
OF STORAGE--
--AND COME
CLUB ME.
BECAUSE THAT'S THE
ONLY WAY ANYONE
IS TAKING--
--MY NXT WOMEN'S
CHAMPIONSHIP.

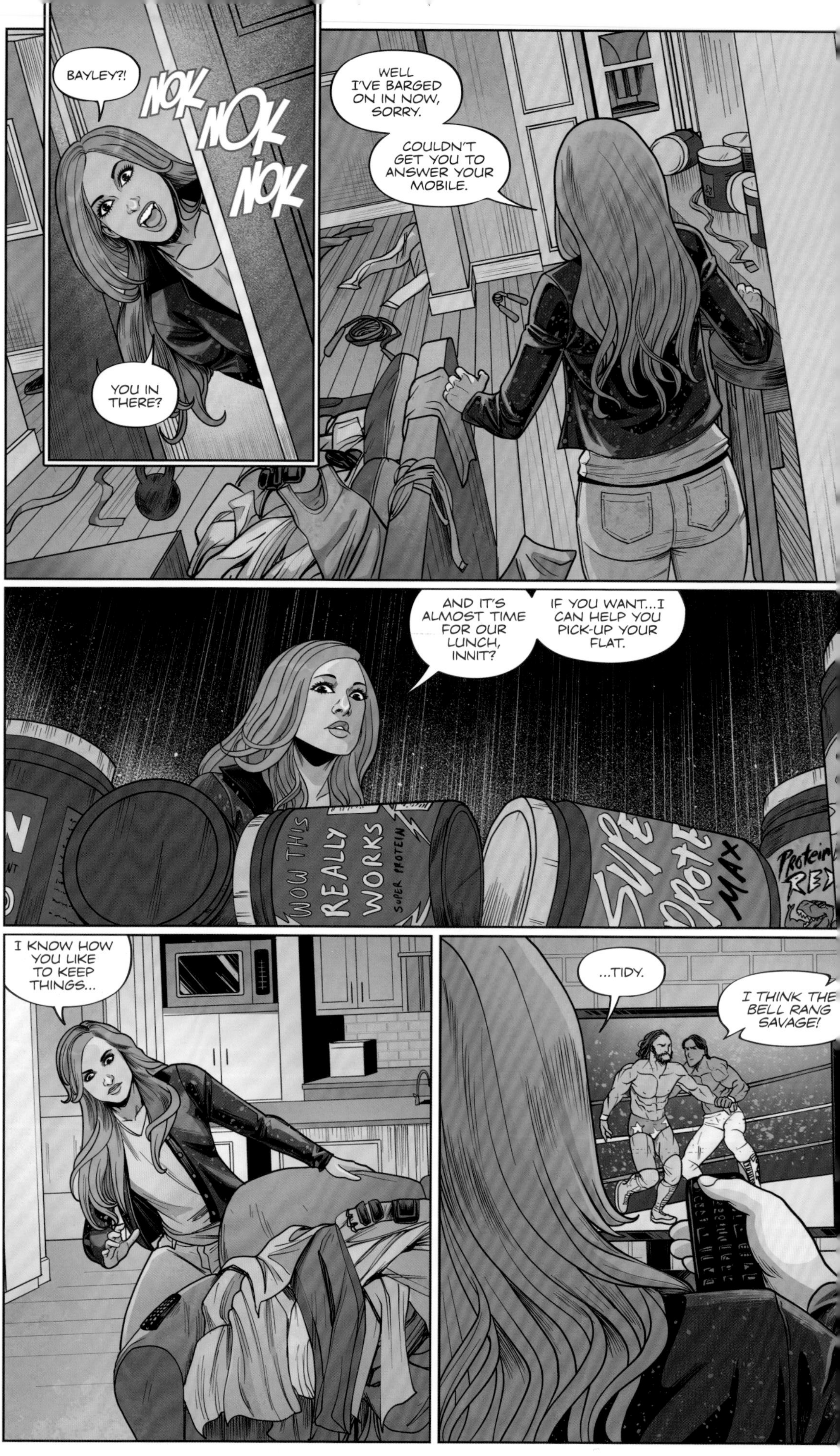
BAYLEY?!
NOK NOK NOK
YOU IN THERE?
WELL I'VE BARGED ON IN NOW, SORRY.
COULDN'T GET YOU TO ANSWER YOUR MOBILE.
AND IT'S ALMOST TIME FOR OUR LUNCH, INNIT?
IF YOU WANT...I CAN HELP YOU PICK-UP YOUR FLAT.
WOW THIS REALLY WORKS
SUPER PROTEIN
MAX
I KNOW HOW YOU LIKE TO KEEP THINGS...
...TIDY.
I THINK THE BELL RANG SAVAGE!

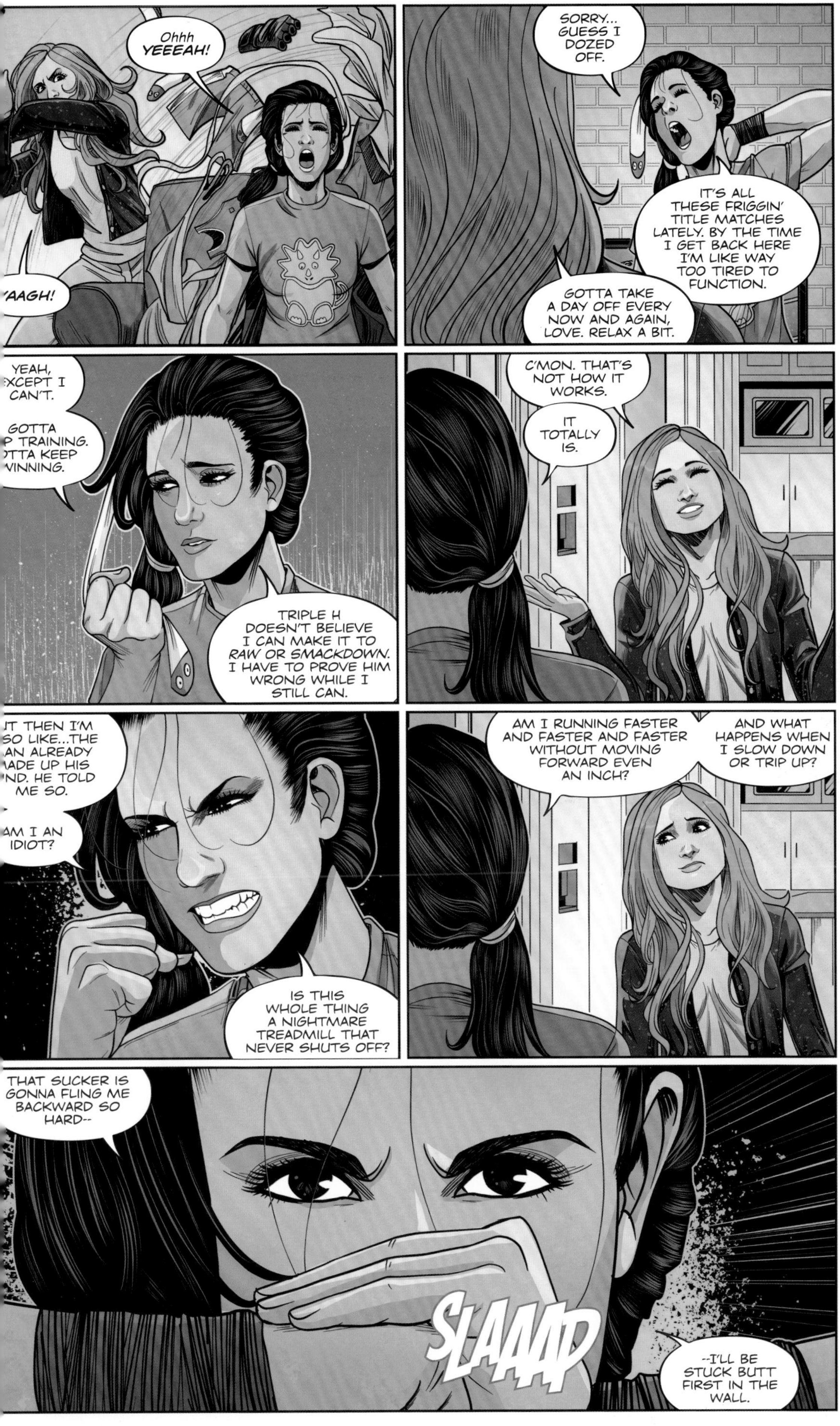

Ohhh YEEEAH!
YAAGH!
SORRY... GUESS I DOZED OFF.
IT'S ALL THESE FRIGGIN' TITLE MATCHES LATELY. BY THE TIME I GET BACK HERE I'M LIKE WAY TOO TIRED TO FUNCTION.
GOTTA TAKE A DAY OFF EVERY NOW AND AGAIN, LOVE. RELAX A BIT.
YEAH, EXCEPT I CAN'T.
GOTTA P TRAINING. OTTA KEEP VINNING.
TRIPLE H DOESN'T BELIEVE I CAN MAKE IT TO *RAW* OR *SMACKDOWN*. I HAVE TO PROVE HIM WRONG WHILE I STILL CAN.
C'MON. THAT'S NOT HOW IT WORKS.
IT TOTALLY IS.
IT THEN I'M SO LIKE...THE AN ALREADY ADE UP HIS ND. HE TOLD ME SO.
AM I AN IDIOT?
IS THIS WHOLE THING A NIGHTMARE TREADMILL THAT NEVER SHUTS OFF?
AM I RUNNING FASTER AND FASTER AND FASTER WITHOUT MOVING FORWARD EVEN AN INCH?
AND WHAT HAPPENS WHEN I SLOW DOWN OR TRIP UP?
THAT SUCKER IS GONNA FLING ME BACKWARD SO HARD--
SLAAAP
--I'LL BE STUCK BUTT FIRST IN THE WALL.

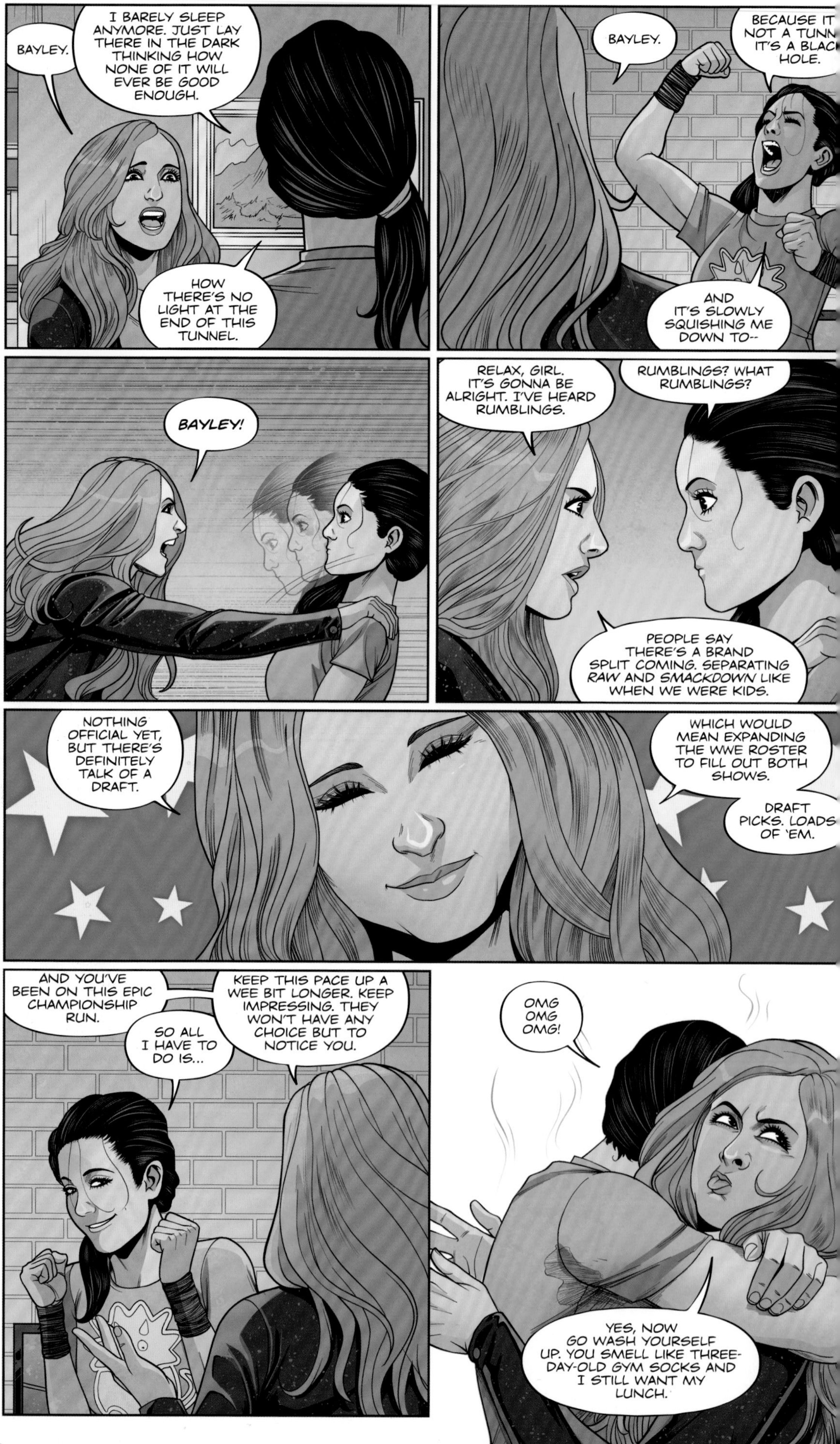
BAYLEY.
I BARELY SLEEP ANYMORE. JUST LAY THERE IN THE DARK THINKING HOW NONE OF IT WILL EVER BE GOOD ENOUGH.
HOW THERE'S NO LIGHT AT THE END OF THIS TUNNEL.
BAYLEY.
AND IT'S SLOWLY SQUISHING ME DOWN TO--
BAYLEY!
RELAX, GIRL. IT'S GONNA BE ALRIGHT. I'VE HEARD RUMBLINGS.
RUMBLINGS? WHAT RUMBLINGS?
PEOPLE SAY THERE'S A BRAND SPLIT COMING. SEPARATING *RAW* AND *SMACKDOWN* LIKE WHEN WE WERE KIDS.
NOTHING OFFICIAL YET, BUT THERE'S DEFINITELY TALK OF A DRAFT.
WHICH WOULD MEAN EXPANDING THE WWE ROSTER TO FILL OUT BOTH SHOWS.
AND YOU'VE BEEN ON THIS EPIC CHAMPIONSHIP RUN.
KEEP THIS PACE UP A WEE BIT LONGER. KEEP IMPRESSING. THEY WON'T HAVE ANY CHOICE BUT TO NOTICE YOU.
SO ALL I HAVE TO DO IS...
OMG OMG OMG!
YES, NOW GO WASH YOURSELF UP. YOU SMELL LIKE THREE-DAY-OLD GYM SOCKS AND I STILL WANT MY LUNCH.

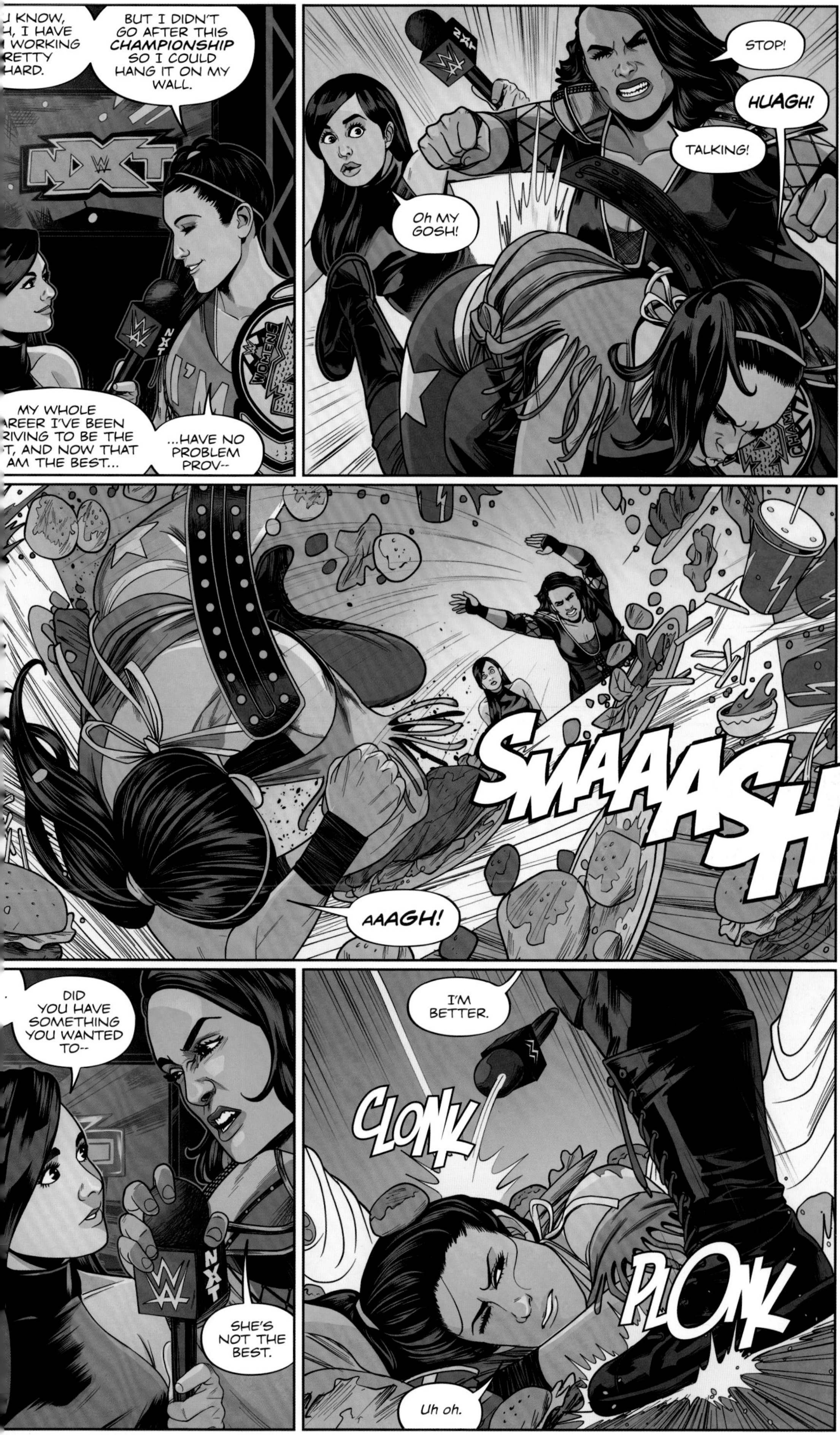

U KNOW, H, I HAVE WORKING RETTY HARD.
BUT I DIDN'T GO AFTER THIS CHAMPIONSHIP SO I COULD HANG IT ON MY WALL.
MY WHOLE AREER I'VE BEEN RIVING TO BE THE T, AND NOW THAT AM THE BEST...
...HAVE NO PROBLEM PROV--
STOP!
HUAGH!
TALKING!
Oh MY GOSH!
SMAAAASH
AAAGH!
DID YOU HAVE SOMETHING YOU WANTED TO--
SHE'S NOT THE BEST.
I'M BETTER.
CLONK
PLONK
Uh oh.

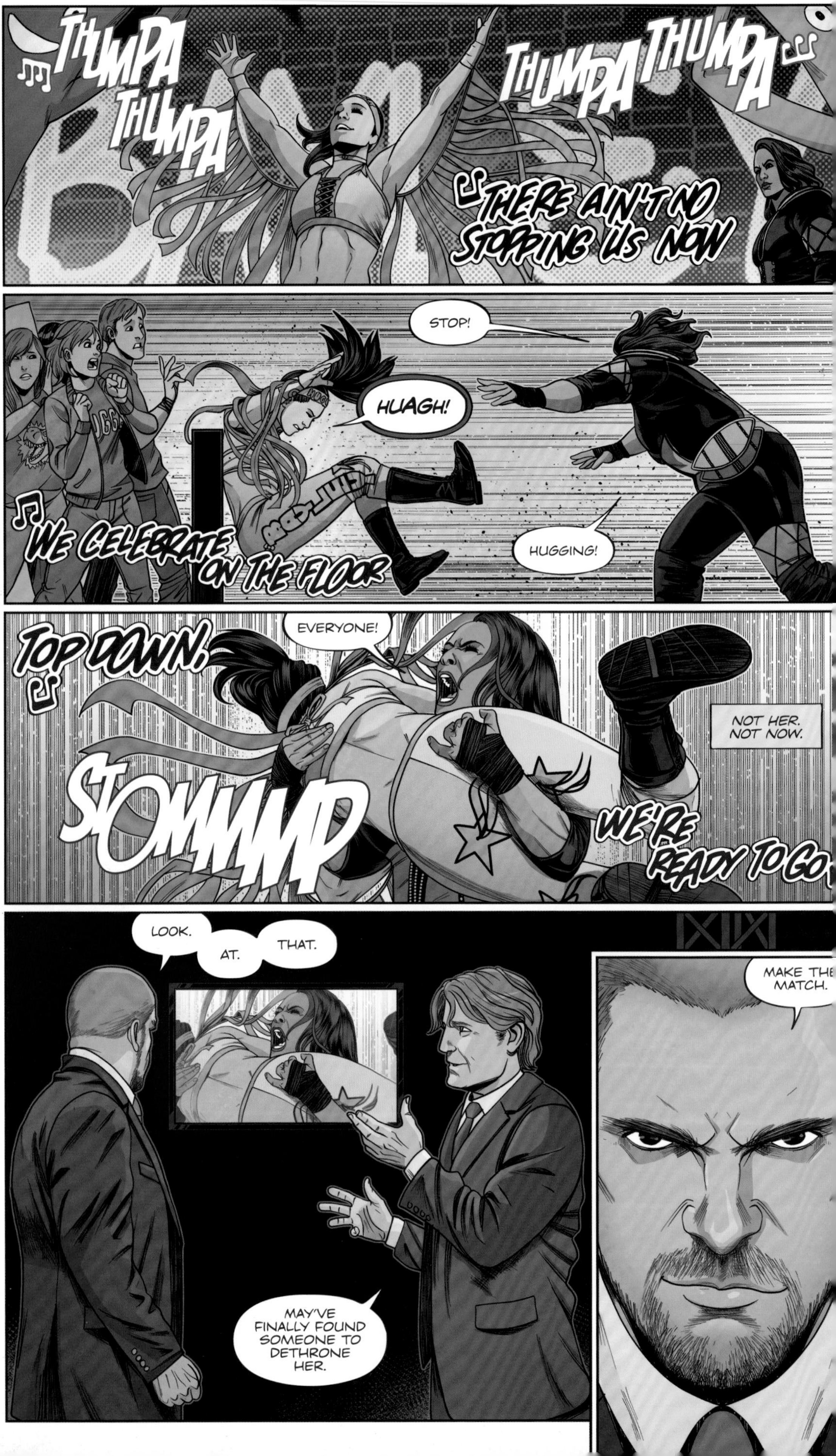
THUMPA THUMPA
THUMPA THUMPA
THERE AIN'T NO STOPPING US NOW
STOP!
HUAGH!
WE CELEBRATE ON THE FLOOR
HUGGING!
TOP DOWN,
EVERYONE!
NOT HER. NOT NOW.
STOMMMP
WE'RE READY TO GO
LOOK.
AT.
THAT.
MAKE THE MATCH.
MAY'VE FINALLY FOUND SOMEONE TO DETHRONE HER.

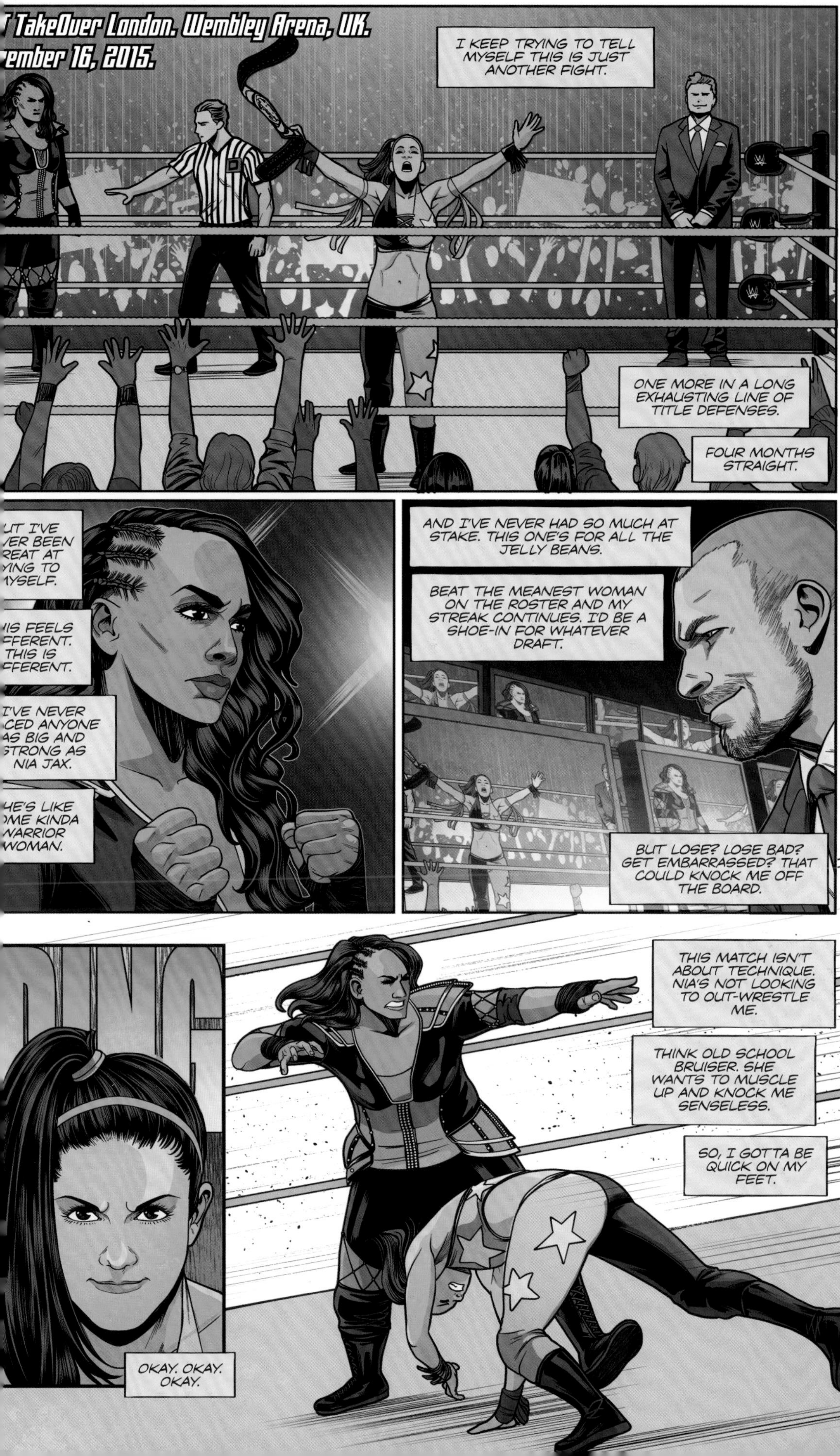
T TakeOver London. Wembley Arena, UK.
ember 16, 2015.
I KEEP TRYING TO TELL MYSELF THIS IS JUST ANOTHER FIGHT.
ONE MORE IN A LONG EXHAUSTING LINE OF TITLE DEFENSES.
FOUR MONTHS STRAIGHT.
UT I'VE VER BEEN REAT AT YING TO MYSELF.
IIS FEELS FFERENT. THIS IS FFERENT.
I'VE NEVER CED ANYONE AS BIG AND STRONG AS NIA JAX.
HE'S LIKE OME KINDA WARRIOR WOMAN.
AND I'VE NEVER HAD SO MUCH AT STAKE. THIS ONE'S FOR ALL THE JELLY BEANS.
BEAT THE MEANEST WOMAN ON THE ROSTER AND MY STREAK CONTINUES. I'D BE A SHOE-IN FOR WHATEVER DRAFT.
BUT LOSE? LOSE BAD? GET EMBARRASSED? THAT COULD KNOCK ME OFF THE BOARD.
OKAY. OKAY. OKAY.
THIS MATCH ISN'T ABOUT TECHNIQUE. NIA'S NOT LOOKING TO OUT-WRESTLE ME.
THINK OLD SCHOOL BRUISER. SHE WANTS TO MUSCLE UP AND KNOCK ME SENSELESS.
SO, I GOTTA BE QUICK ON MY FEET.

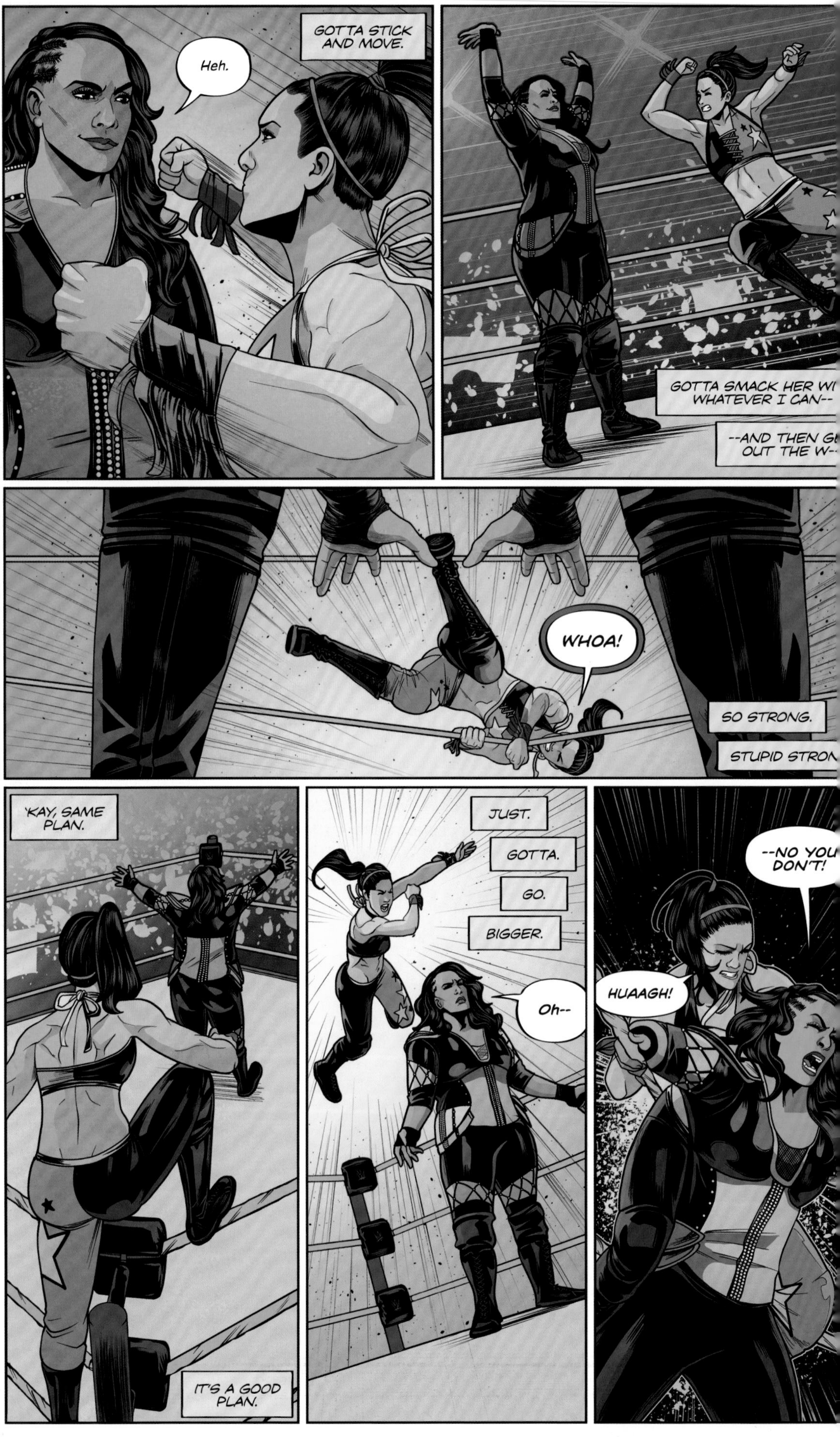
GOTTA STICK AND MOVE.
Heh.
GOTTA SMACK HER WI WHATEVER I CAN--
--AND THEN G OUT THE W--
WHOA!
SO STRONG.
STUPID STRON
'KAY, SAME PLAN.
IT'S A GOOD PLAN.
JUST.
GOTTA.
GO.
BIGGER.
Oh--
--NO YOU DON'T!
HUAAGH!

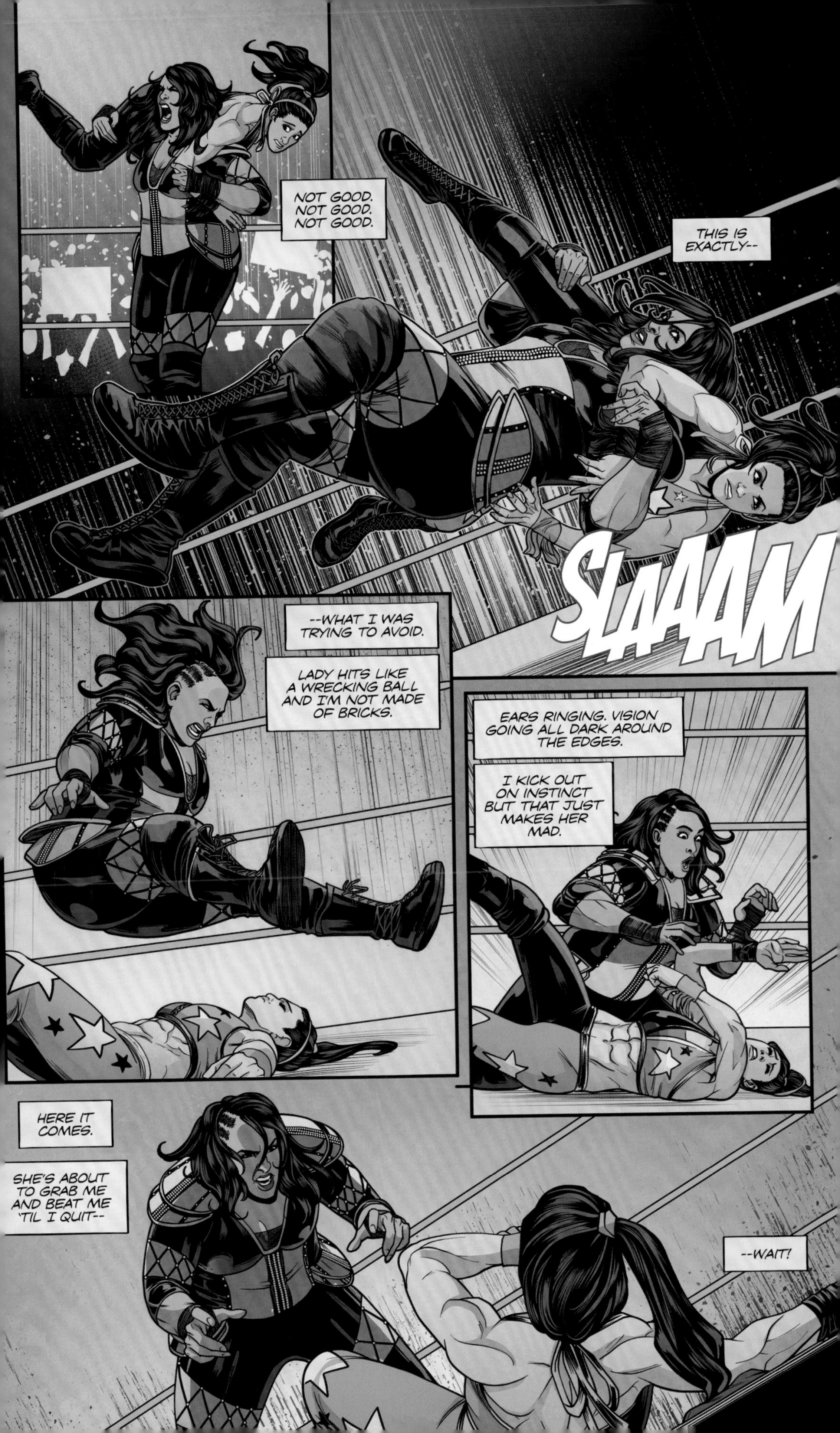
NOT GOOD. NOT GOOD. NOT GOOD.
THIS IS EXACTLY--
SLAAAAM
--WHAT I WAS TRYING TO AVOID.
LADY HITS LIKE A WRECKING BALL AND I'M NOT MADE OF BRICKS.
EARS RINGING. VISION GOING ALL DARK AROUND THE EDGES.
I KICK OUT ON INSTINCT BUT THAT JUST MAKES HER MAD.
HERE IT COMES.
SHE'S ABOUT TO GRAB ME AND BEAT ME 'TIL I QUIT--
--WAIT!

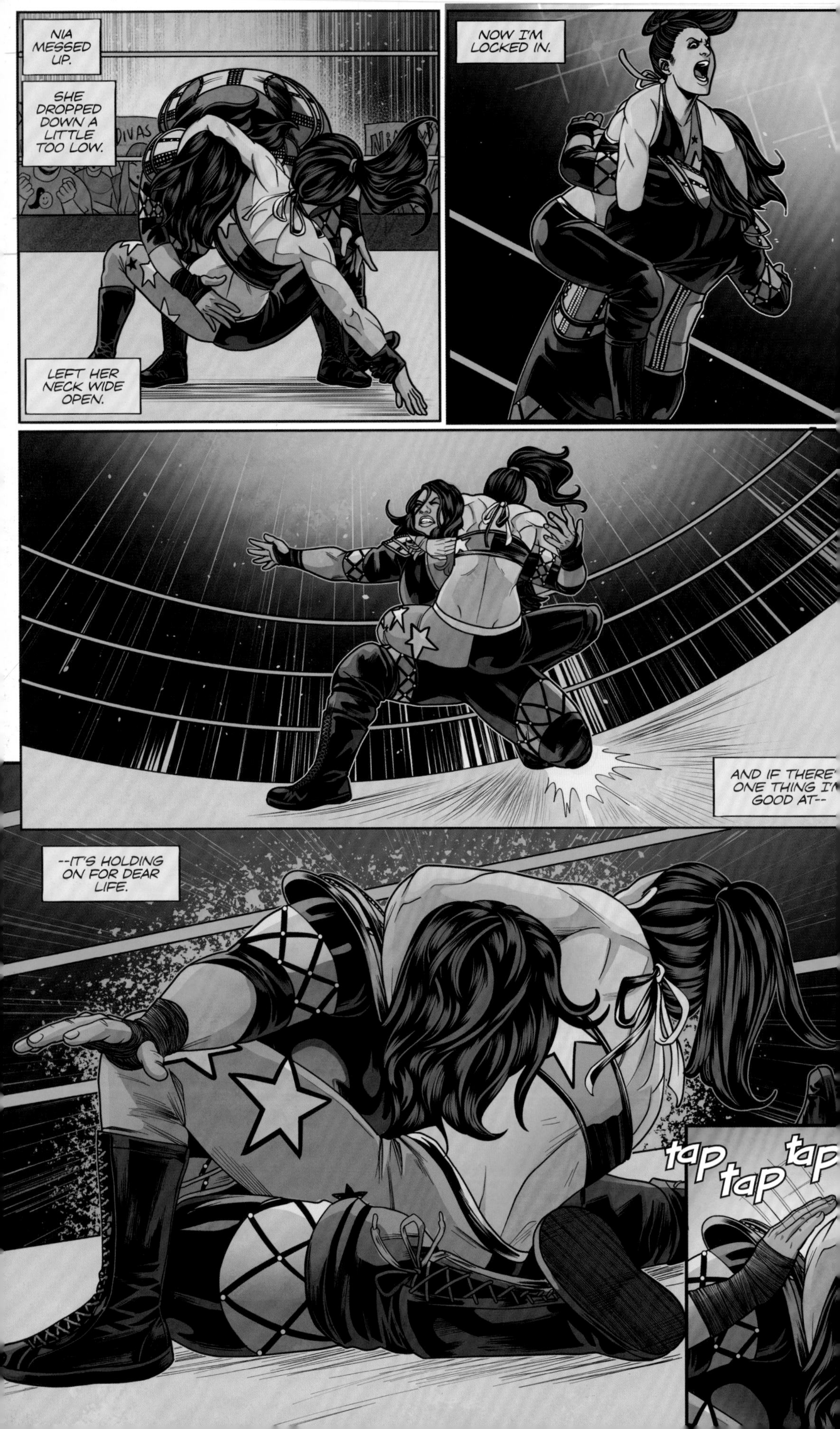

NIA MESSED UP.
SHE DROPPED DOWN A LITTLE TOO LOW.
LEFT HER NECK WIDE OPEN.
NOW I'M LOCKED IN.
AND IF THERE'S ONE THING I'M GOOD AT--
--IT'S HOLDING ON FOR DEAR LIFE.
tap tap tap

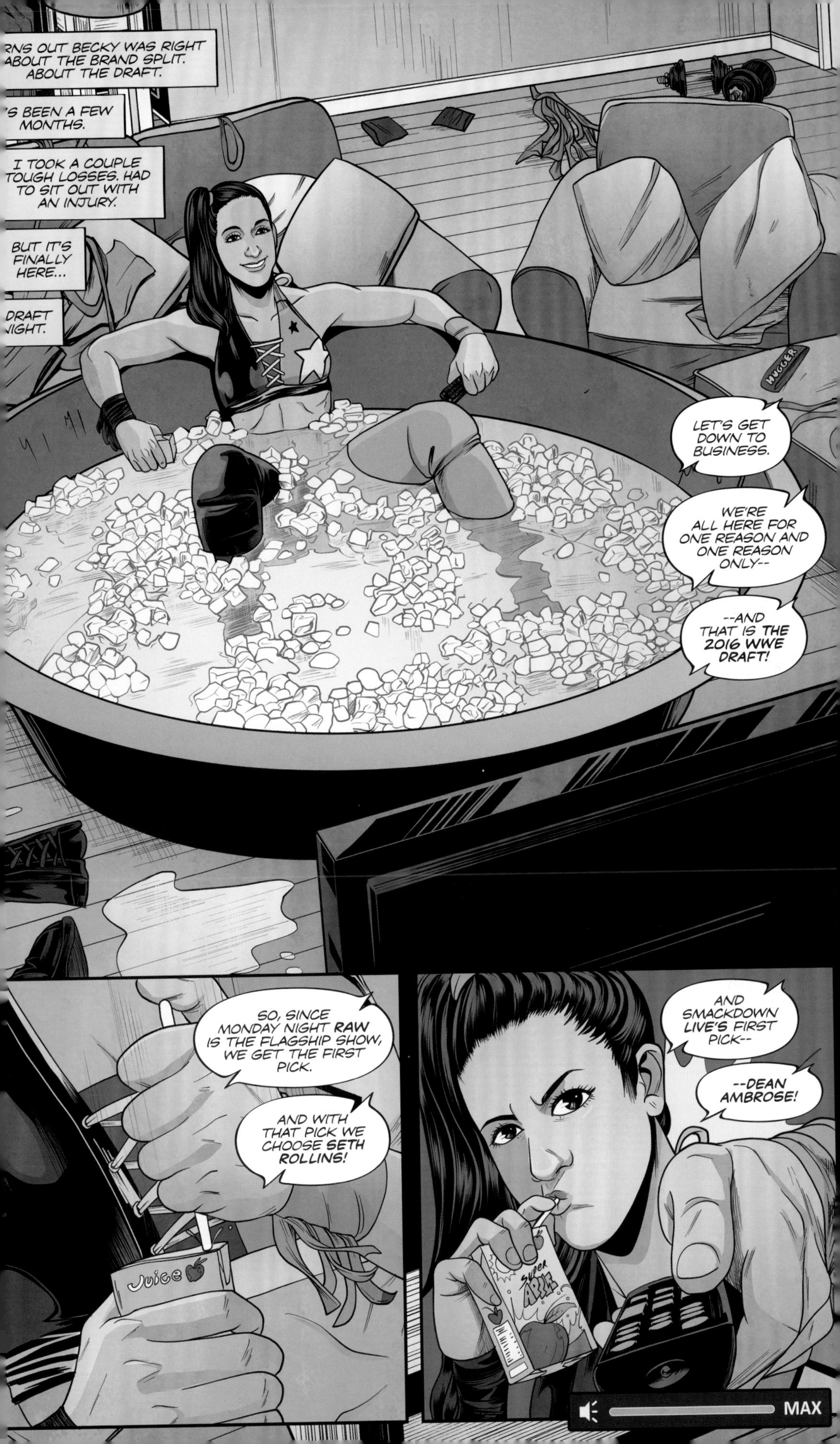
RNS OUT BECKY WAS RIGHT ABOUT THE BRAND SPLIT. ABOUT THE DRAFT.
'S BEEN A FEW MONTHS.
I TOOK A COUPLE TOUGH LOSSES. HAD TO SIT OUT WITH AN INJURY.
BUT IT'S FINALLY HERE...
DRAFT IGHT.
HUGGER
LET'S GET DOWN TO BUSINESS.
WE'RE ALL HERE FOR ONE REASON AND ONE REASON ONLY--
--AND THAT IS THE 2016 WWE DRAFT!
SO, SINCE MONDAY NIGHT RAW IS THE FLAGSHIP SHOW, WE GET THE FIRST PICK.
AND WITH THAT PICK WE CHOOSE SETH ROLLINS!
Juice
AND SMACKDOWN LIVE'S FIRST PICK--
--DEAN AMBROSE!
SUPER APPLE
MAX

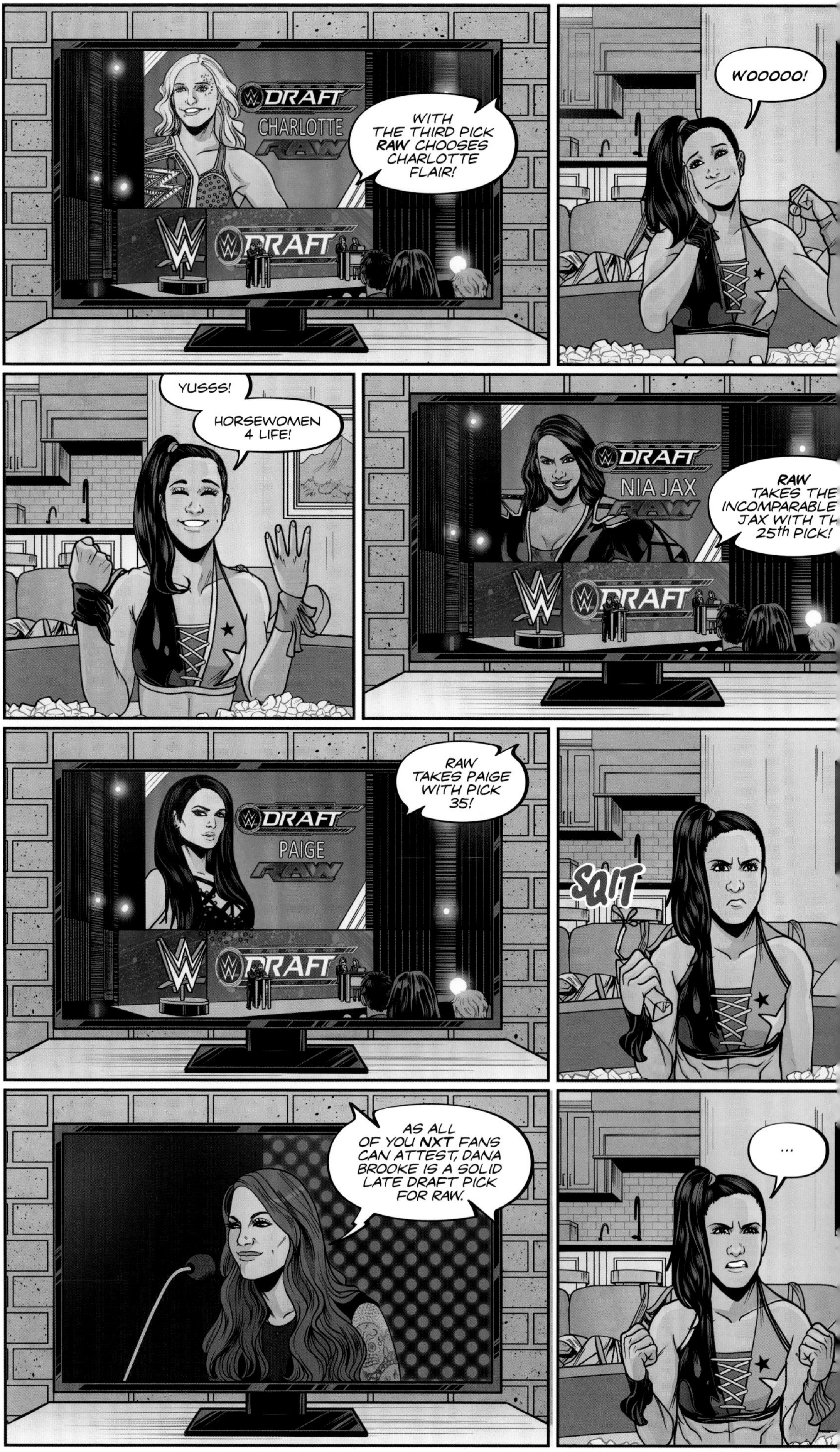
DRAFT
CHARLOTTE
RAW
DRAFT
WITH THE THIRD PICK RAW CHOOSES CHARLOTTE FLAIR!
WOOOOO!
YUSSS!
HORSEWOMEN 4 LIFE!
DRAFT
NIA JAX
RAW
DRAFT
RAW TAKES THE INCOMPARABLE JAX WITH TH 25th PICK!
DRAFT
PAIGE
RAW
DRAFT
RAW TAKES PAIGE WITH PICK 35!
SQIT
AS ALL OF YOU NXT FANS CAN ATTEST, DANA BROOKE IS A SOLID LATE DRAFT PICK FOR RAW.
...

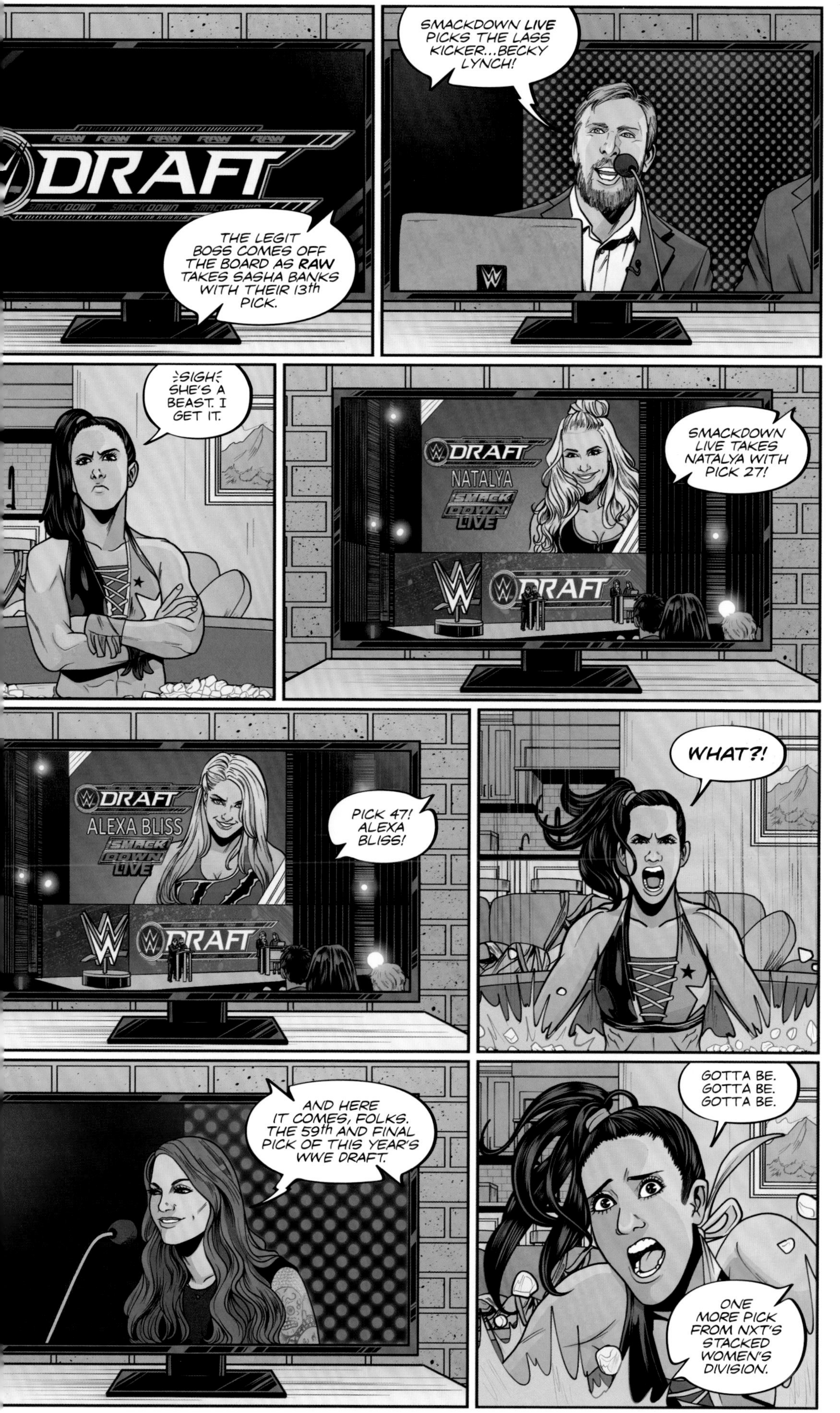
RAW RAW RAW RAW RAW
DRAFT
SMACKDOWN SMACKDOWN
THE LEGIT BOSS COMES OFF THE BOARD AS RAW TAKES SASHA BANKS WITH THEIR 13th PICK.
SMACKDOWN LIVE PICKS THE LASS KICKER...BECKY LYNCH!
SIGH SHE'S A BEAST. I GET IT.
DRAFT
NATALYA
SMACK DOWN LIVE
DRAFT
SMACKDOWN LIVE TAKES NATALYA WITH PICK 27!
DRAFT
ALEXA BLISS
SMACK DOWN LIVE
DRAFT
PICK 47! ALEXA BLISS!
WHAT?!
AND HERE IT COMES, FOLKS. THE 59th AND FINAL PICK OF THIS YEAR'S WWE DRAFT.
GOTTA BE. GOTTA BE. GOTTA BE.
ONE MORE PICK FROM NXT'S STACKED WOMEN'S DIVISION.

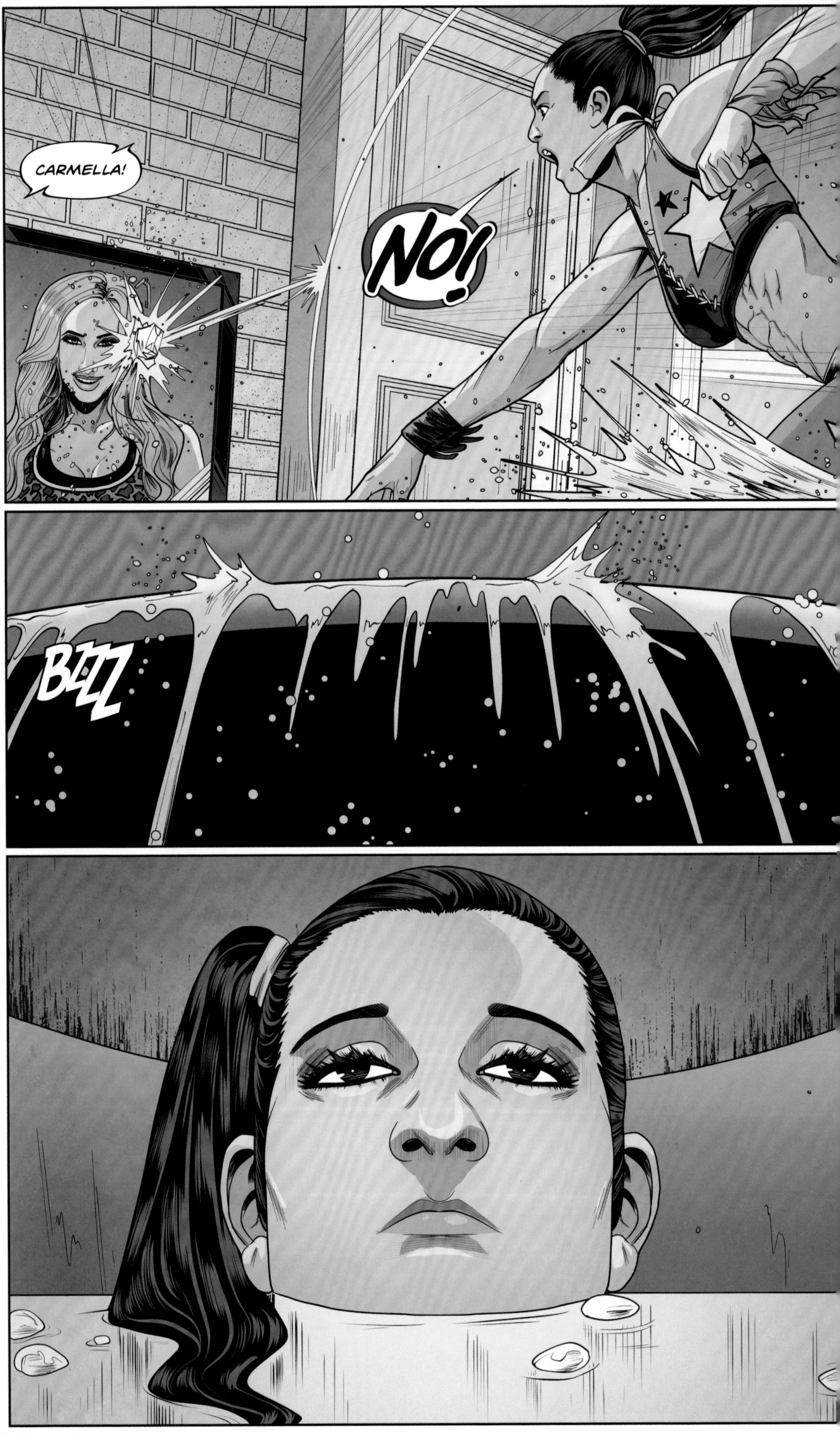
CARMELLA!
NO!
BZZZ

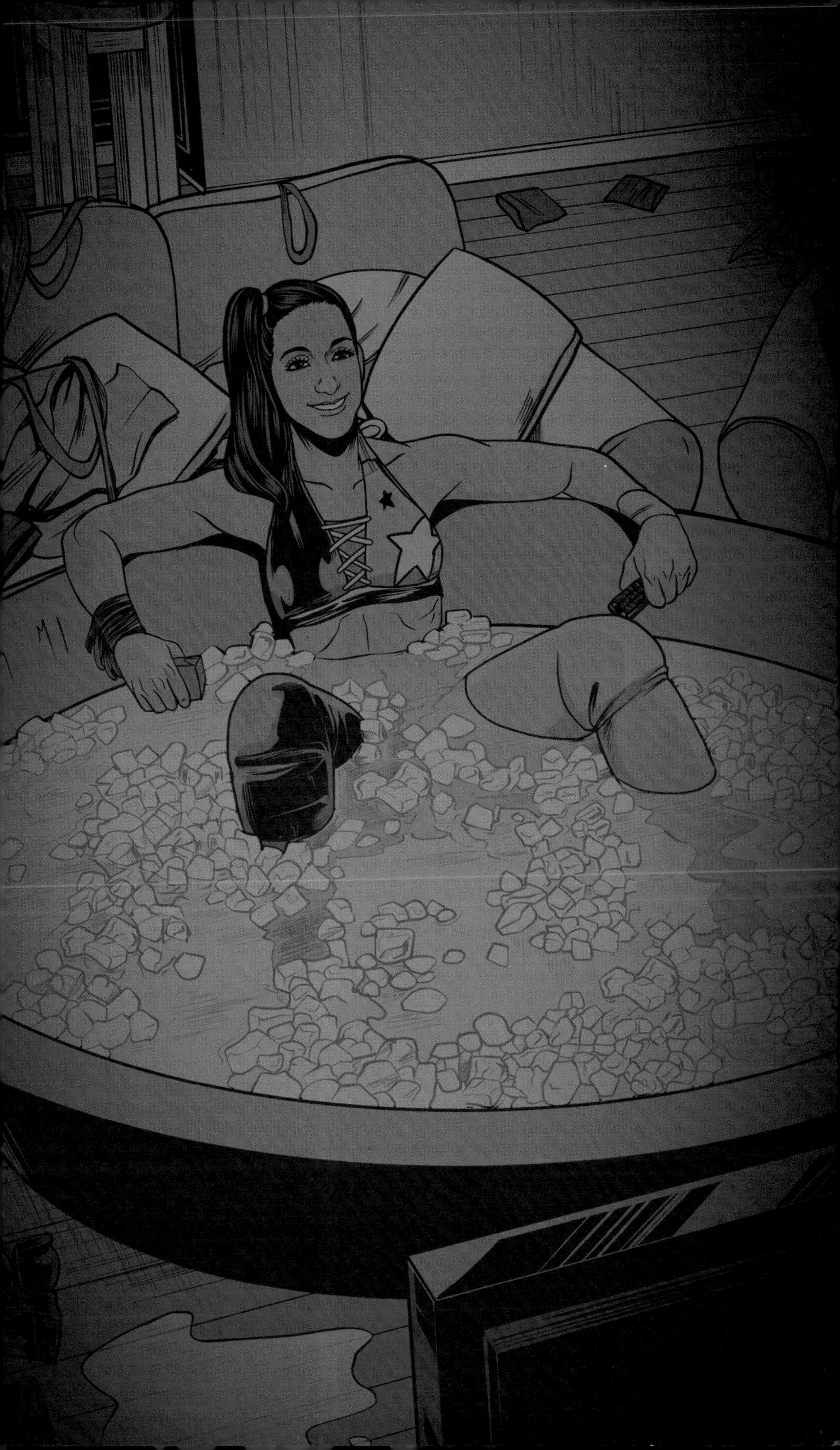

CHAPTER FOUR

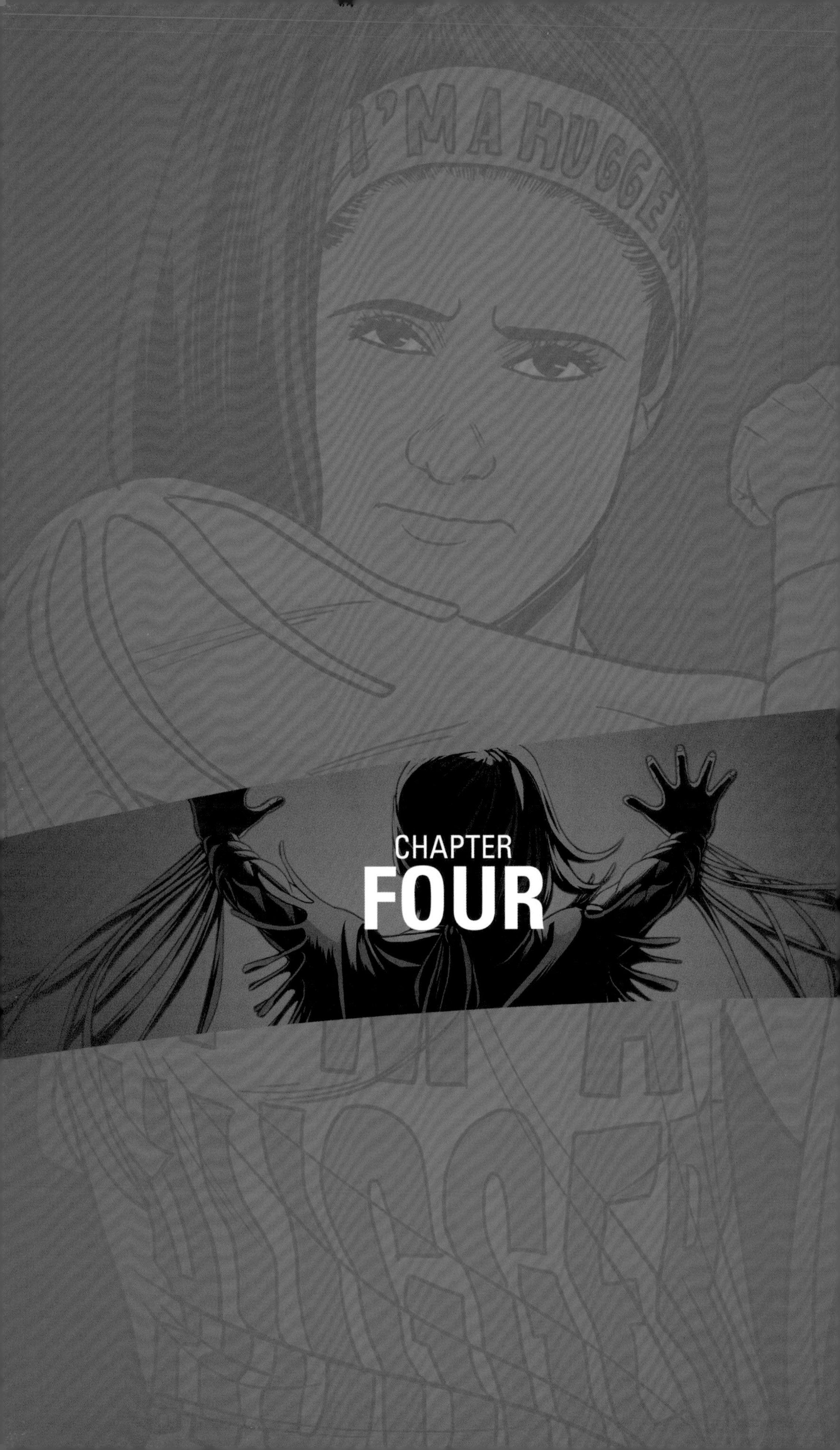
I'M A HUGGER

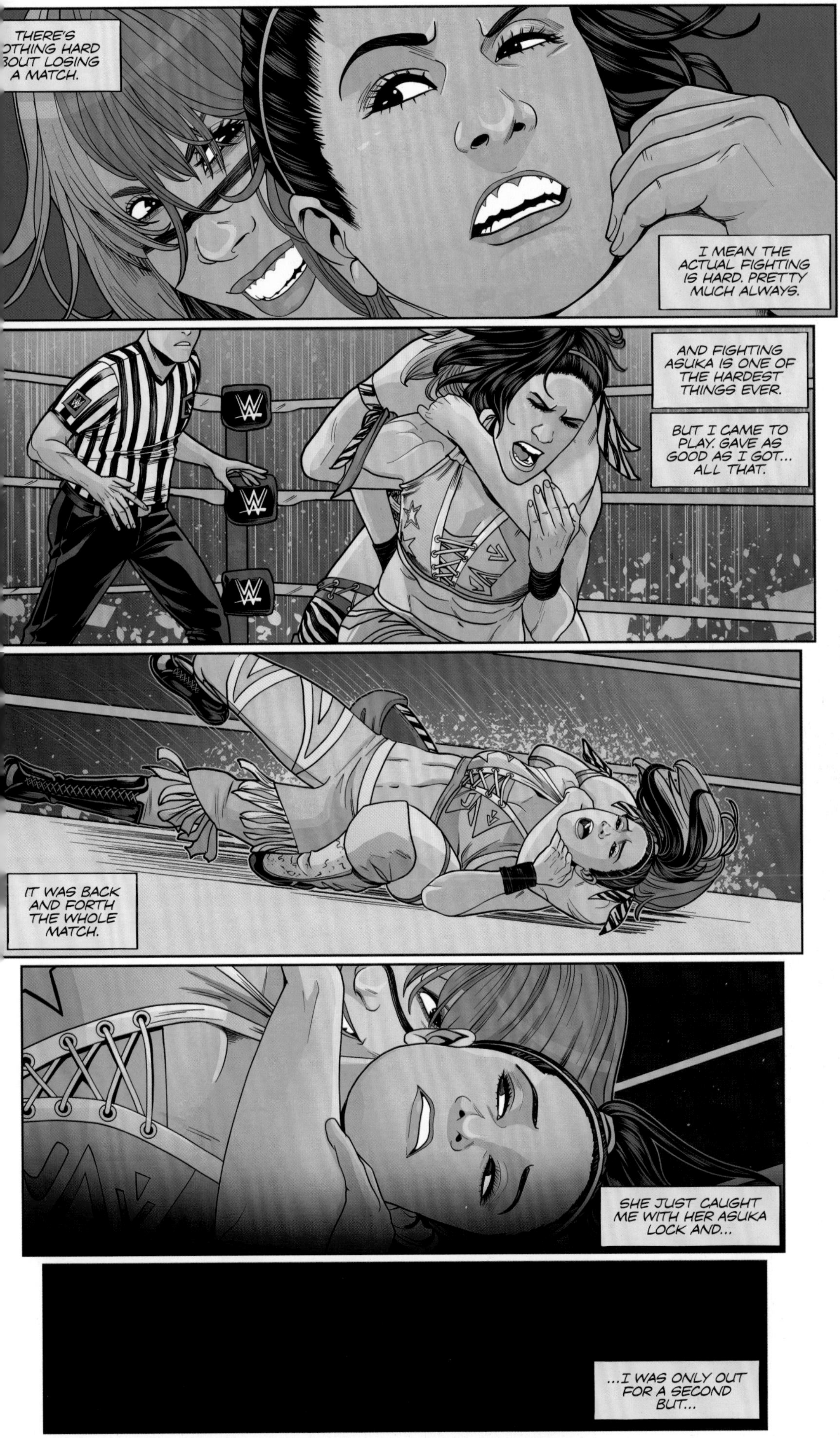
THERE'S
OTHING HARD
BOUT LOSING
A MATCH.
I MEAN THE ACTUAL FIGHTING IS HARD. PRETTY MUCH ALWAYS.
AND FIGHTING ASUKA IS ONE OF THE HARDEST THINGS EVER.
BUT I CAME TO PLAY. GAVE AS GOOD AS I GOT... ALL THAT.
IT WAS BACK AND FORTH THE WHOLE MATCH.
SHE JUST CAUGHT ME WITH HER ASUKA LOCK AND...
...I WAS ONLY OUT FOR A SECOND BUT...

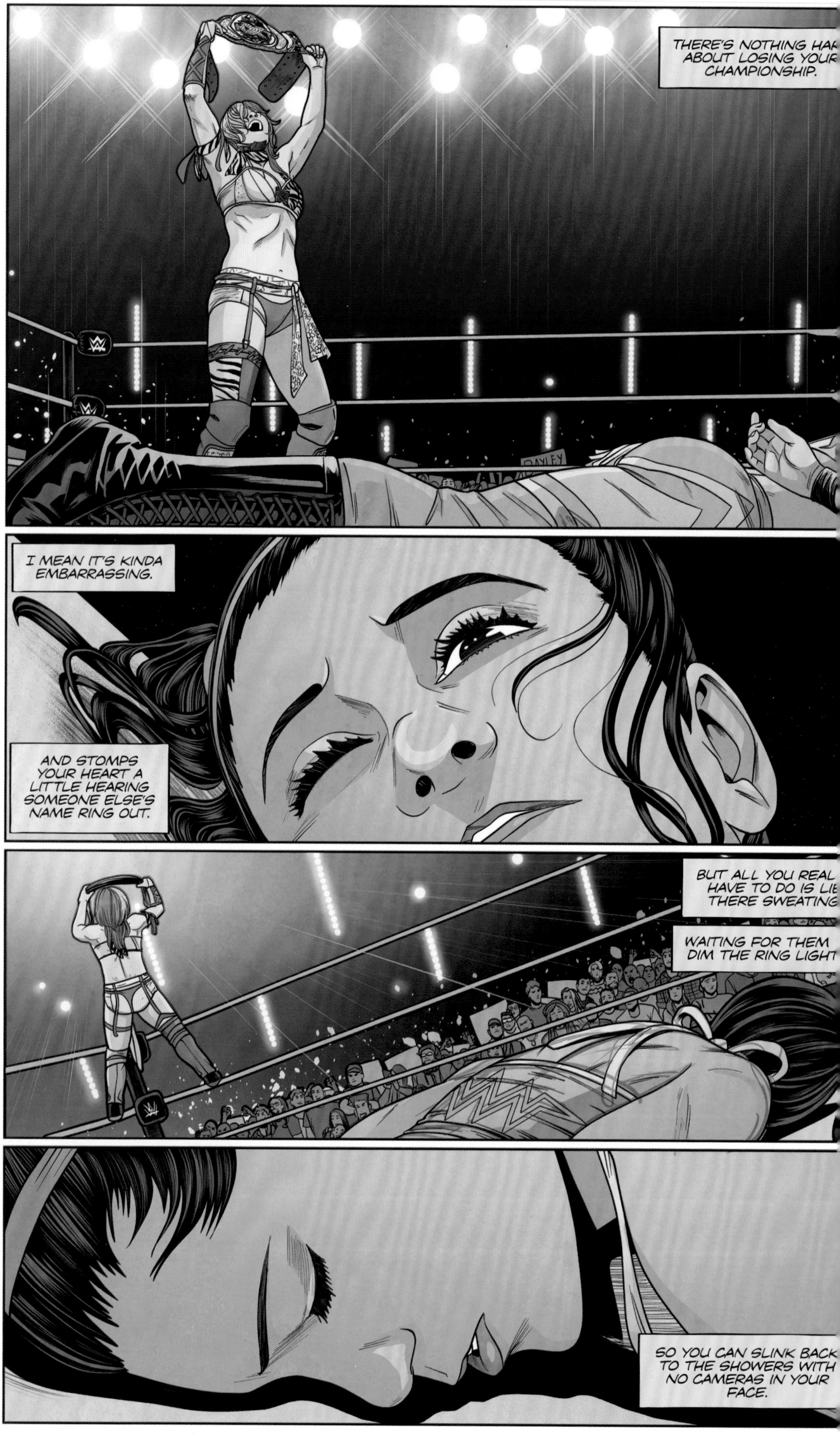
THERE'S NOTHING HAR
ABOUT LOSING YOUR
CHAMPIONSHIP.
I MEAN IT'S KINDA EMBARRASSING.
AND STOMPS YOUR HEART A LITTLE HEARING SOMEONE ELSE'S NAME RING OUT.
BUT ALL YOU REAL
HAVE TO DO IS LIE
THERE SWEATING
WAITING FOR THEM
DIM THE RING LIGHT
SO YOU CAN SLINK BACK TO THE SHOWERS WITH NO CAMERAS IN YOUR FACE.

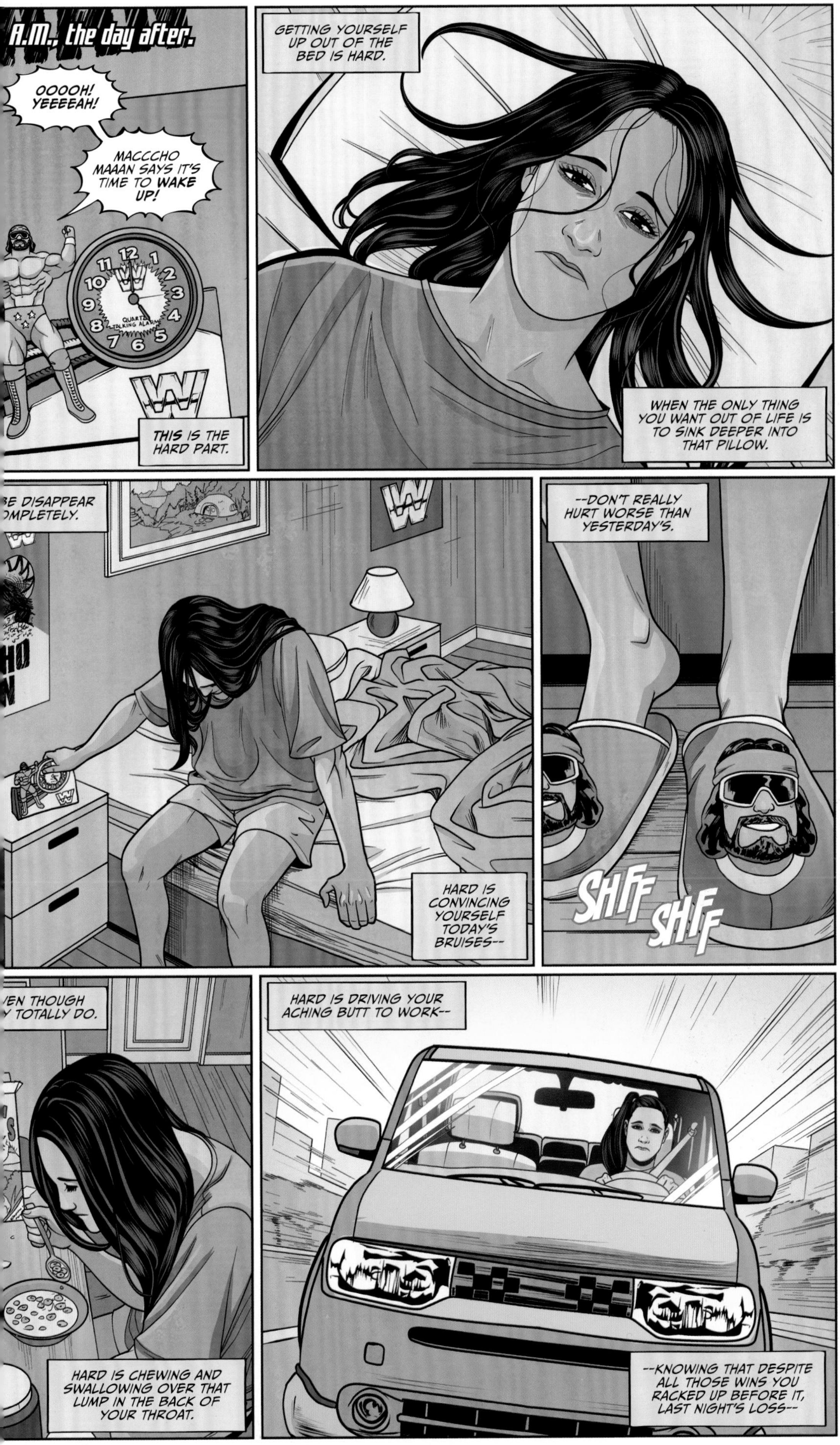
A.M., the day after.
OOOOH! YEEEEAH!
MACCCHO MAAAN SAYS IT'S TIME TO WAKE UP!
QUARTZ TALKING ALARM
THIS IS THE HARD PART.
GETTING YOURSELF UP OUT OF THE BED IS HARD.
WHEN THE ONLY THING YOU WANT OUT OF LIFE IS TO SINK DEEPER INTO THAT PILLOW.
BE DISAPPEAR OMPLETELY.
HARD IS CONVINCING YOURSELF TODAY'S BRUISES--
--DON'T REALLY HURT WORSE THAN YESTERDAY'S.
SHFF SHFF
VEN THOUGH Y TOTALLY DO.
HARD IS CHEWING AND SWALLOWING OVER THAT LUMP IN THE BACK OF YOUR THROAT.
HARD IS DRIVING YOUR ACHING BUTT TO WORK--
--KNOWING THAT DESPITE ALL THOSE WINS YOU RACKED UP BEFORE IT, LAST NIGHT'S LOSS--

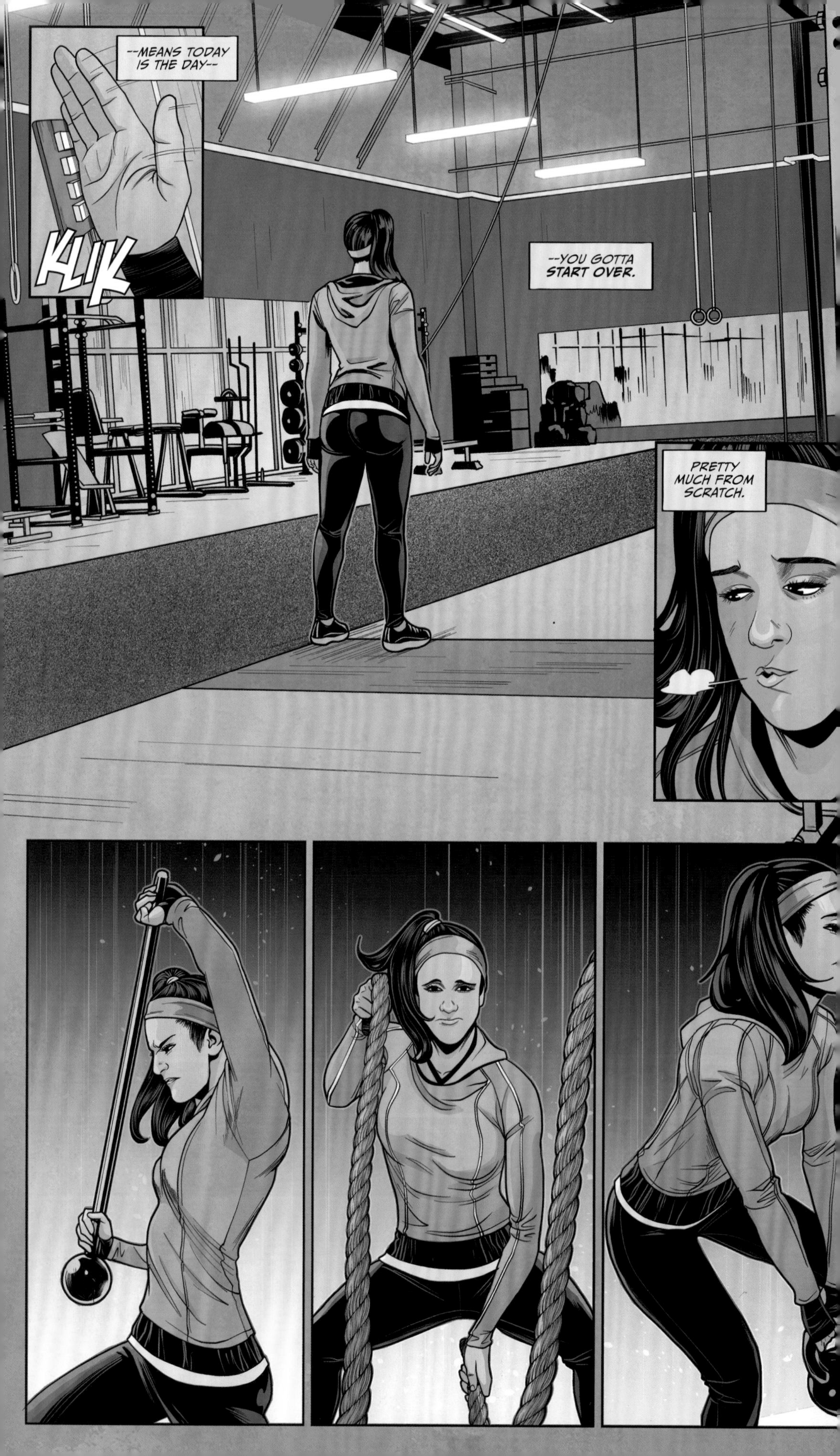
--MEANS TODAY IS THE DAY--
KLIK
--YOU GOTTA START OVER.
PRETTY MUCH FROM SCRATCH.

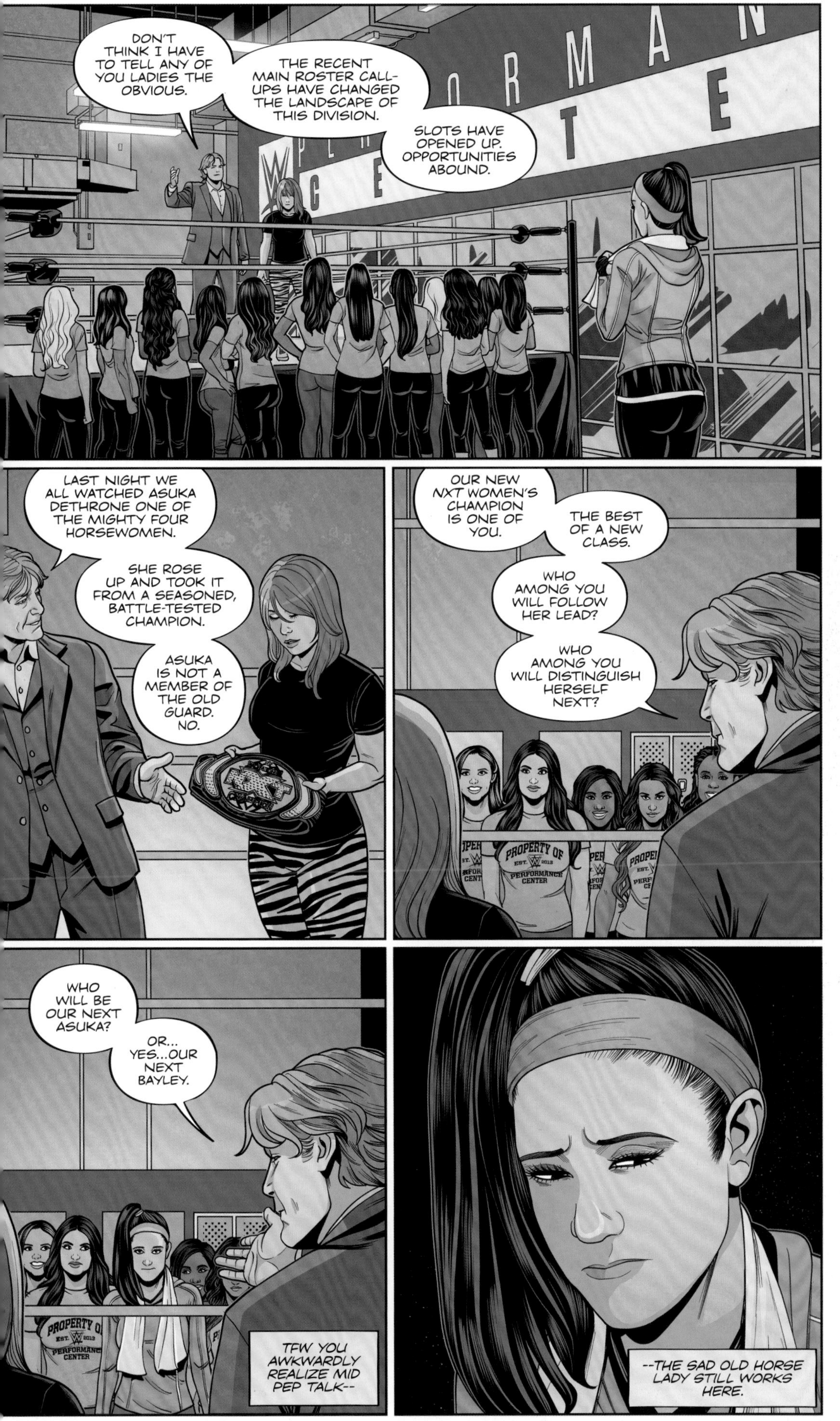
DON'T THINK I HAVE TO TELL ANY OF YOU LADIES THE OBVIOUS.
THE RECENT MAIN ROSTER CALL-UPS HAVE CHANGED THE LANDSCAPE OF THIS DIVISION.
SLOTS HAVE OPENED UP. OPPORTUNITIES ABOUND.
LAST NIGHT WE ALL WATCHED ASUKA DETHRONE ONE OF THE MIGHTY FOUR HORSEWOMEN.
SHE ROSE UP AND TOOK IT FROM A SEASONED, BATTLE-TESTED CHAMPION.
ASUKA IS NOT A MEMBER OF THE OLD GUARD. NO.
OUR NEW NXT WOMEN'S CHAMPION IS ONE OF YOU.
THE BEST OF A NEW CLASS.
WHO AMONG YOU WILL FOLLOW HER LEAD?
WHO AMONG YOU WILL DISTINGUISH HERSELF NEXT?
WHO WILL BE OUR NEXT ASUKA?
OR... YES...OUR NEXT BAYLEY.
TFW YOU AWKWARDLY REALIZE MID PEP TALK--
--THE SAD OLD HORSE LADY STILL WORKS HERE.

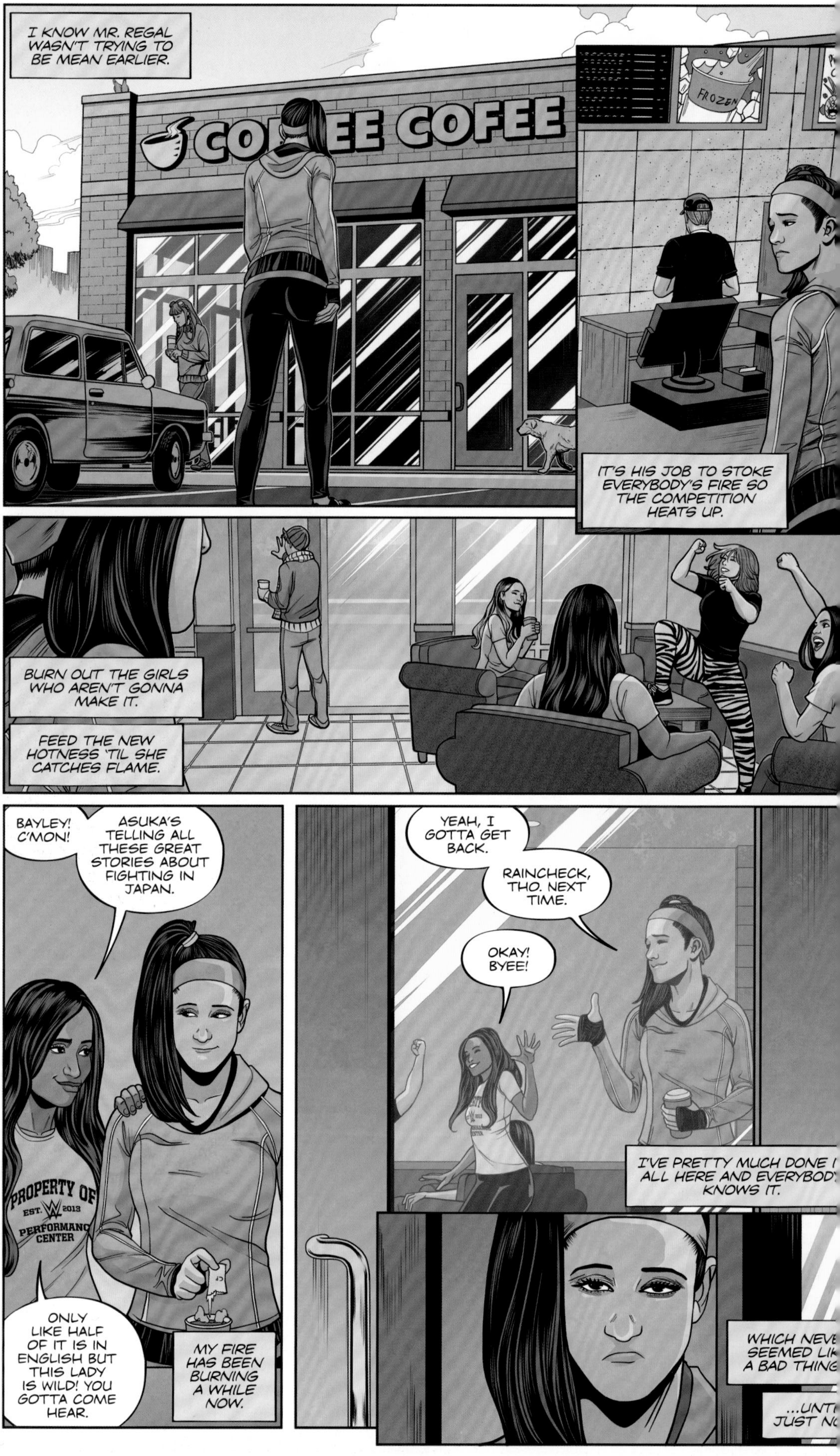

I KNOW MR. REGAL WASN'T TRYING TO BE MEAN EARLIER.
COFFEE COFEE
FROZEN
IT'S HIS JOB TO STOKE EVERYBODY'S FIRE SO THE COMPETITION HEATS UP.
BURN OUT THE GIRLS WHO AREN'T GONNA MAKE IT.
FEED THE NEW HOTNESS 'TIL SHE CATCHES FLAME.
BAYLEY! C'MON!
ASUKA'S TELLING ALL THESE GREAT STORIES ABOUT FIGHTING IN JAPAN.
PROPERTY OF
EST. 2013
PERFORMANC
CENTER
ONLY LIKE HALF OF IT IS IN ENGLISH BUT THIS LADY IS WILD! YOU GOTTA COME HEAR.
MY FIRE HAS BEEN BURNING A WHILE NOW.
YEAH, I GOTTA GET BACK.
RAINCHECK, THO. NEXT TIME.
OKAY! BYEE!
I'VE PRETTY MUCH DONE I ALL HERE AND EVERYBOD KNOWS IT.
WHICH NEVE SEEMED LIK A BAD THING
...UNT JUST N

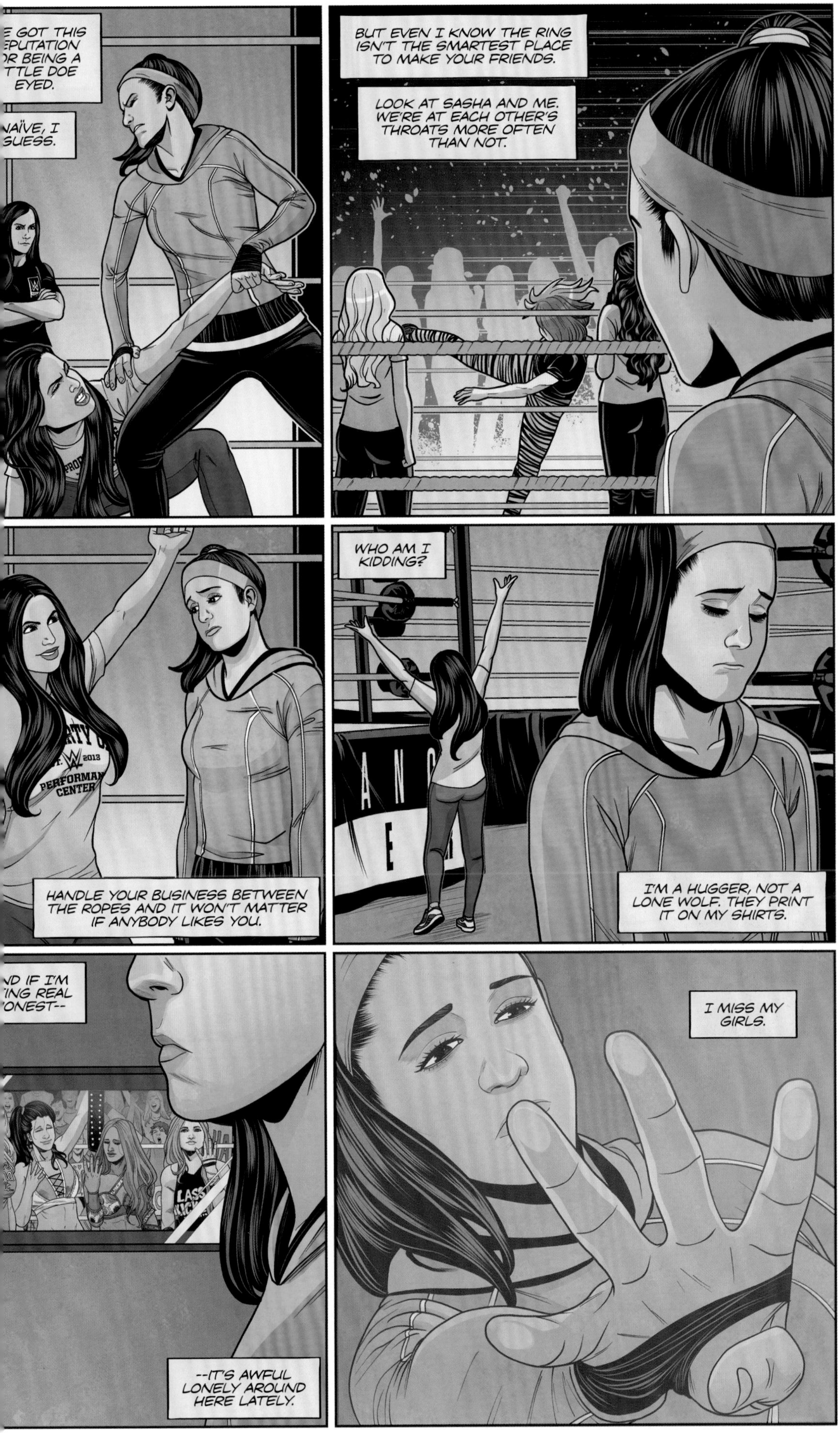
E GOT THIS
EPUTATION
OR BEING A
TTLE DOE
EYED.
NAÏVE, I
GUESS.
BUT EVEN I KNOW THE RING ISN'T THE SMARTEST PLACE TO MAKE YOUR FRIENDS.
LOOK AT SASHA AND ME. WE'RE AT EACH OTHER'S THROATS MORE OFTEN THAN NOT.
PERFORMAN
CENTER
HANDLE YOUR BUSINESS BETWEEN THE ROPES AND IT WON'T MATTER IF ANYBODY LIKES YOU.
WHO AM I KIDDING?
I'M A HUGGER, NOT A LONE WOLF. THEY PRINT IT ON MY SHIRTS.
ND IF I'M
ING REAL
ONEST--
--IT'S AWFUL LONELY AROUND HERE LATELY.
I MISS MY GIRLS.

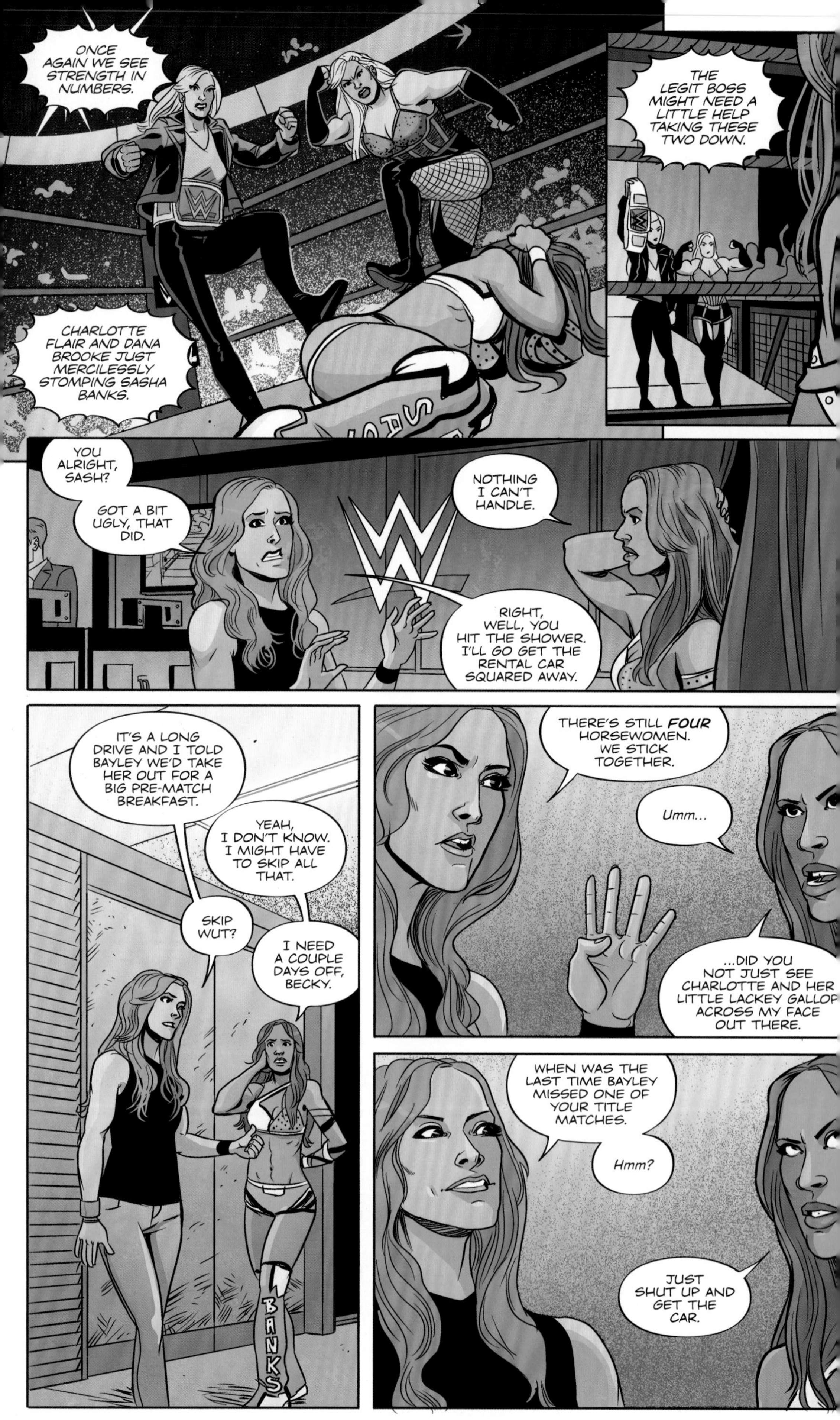
ONCE AGAIN WE SEE STRENGTH IN NUMBERS.
CHARLOTTE FLAIR AND DANA BROOKE JUST MERCILESSLY STOMPING SASHA BANKS.
THE LEGIT BOSS MIGHT NEED A LITTLE HELP TAKING THESE TWO DOWN.
YOU ALRIGHT, SASH?
GOT A BIT UGLY, THAT DID.
NOTHING I CAN'T HANDLE.
RIGHT, WELL, YOU HIT THE SHOWER. I'LL GO GET THE RENTAL CAR SQUARED AWAY.
IT'S A LONG DRIVE AND I TOLD BAYLEY WE'D TAKE HER OUT FOR A BIG PRE-MATCH BREAKFAST.
YEAH, I DON'T KNOW. I MIGHT HAVE TO SKIP ALL THAT.
SKIP WUT?
I NEED A COUPLE DAYS OFF, BECKY.
BANKS
THERE'S STILL **FOUR** HORSEWOMEN. WE STICK TOGETHER.
Umm...
...DID YOU NOT JUST SEE CHARLOTTE AND HER LITTLE LACKEY GALLOP ACROSS MY FACE OUT THERE.
WHEN WAS THE LAST TIME BAYLEY MISSED ONE OF YOUR TITLE MATCHES.
Hmm?
JUST SHUT UP AND GET THE CAR.

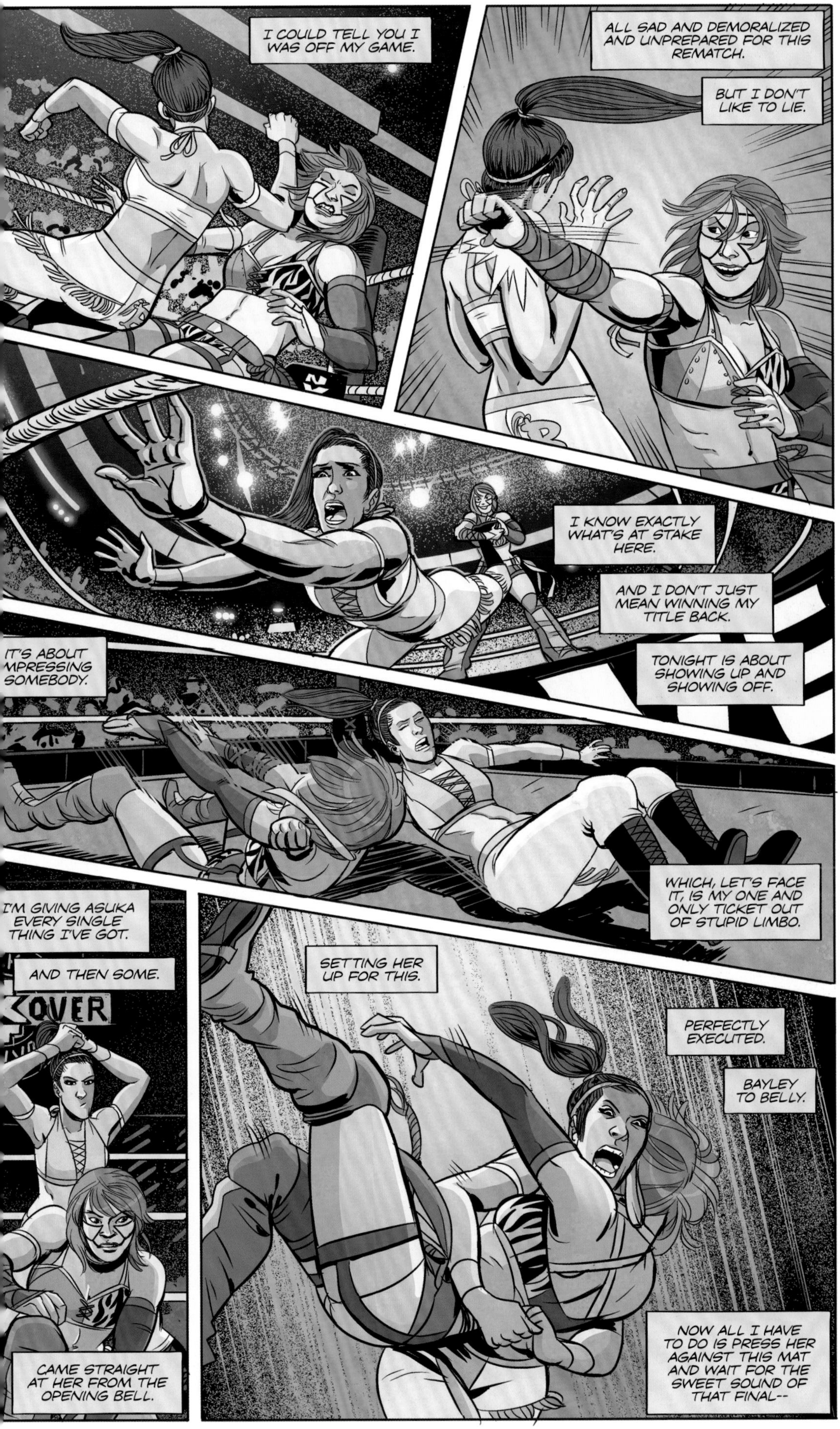
I COULD TELL YOU I WAS OFF MY GAME.
ALL SAD AND DEMORALIZED AND UNPREPARED FOR THIS REMATCH.
BUT I DON'T LIKE TO LIE.
I KNOW EXACTLY WHAT'S AT STAKE HERE.
AND I DON'T JUST MEAN WINNING MY TITLE BACK.
IT'S ABOUT IMPRESSING SOMEBODY.
TONIGHT IS ABOUT SHOWING UP AND SHOWING OFF.
WHICH, LET'S FACE IT, IS MY ONE AND ONLY TICKET OUT OF STUPID LIMBO.
I'M GIVING ASUKA EVERY SINGLE THING I'VE GOT.
AND THEN SOME.
CAME STRAIGHT AT HER FROM THE OPENING BELL.
SETTING HER UP FOR THIS.
PERFECTLY EXECUTED.
BAYLEY TO BELLY.
NOW ALL I HAVE TO DO IS PRESS HER AGAINST THIS MAT AND WAIT FOR THE SWEET SOUND OF THAT FINAL--

THAT'S TWO!

SHE KICKE OUT.

THAK

Uh oh.

DIFFEREN ENDING.

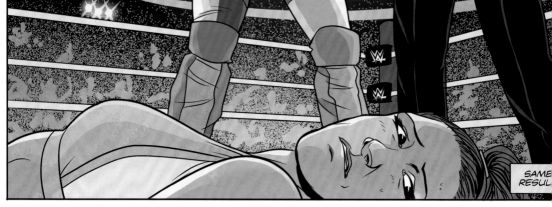

SAME RESUL

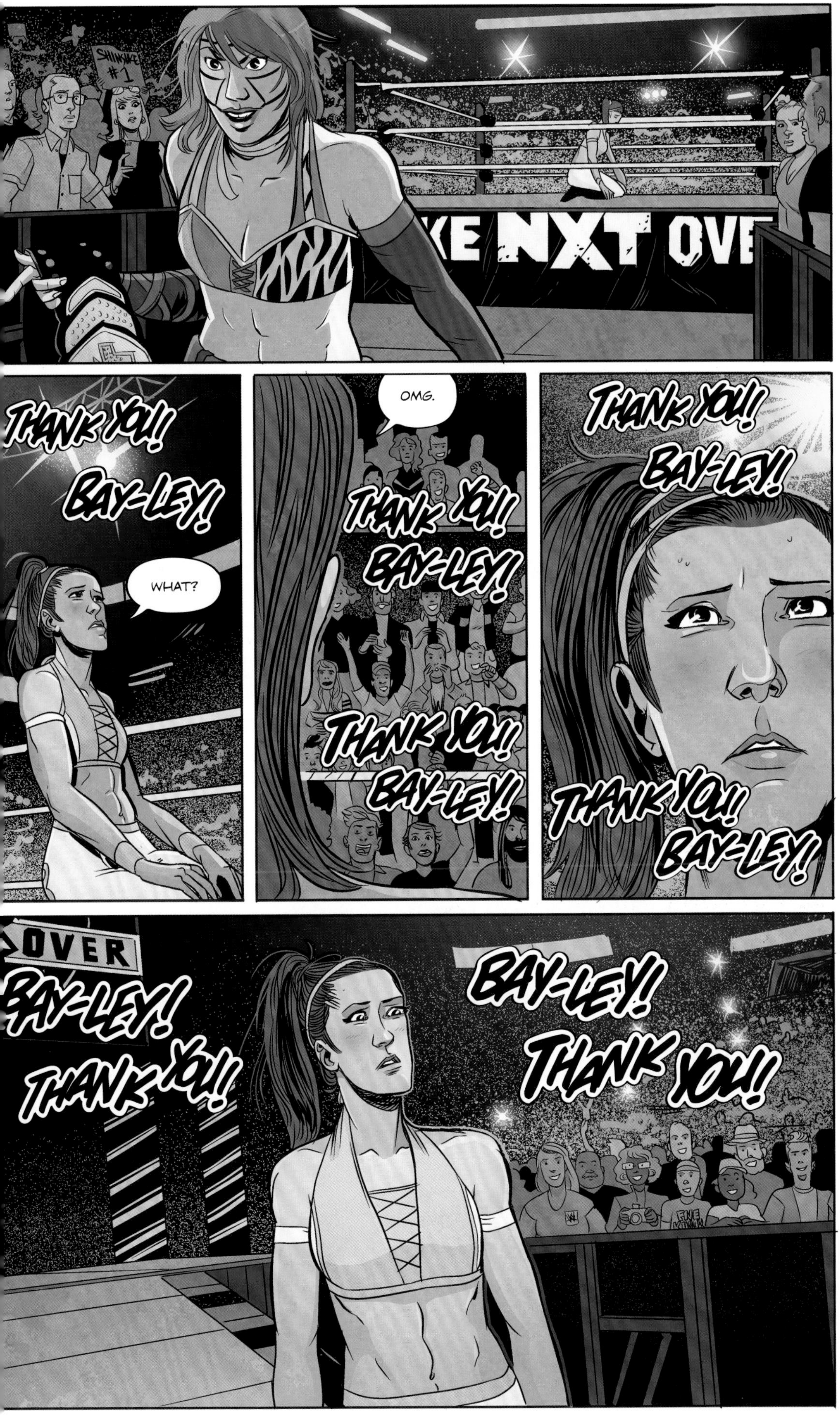
SHINSUKE #1
KE NXT OVE
THANK YOU!
BAY-LEY!
WHAT?
OMG.
THANK YOU!
BAY-LEY!
THANK YOU!
BAY-LEY!
THANK YOU!
BAY-LEY!
THANK YOU!
BAY-LEY!
OVER
BAY-LEY!
THANK YOU!
BAY-LEY!
THANK YOU!

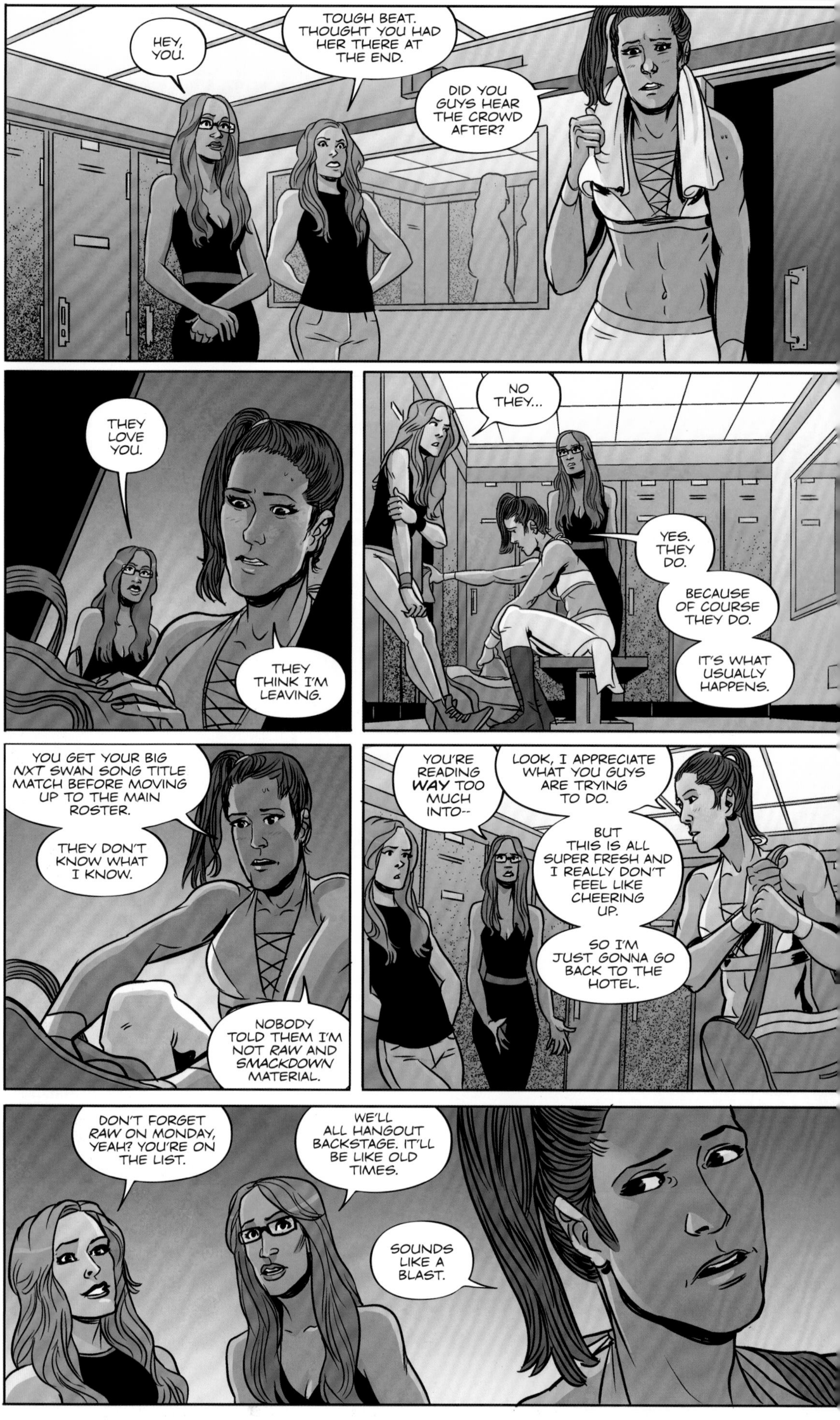
HEY, YOU.
TOUGH BEAT. THOUGHT YOU HAD HER THERE AT THE END.
DID YOU GUYS HEAR THE CROWD AFTER?
THEY LOVE YOU.
THEY THINK I'M LEAVING.
NO THEY...
YES. THEY DO.
BECAUSE OF COURSE THEY DO.
IT'S WHAT USUALLY HAPPENS.
YOU GET YOUR BIG NXT SWAN SONG TITLE MATCH BEFORE MOVING UP TO THE MAIN ROSTER.
THEY DON'T KNOW WHAT I KNOW.
NOBODY TOLD THEM I'M NOT *RAW* AND *SMACKDOWN* MATERIAL.
YOU'RE READING **WAY** TOO MUCH INTO--
LOOK, I APPRECIATE WHAT YOU GUYS ARE TRYING TO DO.
BUT THIS IS ALL SUPER FRESH AND I REALLY DON'T FEEL LIKE CHEERING UP.
SO I'M JUST GONNA GO BACK TO THE HOTEL.
DON'T FORGET *RAW* ON MONDAY, YEAH? YOU'RE ON THE LIST.
WE'LL ALL HANGOUT BACKSTAGE. IT'LL BE LIKE OLD TIMES.
SOUNDS LIKE A BLAST.

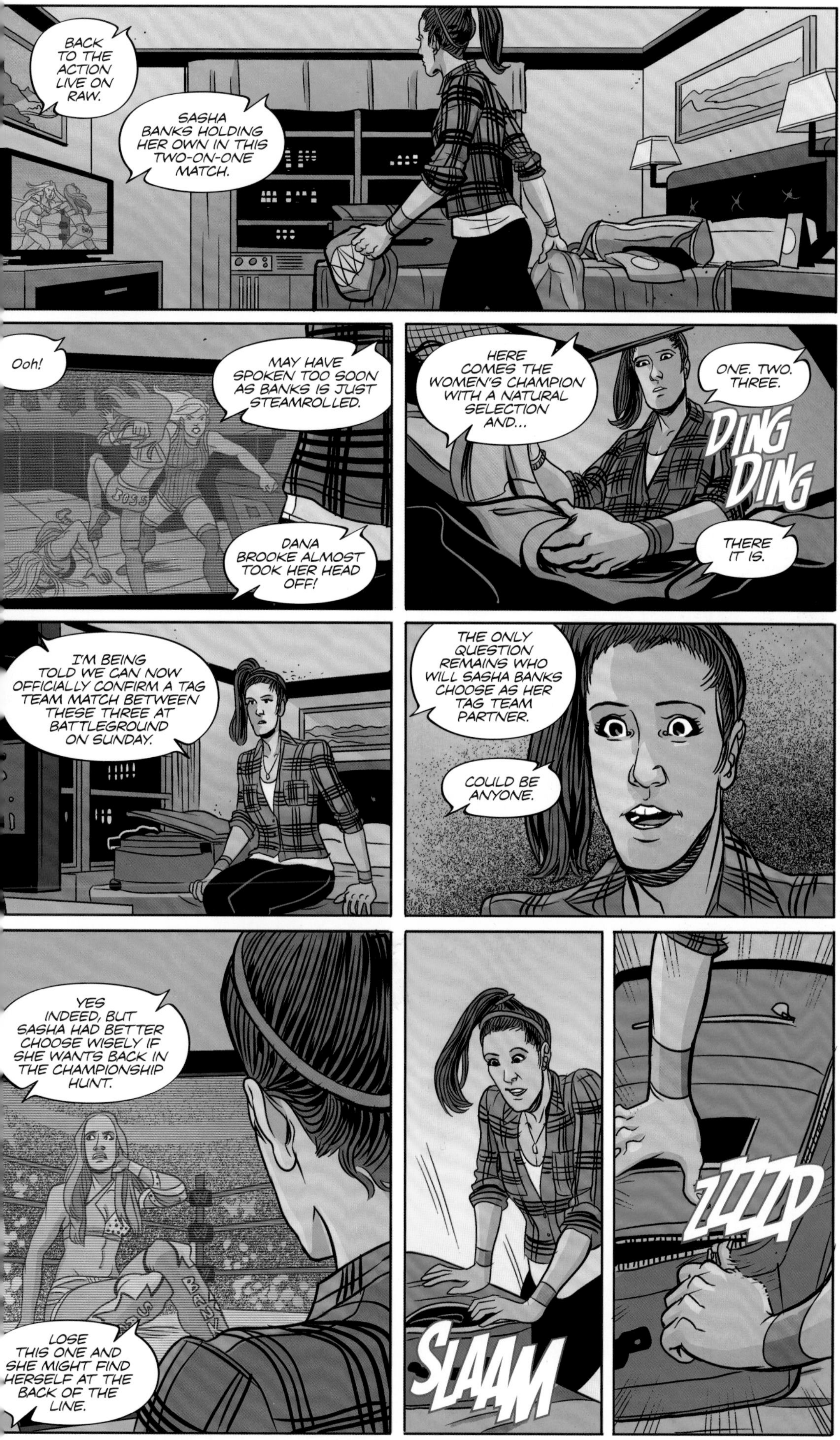
BACK TO THE ACTION LIVE ON RAW.
SASHA BANKS HOLDING HER OWN IN THIS TWO-ON-ONE MATCH.
Ooh!
MAY HAVE SPOKEN TOO SOON AS BANKS IS JUST STEAMROLLED.
DANA BROOKE ALMOST TOOK HER HEAD OFF!
HERE COMES THE WOMEN'S CHAMPION WITH A NATURAL SELECTION AND...
ONE. TWO. THREE.
DING DING
THERE IT IS.
I'M BEING TOLD WE CAN NOW OFFICIALLY CONFIRM A TAG TEAM MATCH BETWEEN THESE THREE AT BATTLEGROUND ON SUNDAY.
THE ONLY QUESTION REMAINS WHO WILL SASHA BANKS CHOOSE AS HER TAG TEAM PARTNER.
COULD BE ANYONE.
YES INDEED, BUT SASHA HAD BETTER CHOOSE WISELY IF SHE WANTS BACK IN THE CHAMPIONSHIP HUNT.
LOSE THIS ONE AND SHE MIGHT FIND HERSELF AT THE BACK OF THE LINE.
SLAAM
ZZZZP

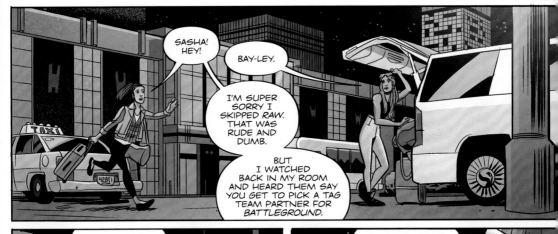

SASHA! HEY!

BAY-LEY.

I'M SUPER SORRY I SKIPPED RAW. THAT WAS RUDE AND DUMB.

BUT I WATCHED BACK IN MY ROOM AND HEARD THEM SAY YOU GET TO PICK A TAG TEAM PARTNER FOR BATTLEGROUND.

AND THERE'S NOTHING IN MY NXT CONTRACT THAT SAYS I CAN'T COME FIGHT WITH YOU.

BAYLEY--

LOOK I KNOW YOU DON'T LIKE TO MESS AROUND WITH YOUR CAREER. AND I KNOW THERE'S A WHOLE LOCKER ROOM FULL OF LIKE SEASONED VETERANS TO CHOOSE FROM.

I WOULD NEVER EVER ASK YOU TO DO ME THIS AS A FAVOR. NEVER EVER.

BUT I AM STUCK IN THE MUD DOWN THERE AND I CAN FEEL IT STARTING TO BAKE DRY.

I'M RUNNING OUT OF WAYS TO PROVE MYSELF.

A BATTLEGROUND MATCH WITH YOU THOUGH...THAT WOULD BE A REAL SHOT TO GIVE IT MY ALL ON THE BIG STAGE WITH THE BRIGHT LIGHTS.

LET THE WWE UNIVERSE DECIDE WHAT KIND OF TALENT I AM.

EITHER WAY, THERE'S NO ONE ELSE ON THE PLANET WHO'S GONNA GIVE YOU MORE THAN ME.

NO ONE ELSE COULD POSSIBLY CARE THIS MUCH.

ALRIGHT, CALM YOURSELF.

PLEASE, SASH. I NE THIS.

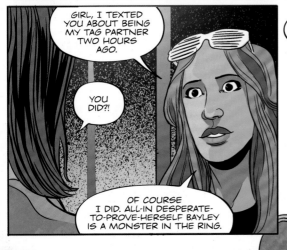

GIRL, I TEXTED YOU ABOUT BEING MY TAG PARTNER TWO HOURS AGO.

YOU DID?!

OF COURSE I DID. ALL-IN DESPERATE-TO-PROVE-HERSELF BAYLEY IS A MONSTER IN THE RING.

EEEEE!

IT'S NOT EVEN A COMPLIMENT. I KNOW THIS FROM RECENT PERSONAL EXPERIENCE.

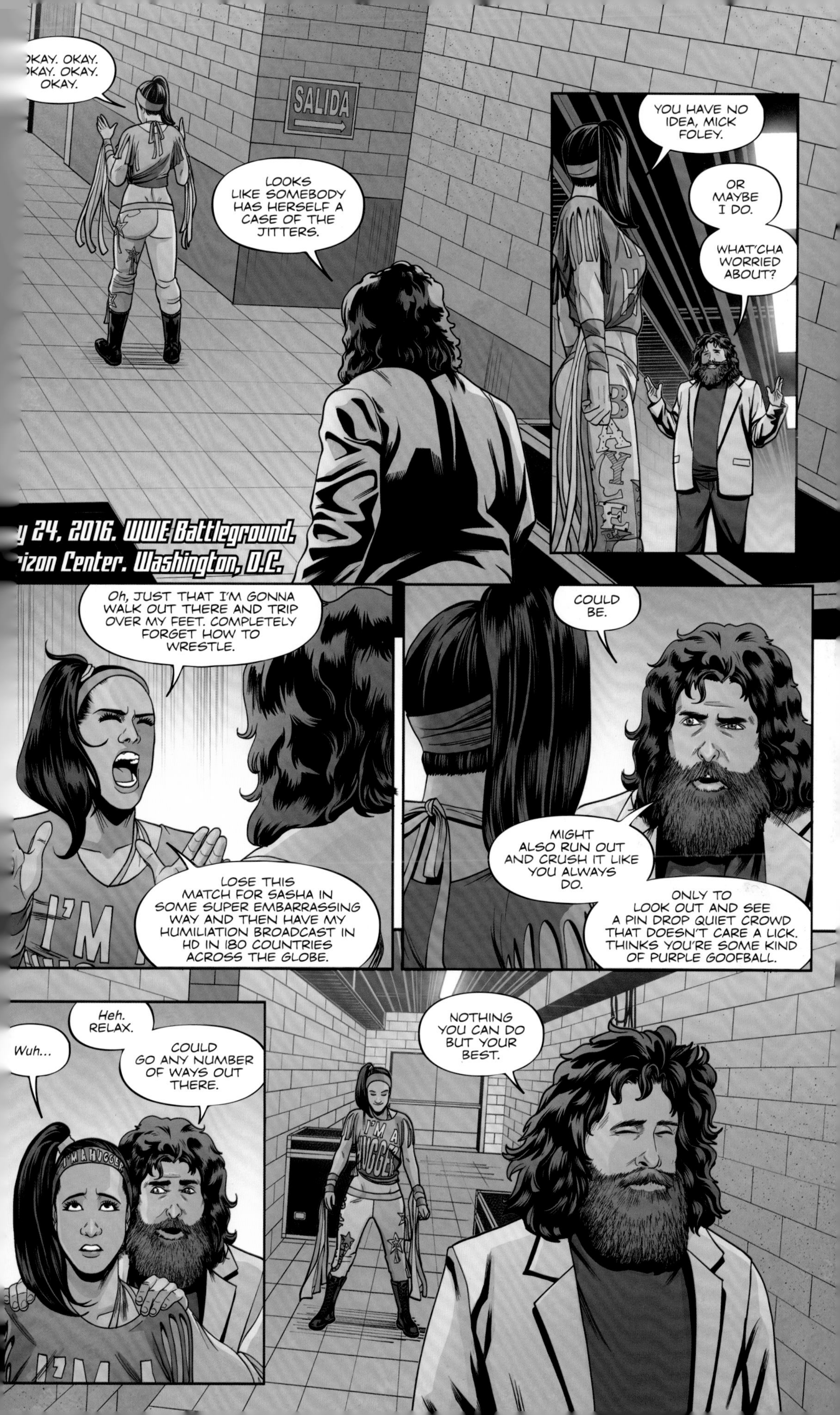
OKAY. OKAY. OKAY. OKAY. OKAY.
SALIDA
LOOKS LIKE SOMEBODY HAS HERSELF A CASE OF THE JITTERS.
y 24, 2016. WWE Battleground. rizon Center. Washington, D.C.
YOU HAVE NO IDEA, MICK FOLEY.
OR MAYBE I DO.
WHAT'CHA WORRIED ABOUT?
Oh, JUST THAT I'M GONNA WALK OUT THERE AND TRIP OVER MY FEET. COMPLETELY FORGET HOW TO WRESTLE.
LOSE THIS MATCH FOR SASHA IN SOME SUPER EMBARRASSING WAY AND THEN HAVE MY HUMILIATION BROADCAST IN HD IN 180 COUNTRIES ACROSS THE GLOBE.
COULD BE.
MIGHT ALSO RUN OUT AND CRUSH IT LIKE YOU ALWAYS DO.
ONLY TO LOOK OUT AND SEE A PIN DROP QUIET CROWD THAT DOESN'T CARE A LICK. THINKS YOU'RE SOME KIND OF PURPLE GOOFBALL.
Wuh...
Heh. RELAX.
COULD GO ANY NUMBER OF WAYS OUT THERE.
NOTHING YOU CAN DO BUT YOUR BEST.

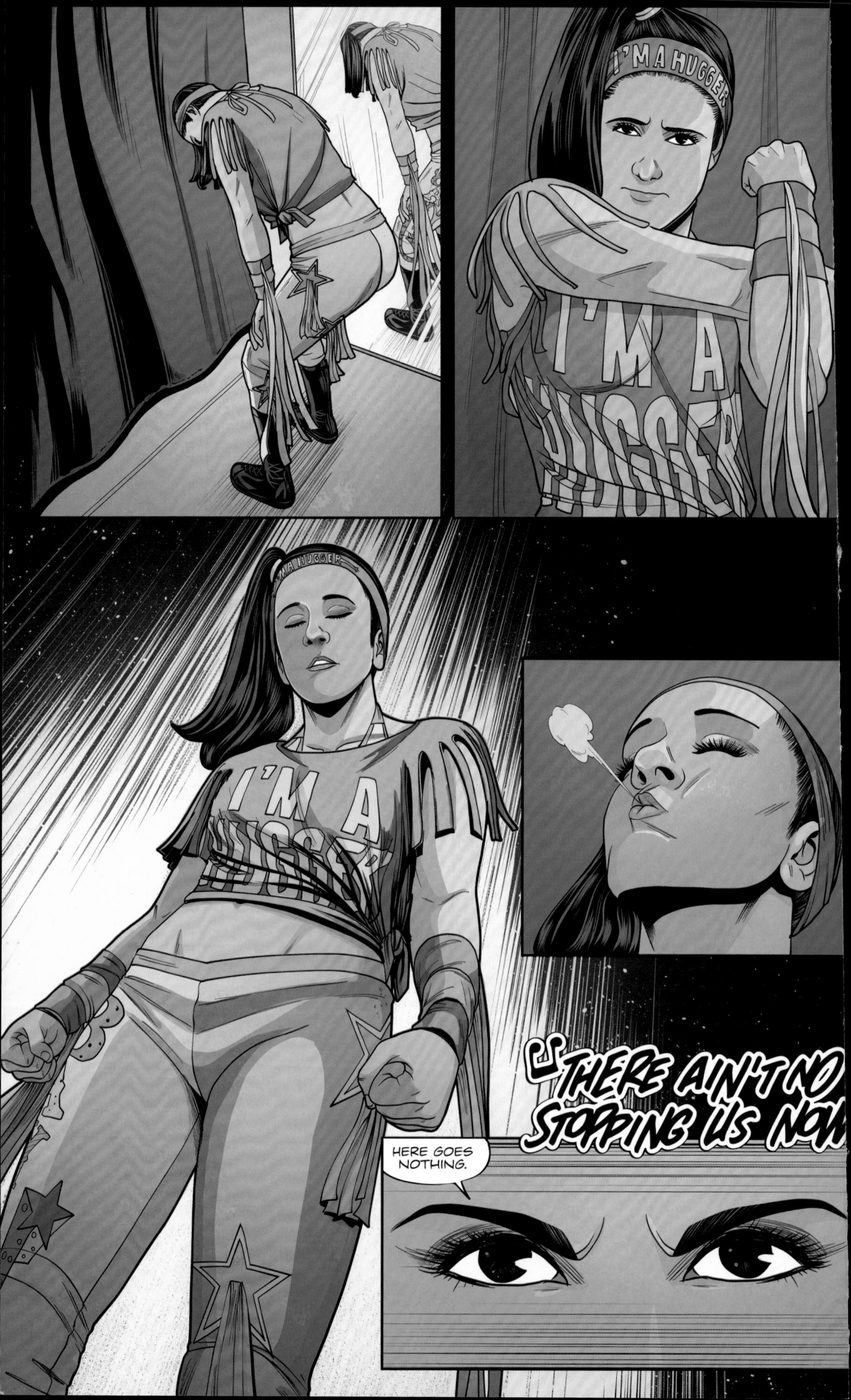
I'M A HUGGER
I'M A HUGGER
♫ THERE AIN'T NO STOPPING US NOW
HERE GOES NOTHING.

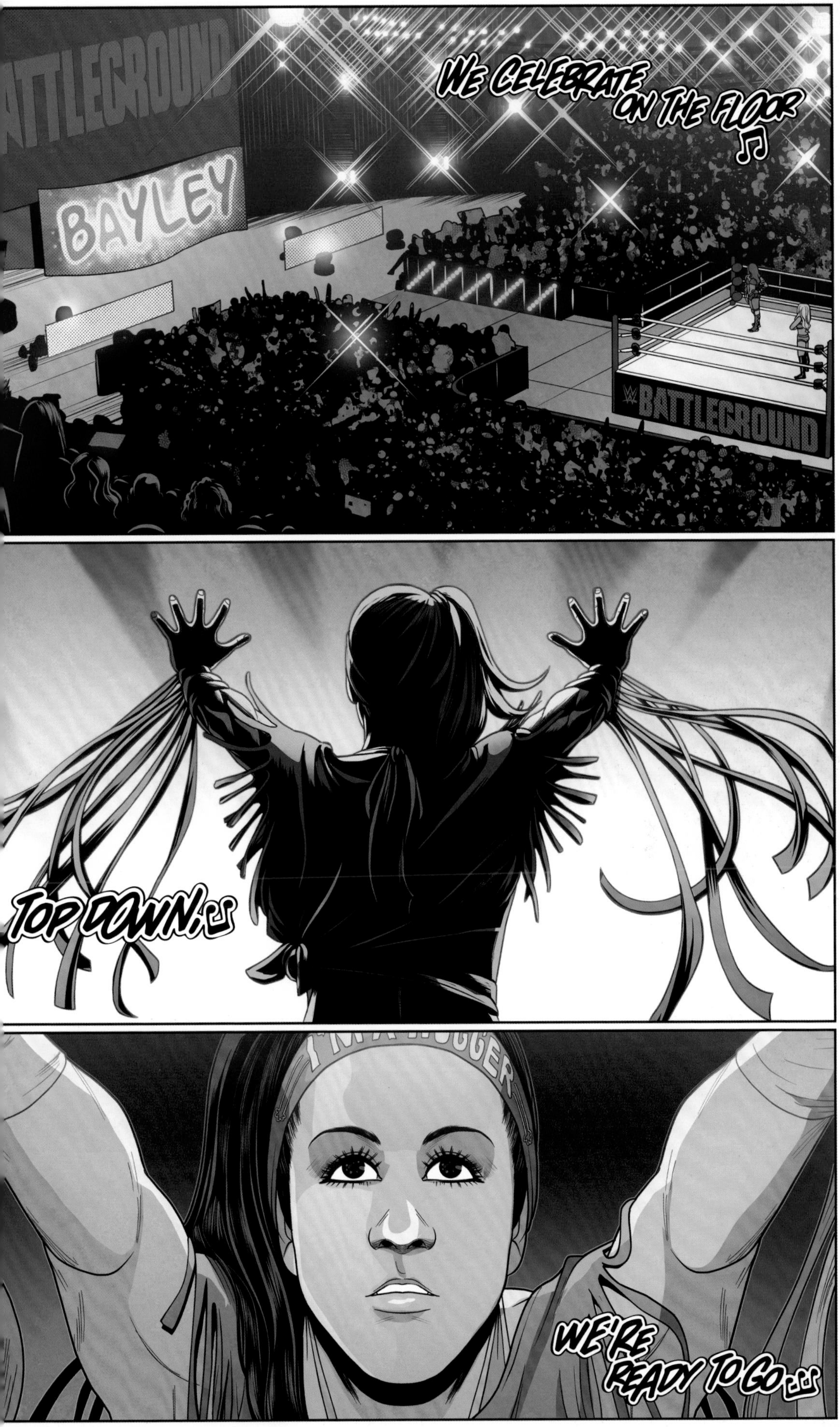
BATTLEGROUND
BAYLEY
WE CELEBRATE ON THE FLOOR ♫
BATTLEGROUND
TOP DOWN,
WE'RE READY TO GO

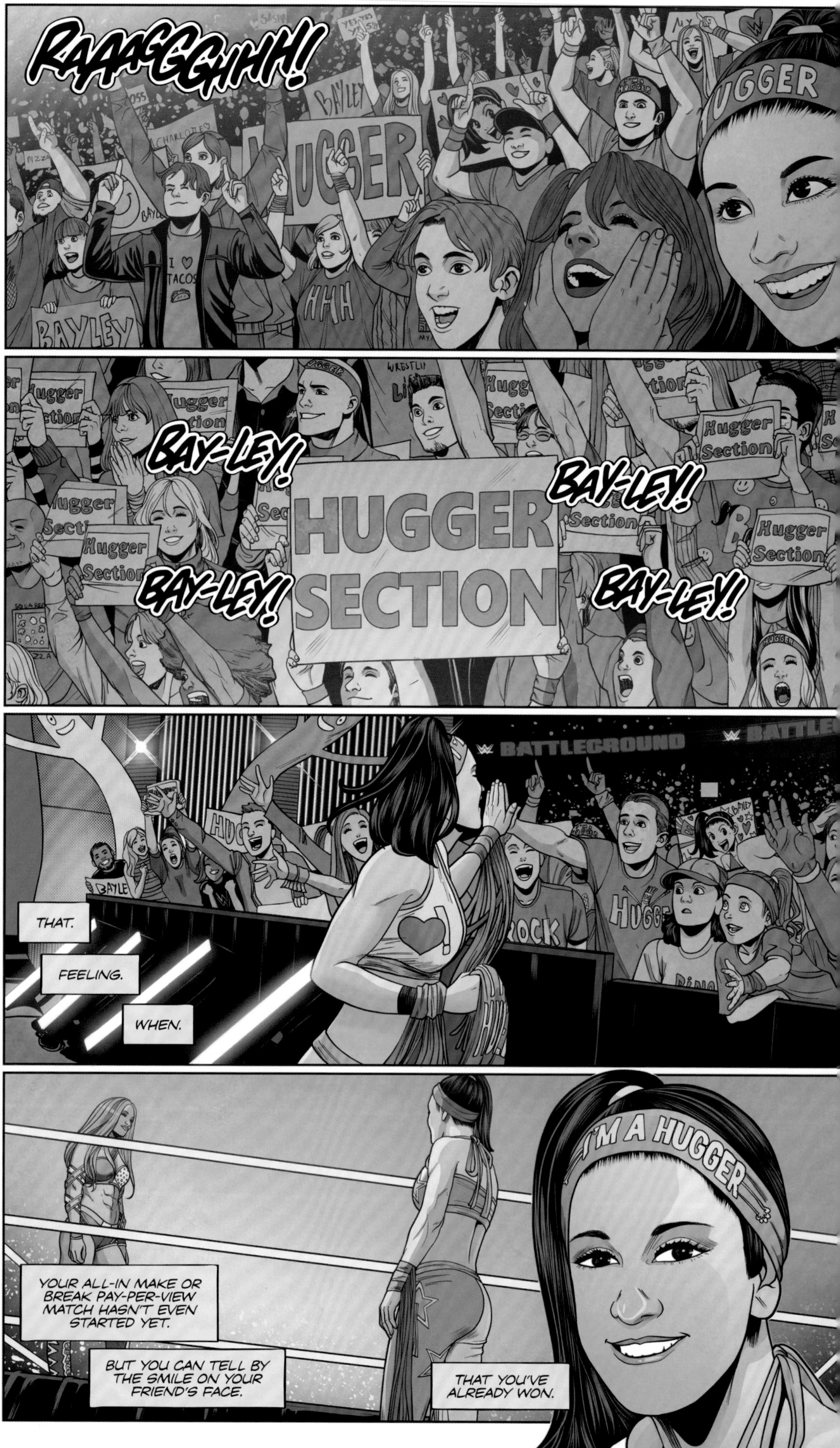

RAAAGGHHH!
HUGGER
BAYLEY
HUGGER
BAY-LEY!
HUGGER SECTION
BAY-LEY!
BAY-LEY!
BAY-LEY!
BATTLEGROUND
THAT.
FEELING.
WHEN.
I'M A HUGGER
YOUR ALL-IN MAKE OR BREAK PAY-PER-VIEW MATCH HASN'T EVEN STARTED YET.
BUT YOU CAN TELL BY THE SMILE ON YOUR FRIEND'S FACE.
THAT YOU'VE ALREADY WON.

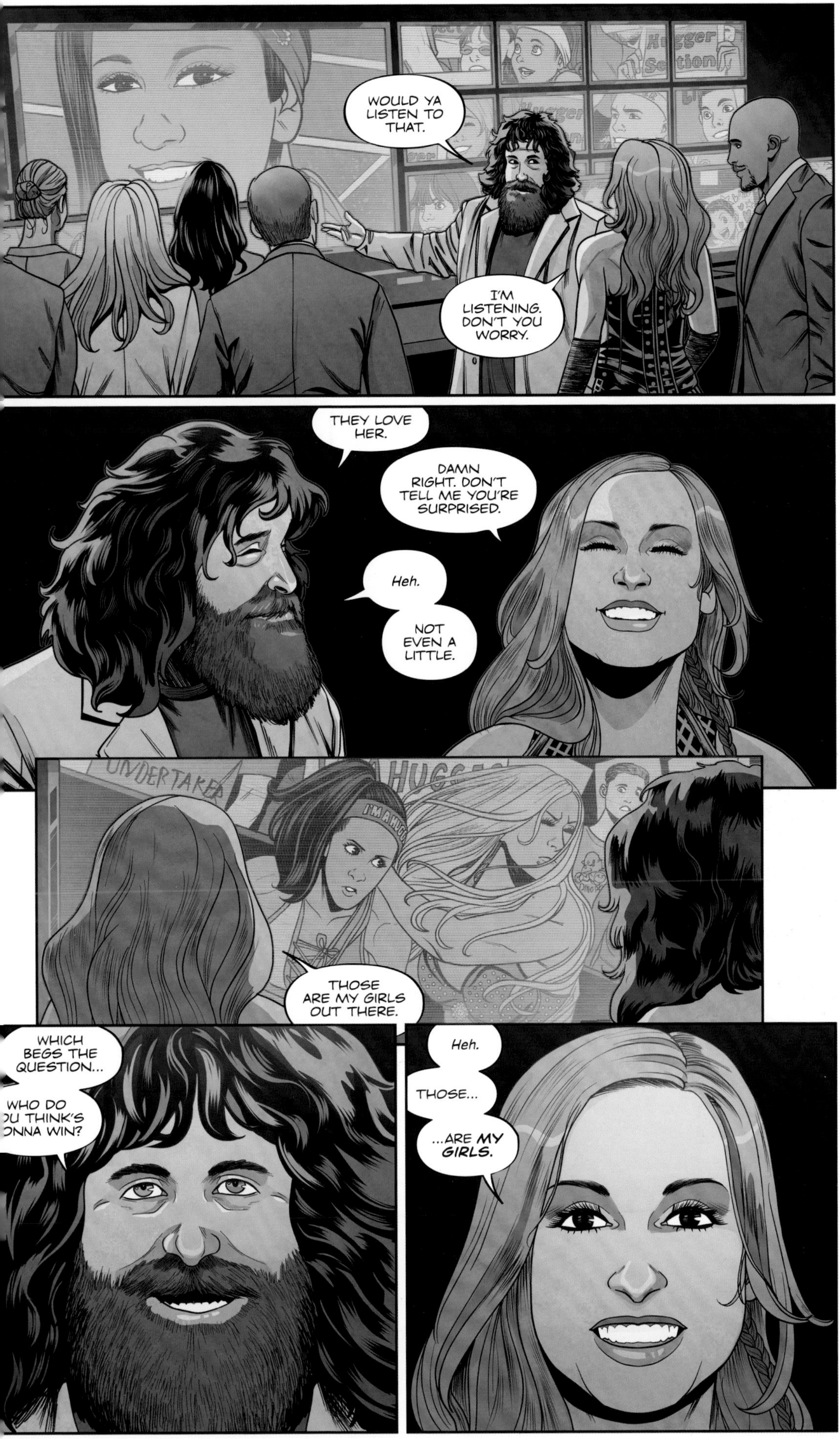

WOULD YA LISTEN TO THAT.
I'M LISTENING. DON'T YOU WORRY.
THEY LOVE HER.
DAMN RIGHT. DON'T TELL ME YOU'RE SURPRISED.
Heh.
NOT EVEN A LITTLE.
UNDERTAKER
THOSE ARE MY GIRLS OUT THERE.
WHICH BEGS THE QUESTION...
WHO DO ...U THINK'S ...ONNA WIN?
Heh.
THOSE...
...ARE MY GIRLS.

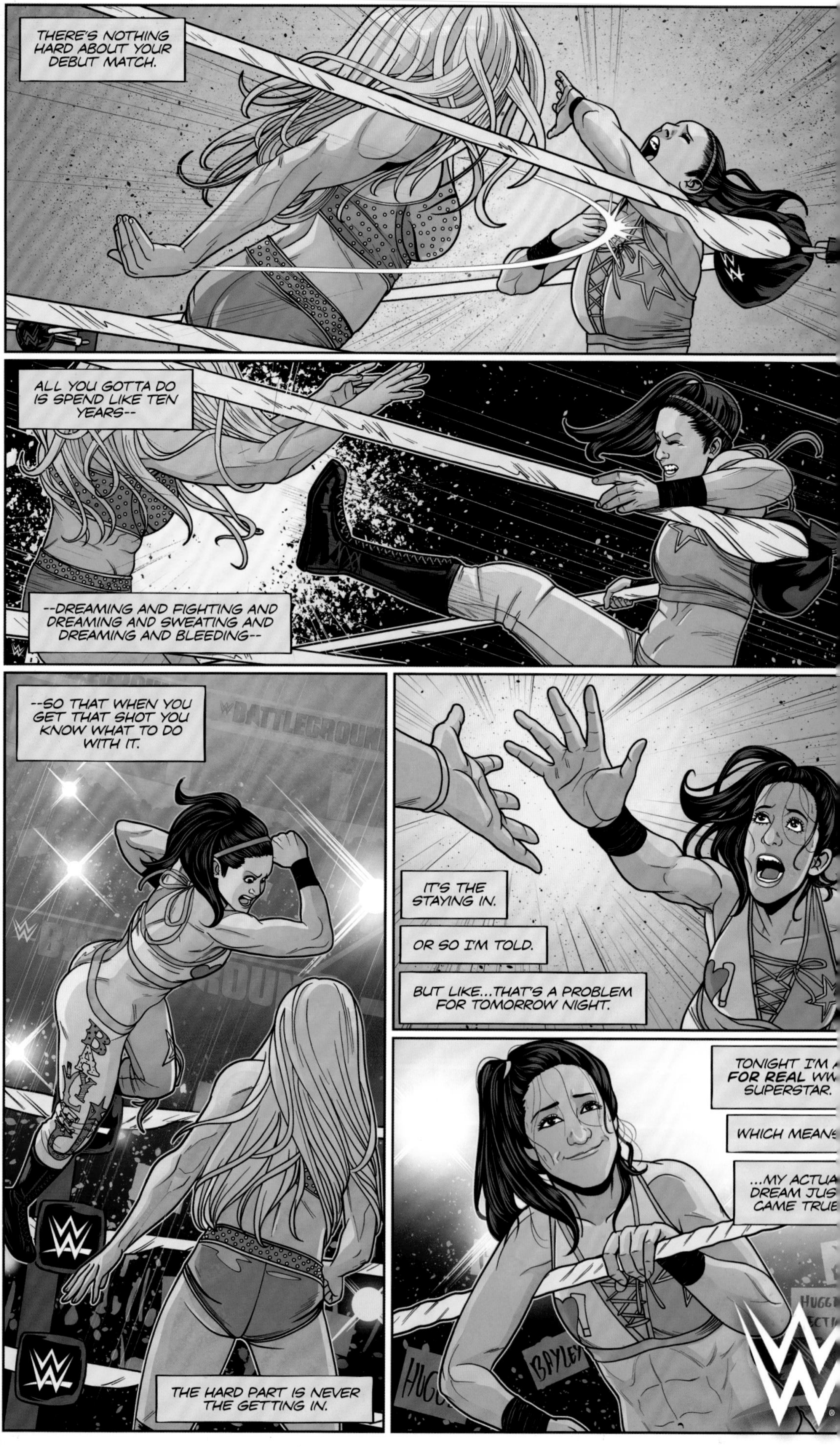
THERE'S NOTHING HARD ABOUT YOUR DEBUT MATCH.
ALL YOU GOTTA DO IS SPEND LIKE TEN YEARS--
--DREAMING AND FIGHTING AND DREAMING AND SWEATING AND DREAMING AND BLEEDING--
--SO THAT WHEN YOU GET THAT SHOT YOU KNOW WHAT TO DO WITH IT.
THE HARD PART IS NEVER THE GETTING IN.
IT'S THE STAYING IN.
OR SO I'M TOLD.
BUT LIKE...THAT'S A PROBLEM FOR TOMORROW NIGHT.
TONIGHT I'M
FOR REAL WW
SUPERSTAR.
WHICH MEAN
...MY ACTUA
DREAM JUS
CAME TRUE

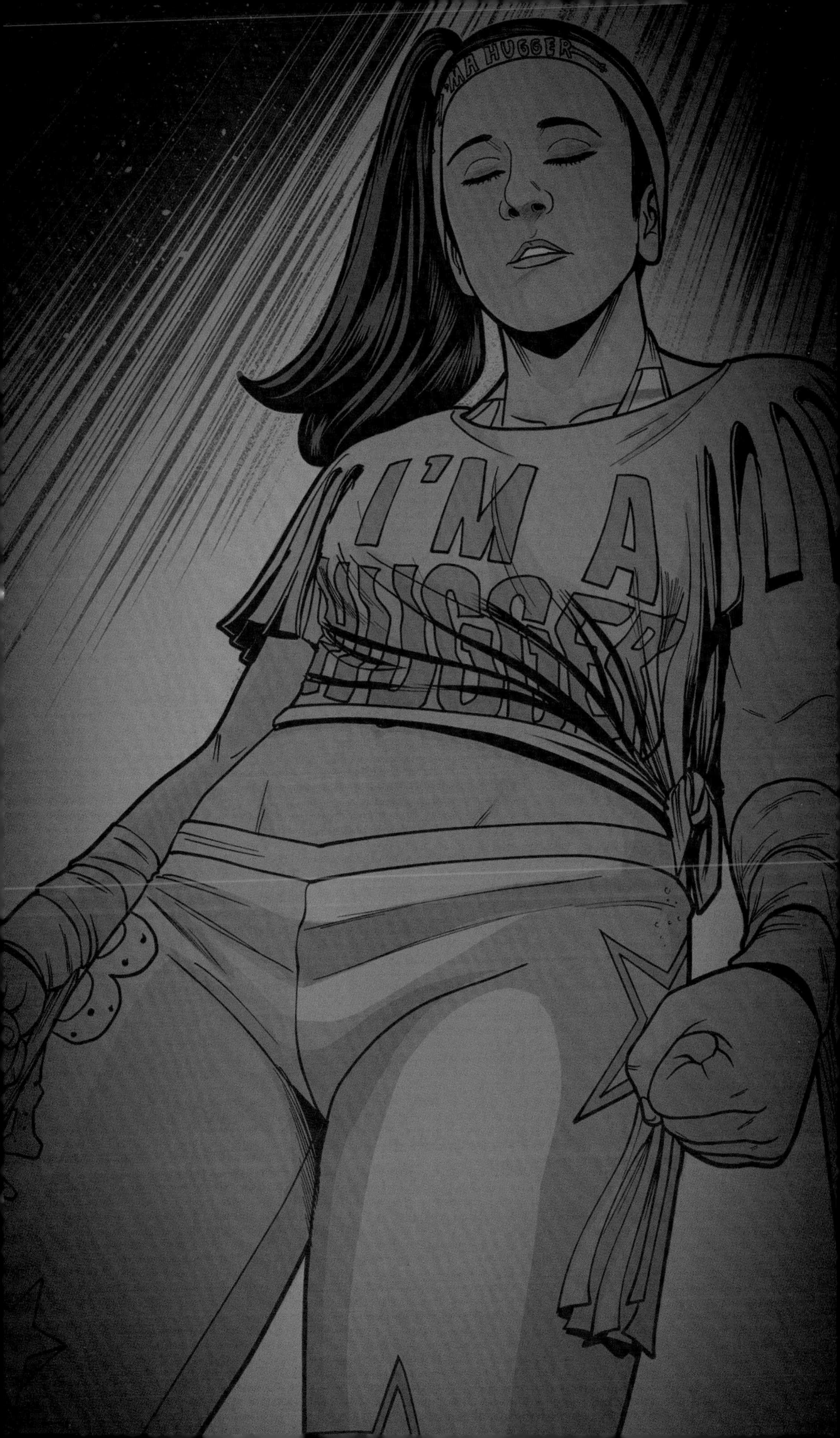
I'MA HUGGER
I'M A HUGGER

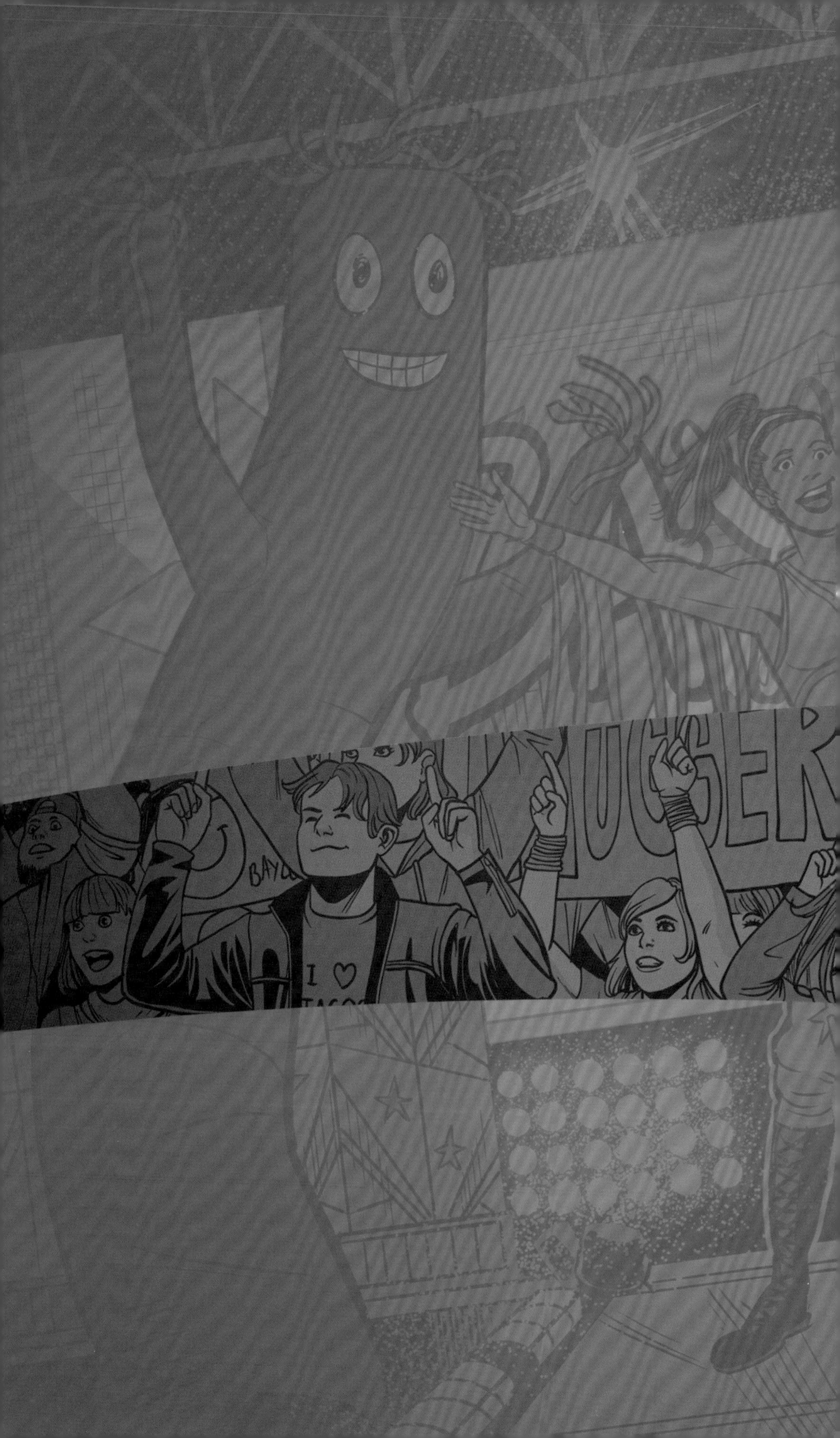

COVER GALLERY

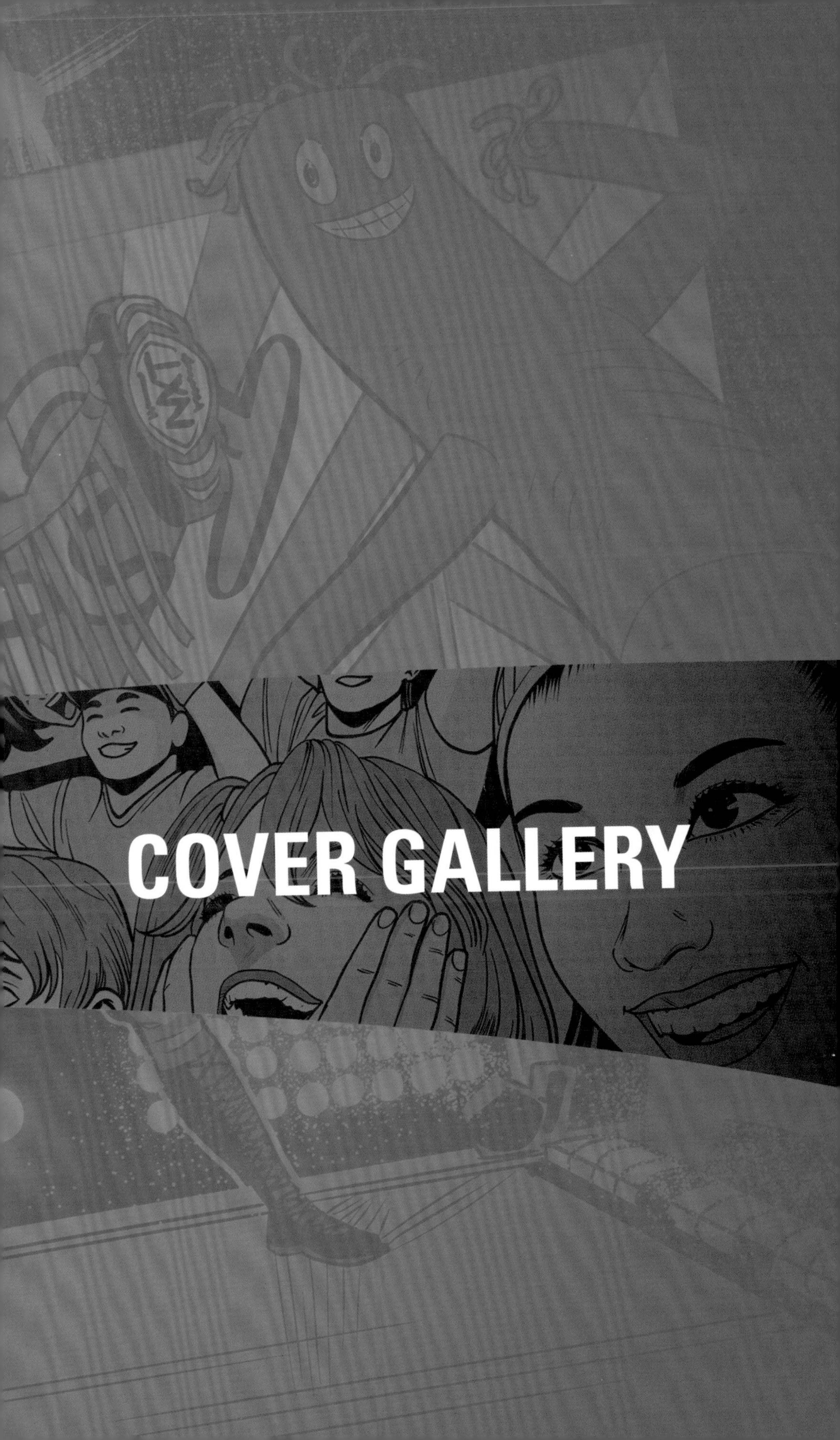

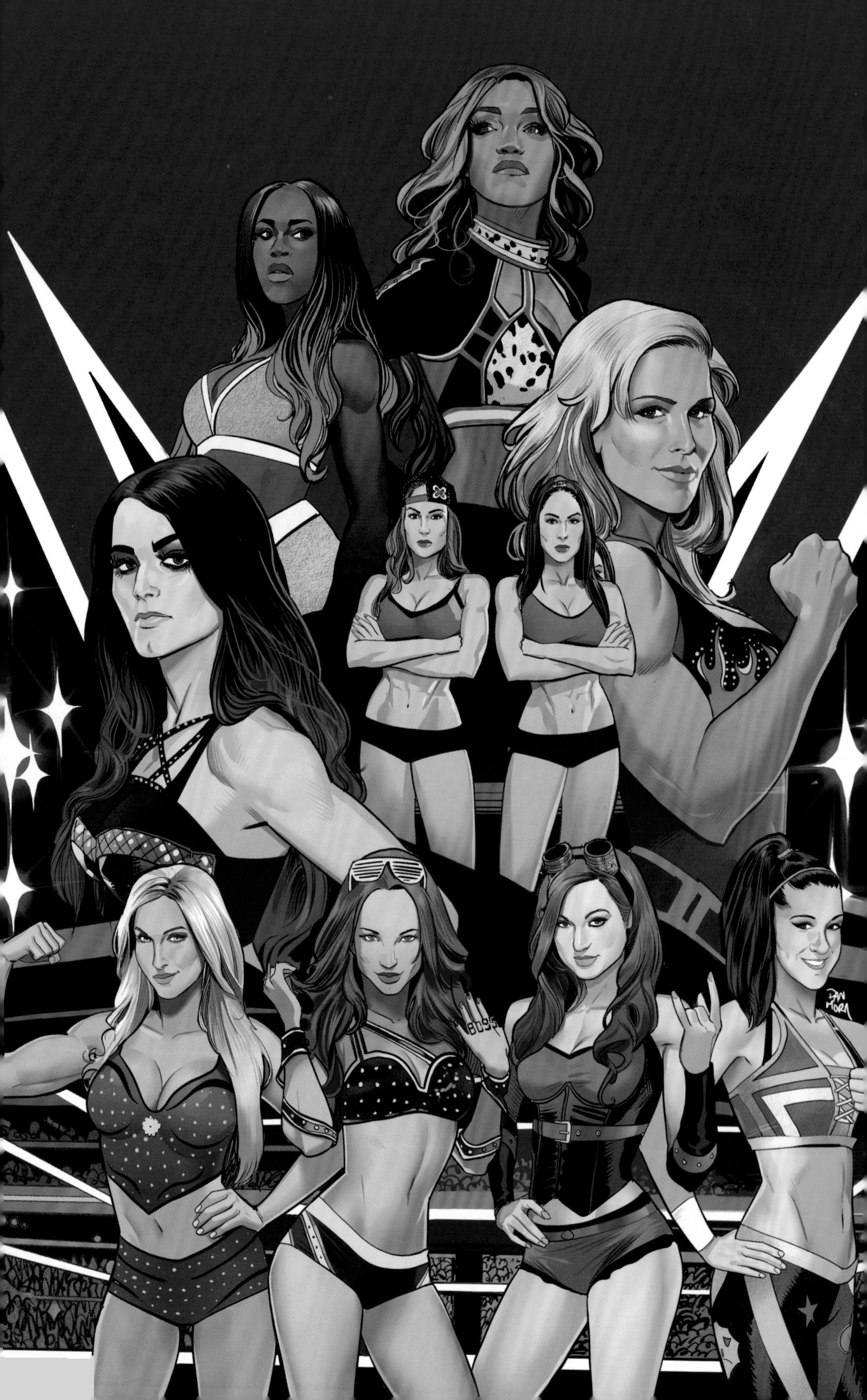
DAN MORA

WWE #14
COVER BY
DAN MORA

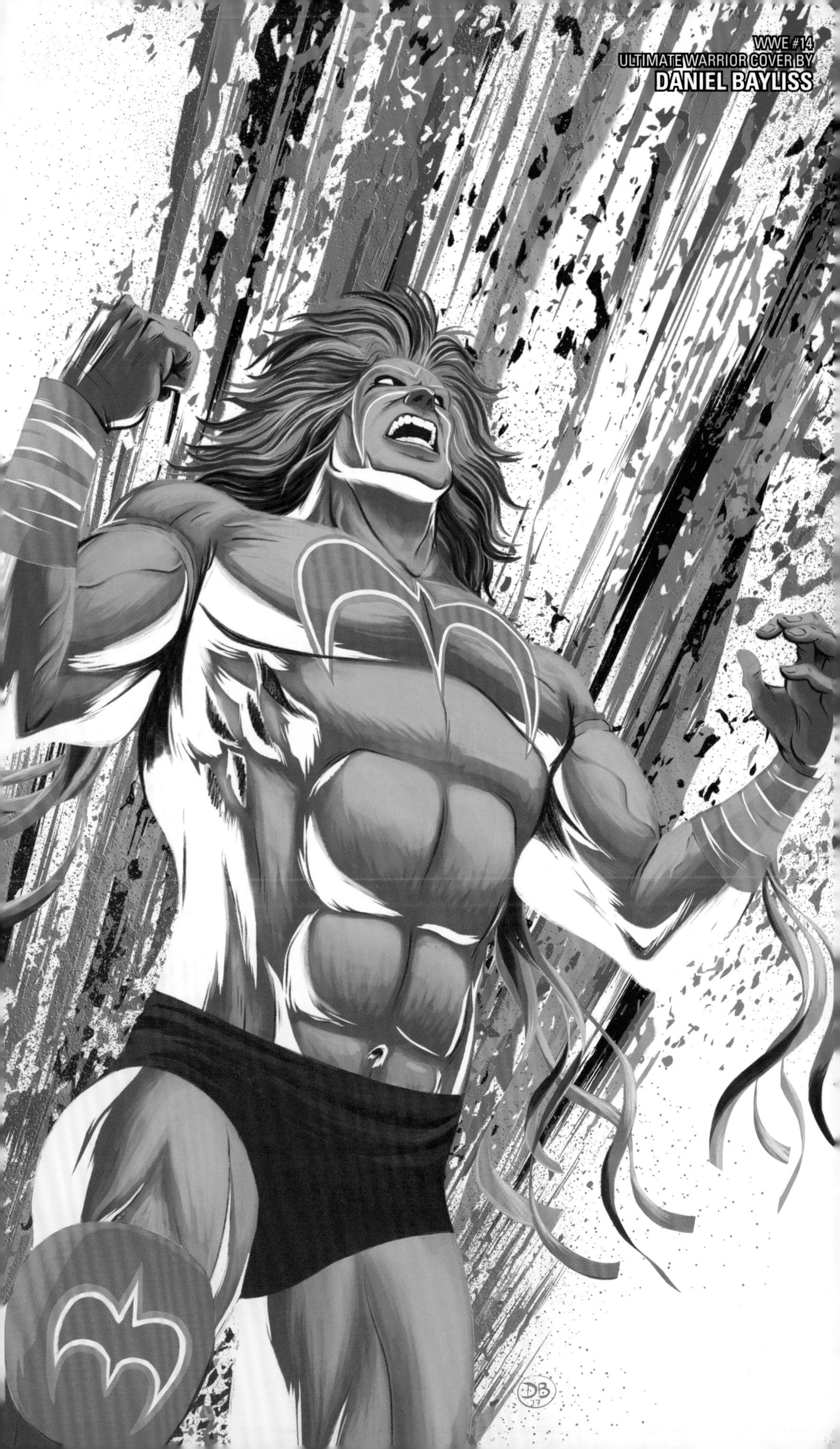

WWE #14
ULTIMATE WARRIOR COVER BY
DANIEL BAYLISS

WWE #14
ALEXA BLISS FRIENDLY NEIGHBORHOOD
COMICS EXCLUSIVE COVERS BY
AUDREY MOK

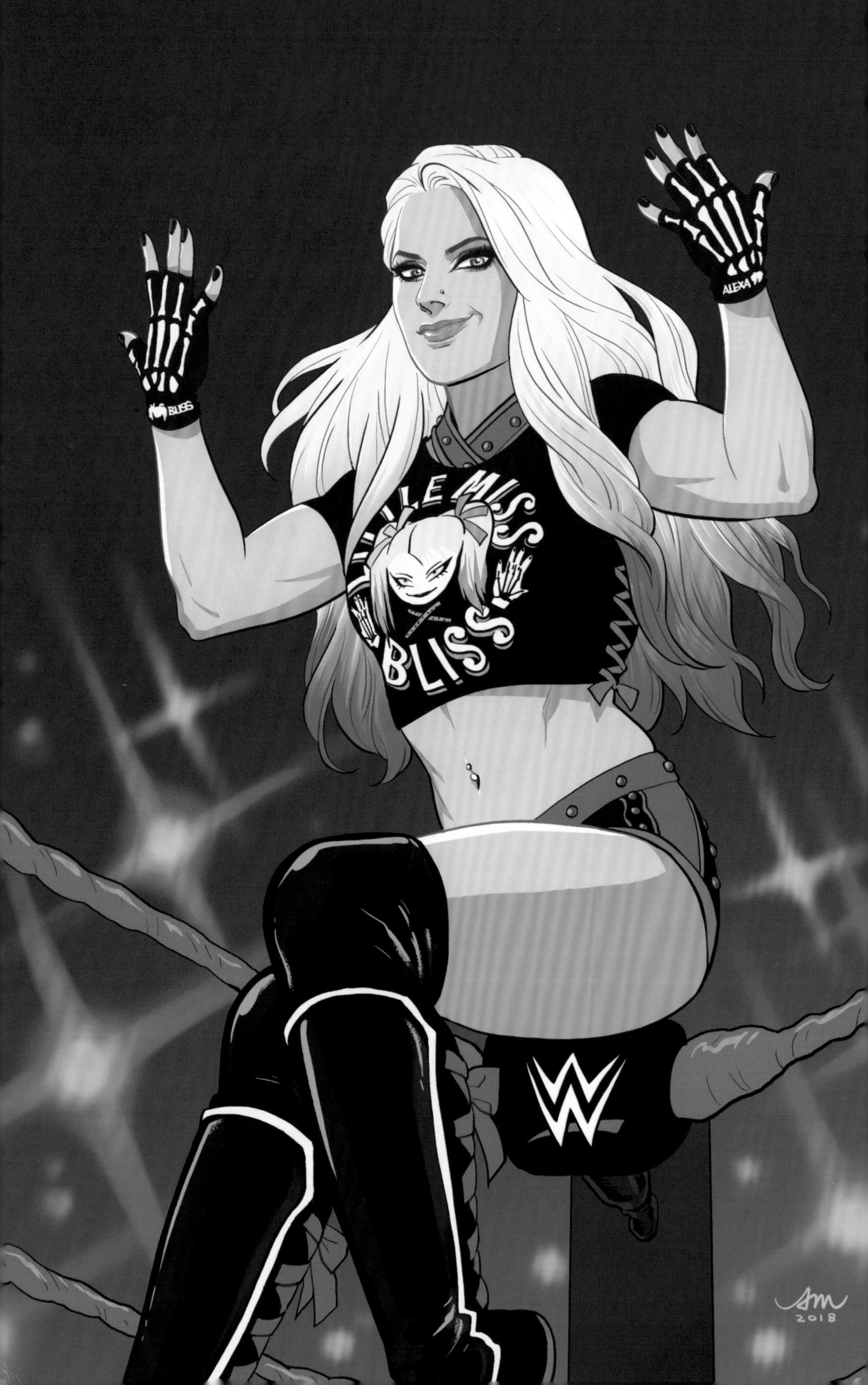
BLISS
ALEXA
BLISS
2018

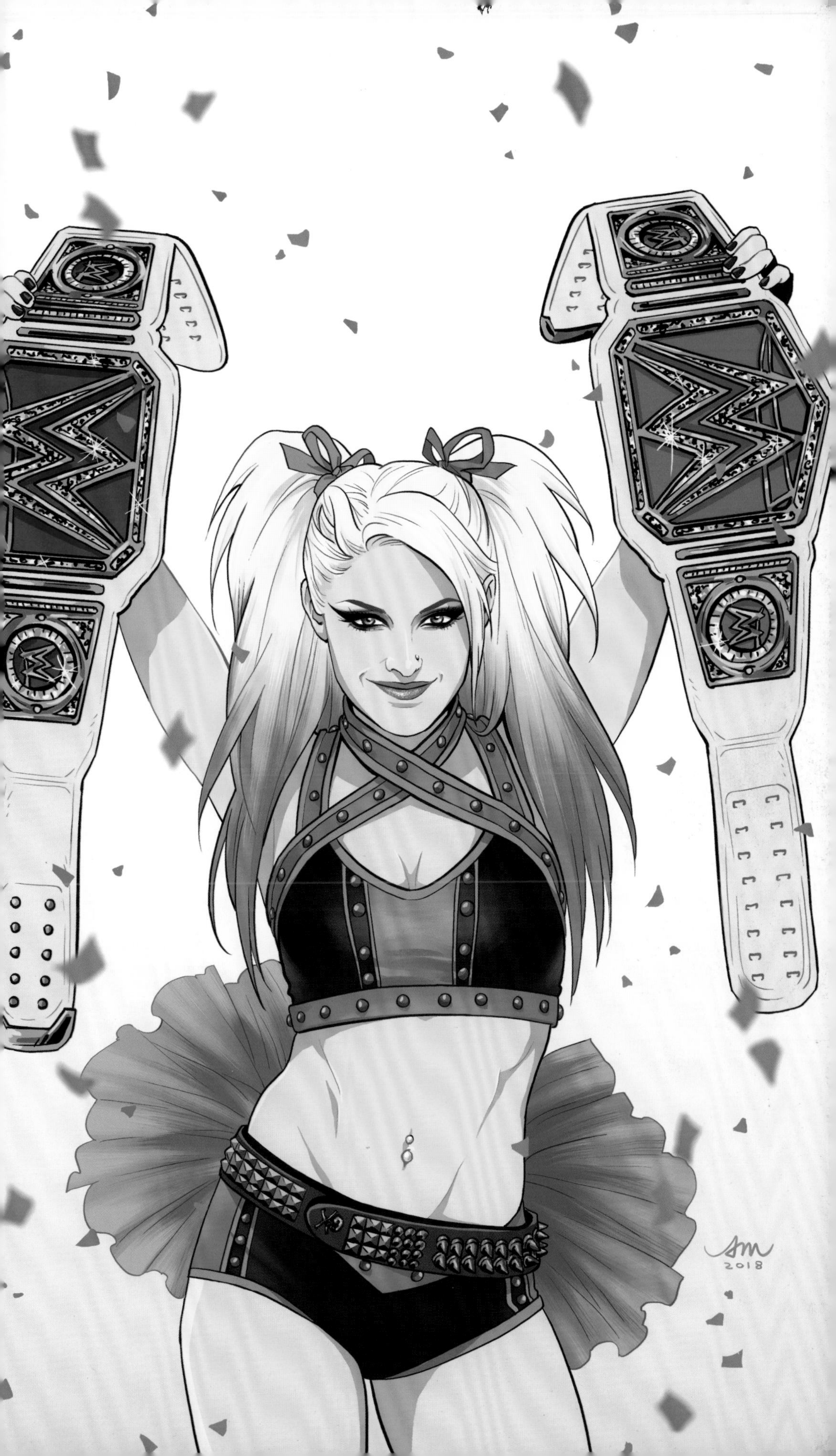
2018

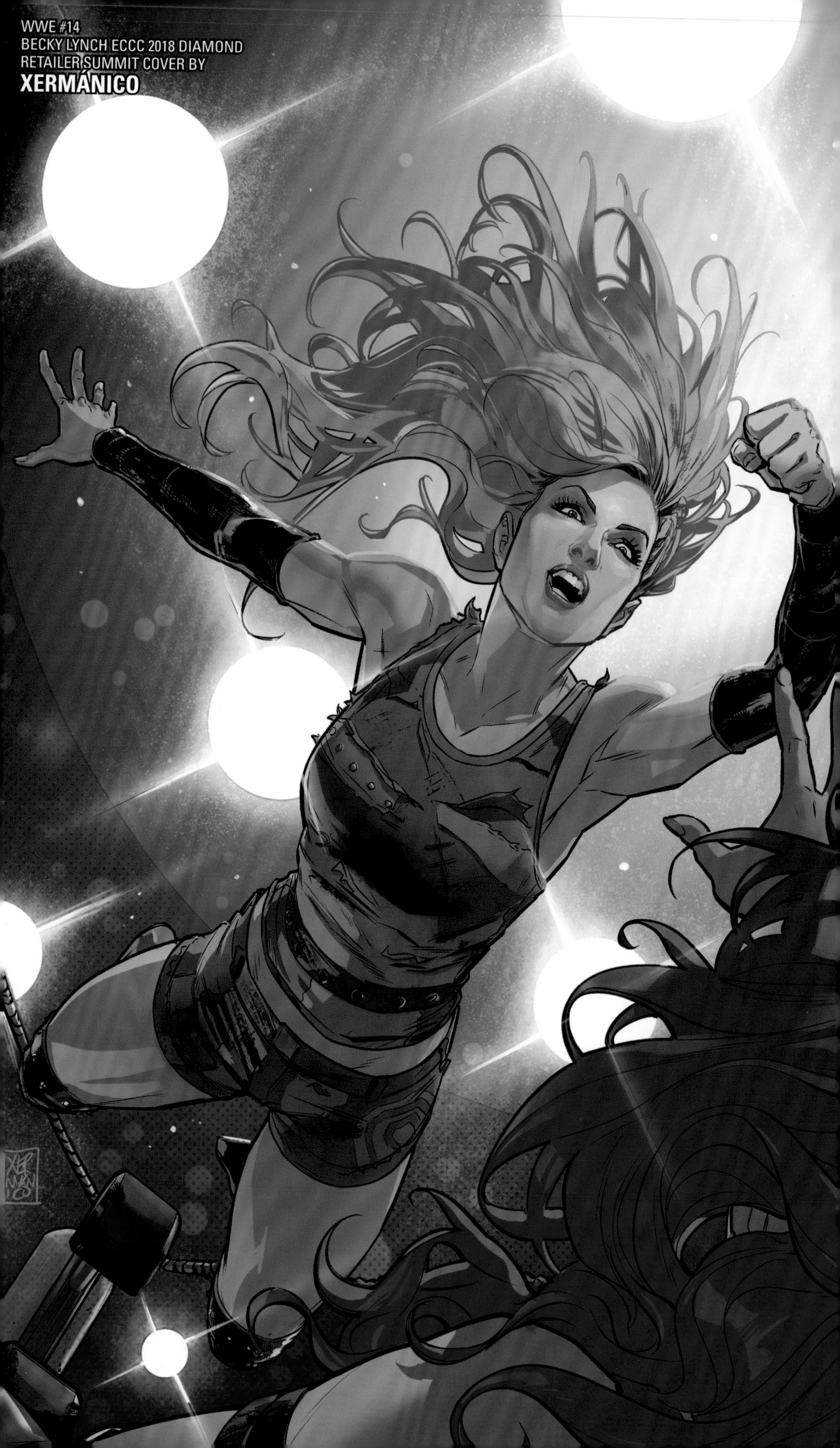

WWE #14
BECKY LYNCH ECCC 2018 DIAMOND
RETAILER SUMMIT COVER BY
XERMÁNICO

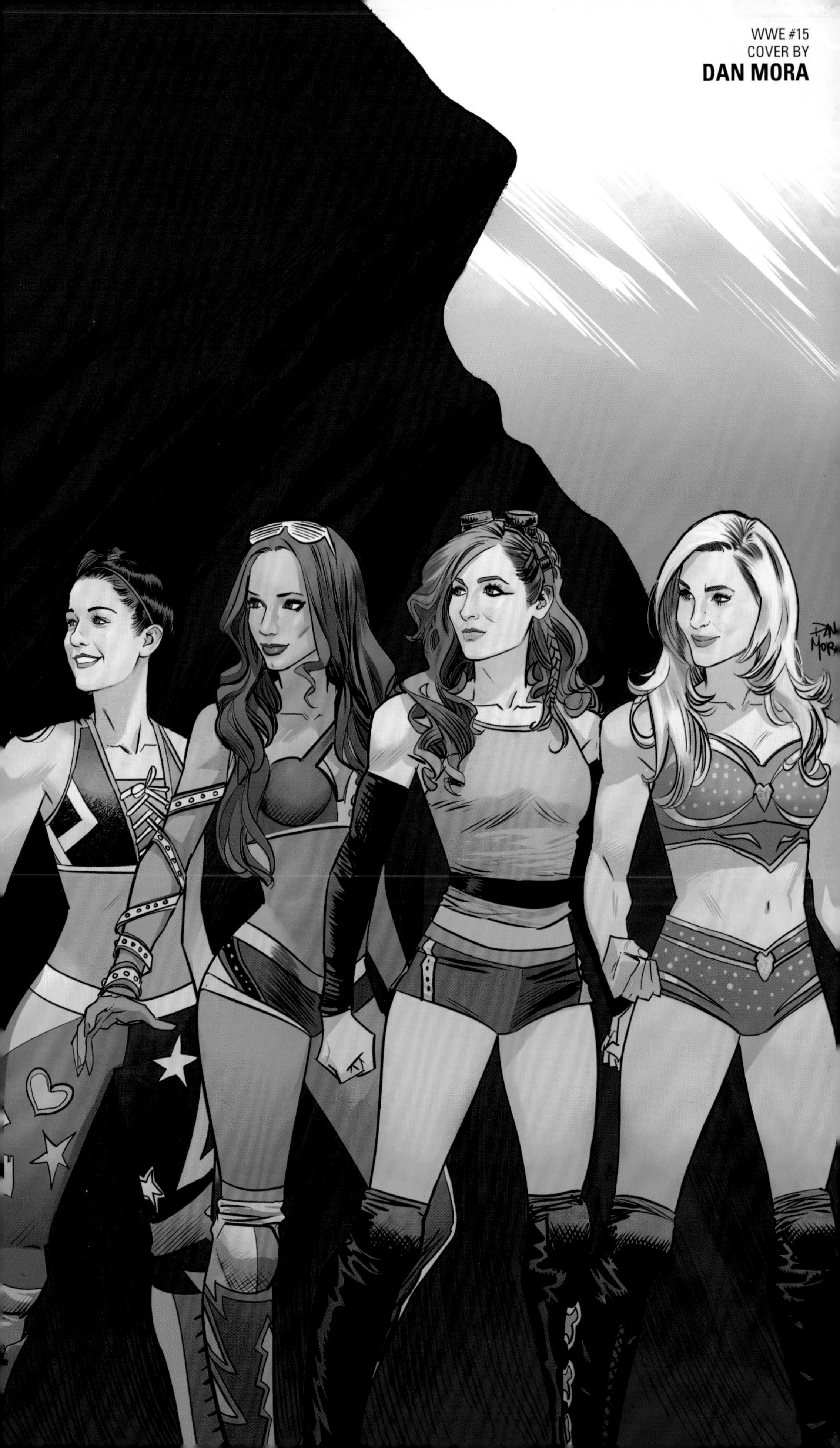

WWE #15
COVER BY
DAN MORA

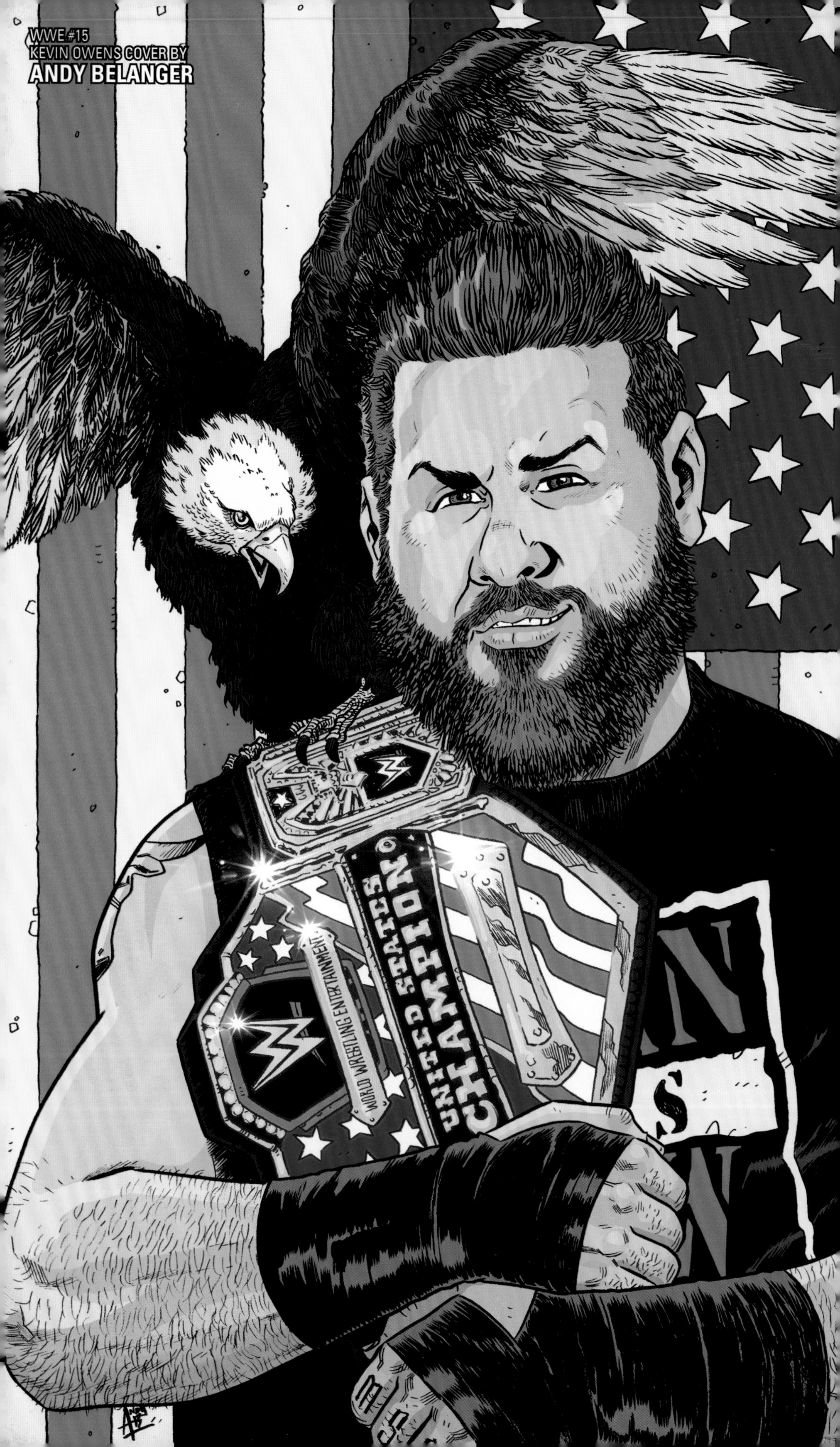
UNITED STATES
CHAMPION
WORLD WRESTLING ENTERTAINMENT

WWE #15
KEVIN OWENS COVER BY
ANDY BELANGER

WWE #16
COVER BY
DAN MORA

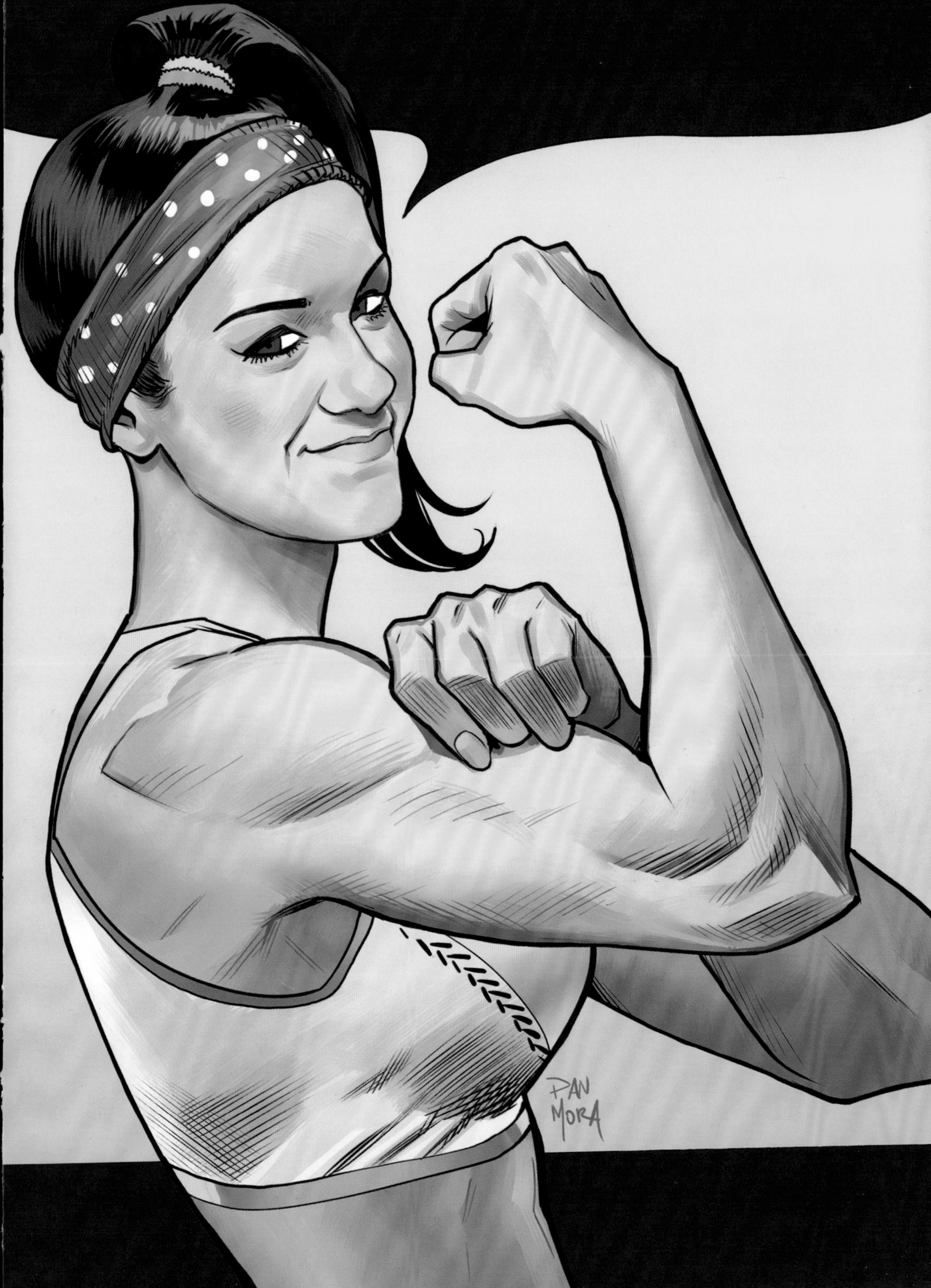
DAN
MORA

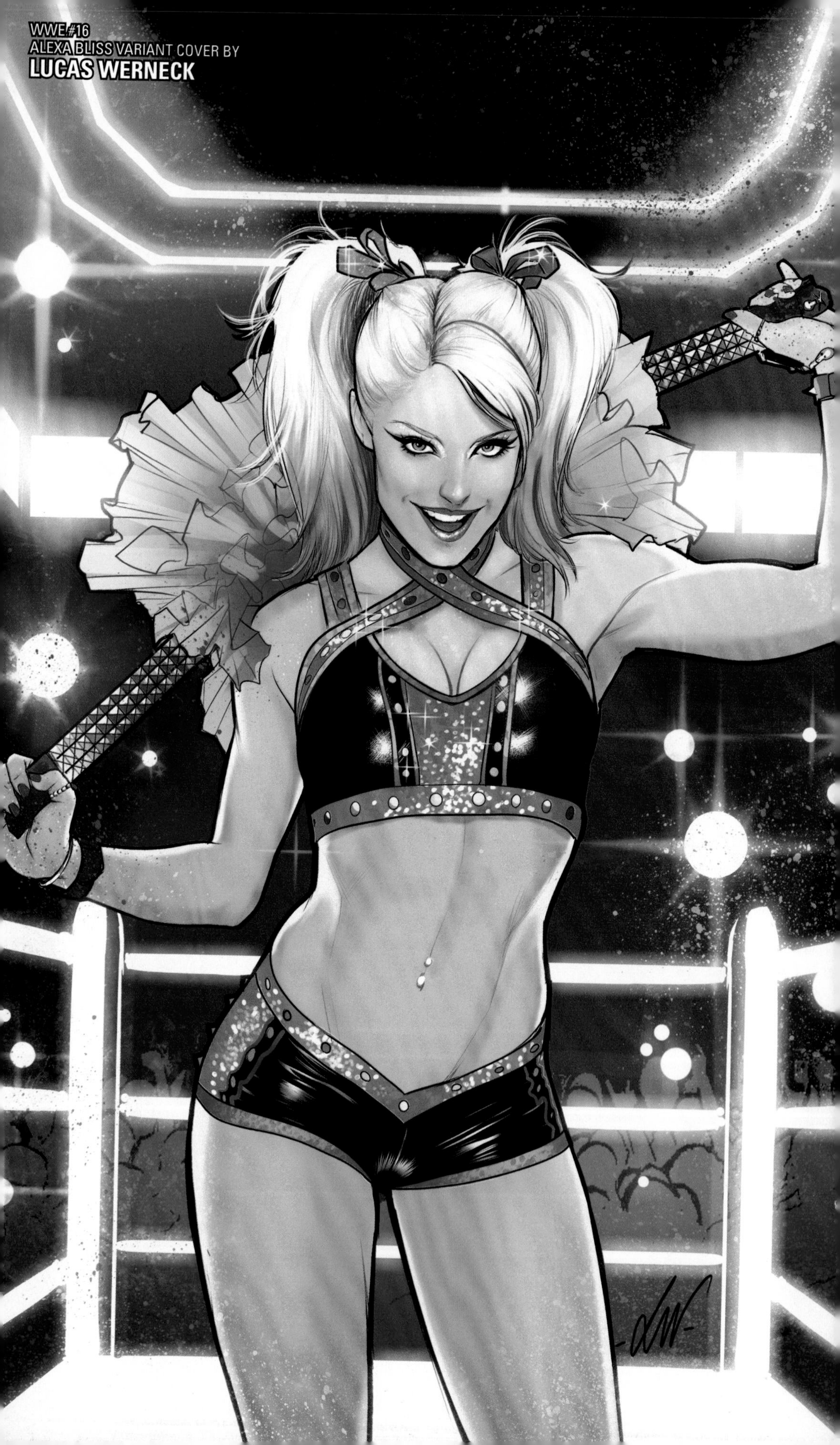

WWE #16
ALEXA BLISS VARIANT COVER BY
LUCAS WERNECK

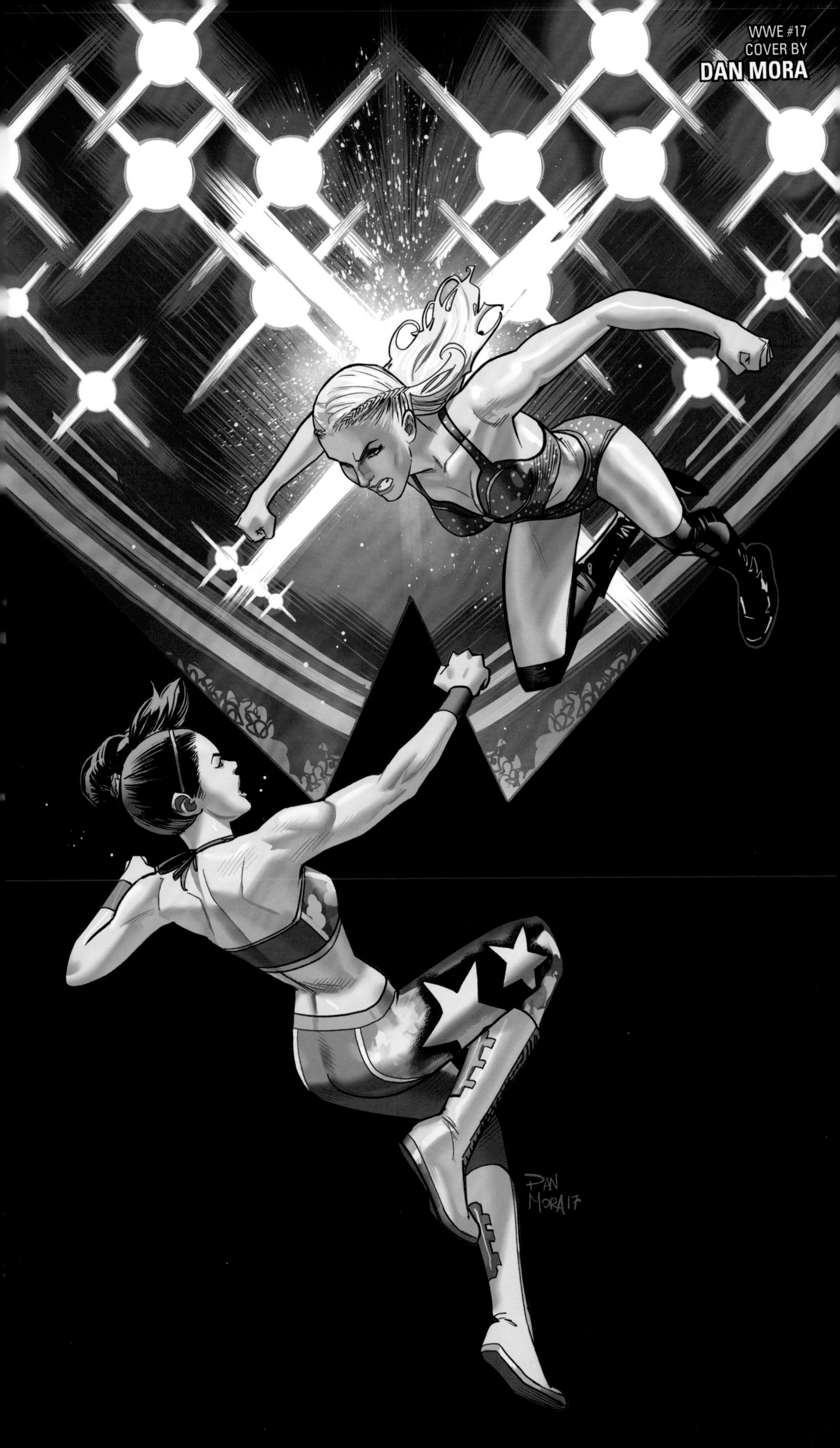
DAN
MORA17

WWE #17
COVER BY
DAN MORA

WWE #17
ASUKA COVER BY
HYEONJIN KIM

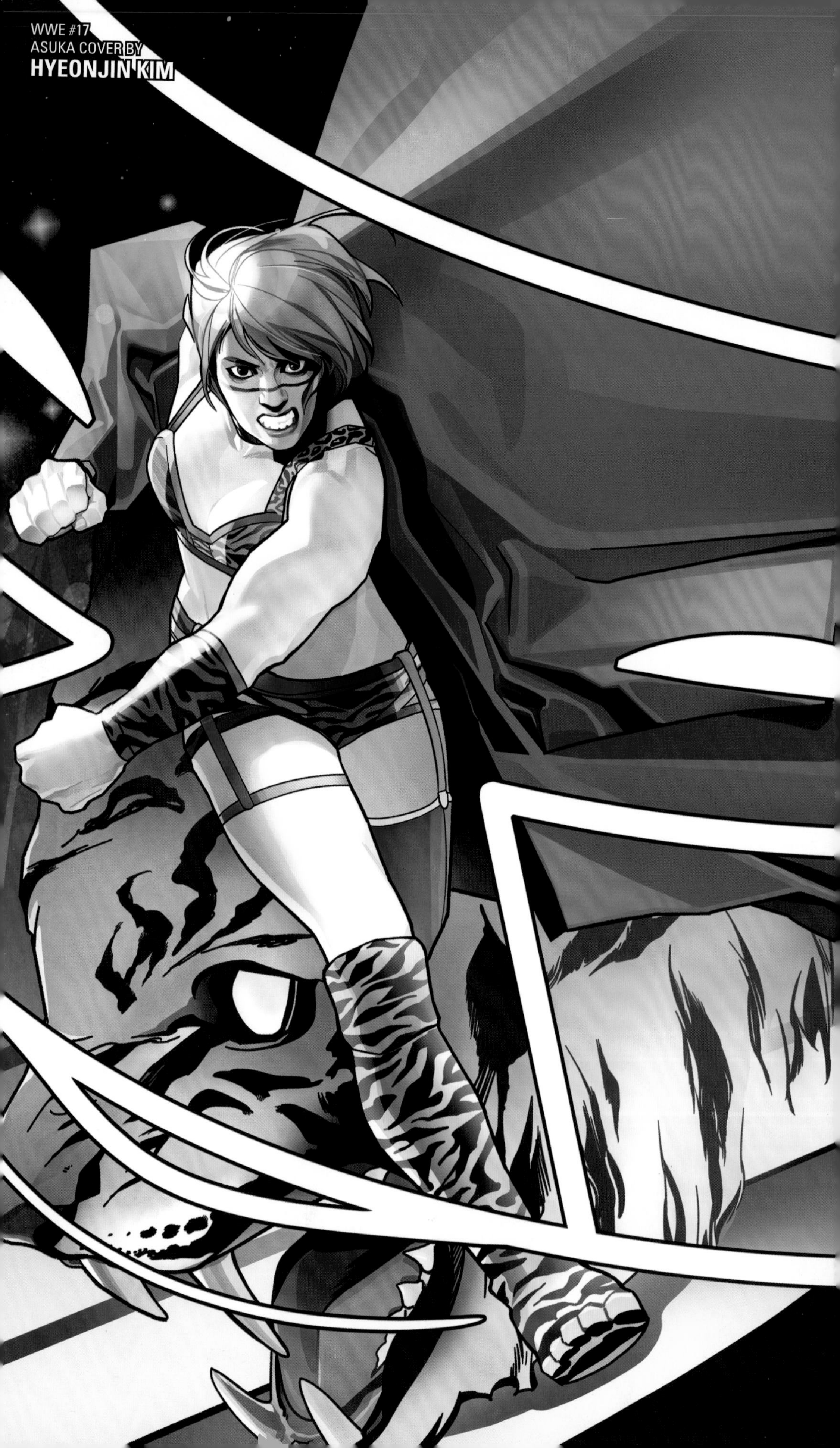

WWE #14
JINDER MAHAL ACTION FIGURE COVER BY
ADAM RICHES

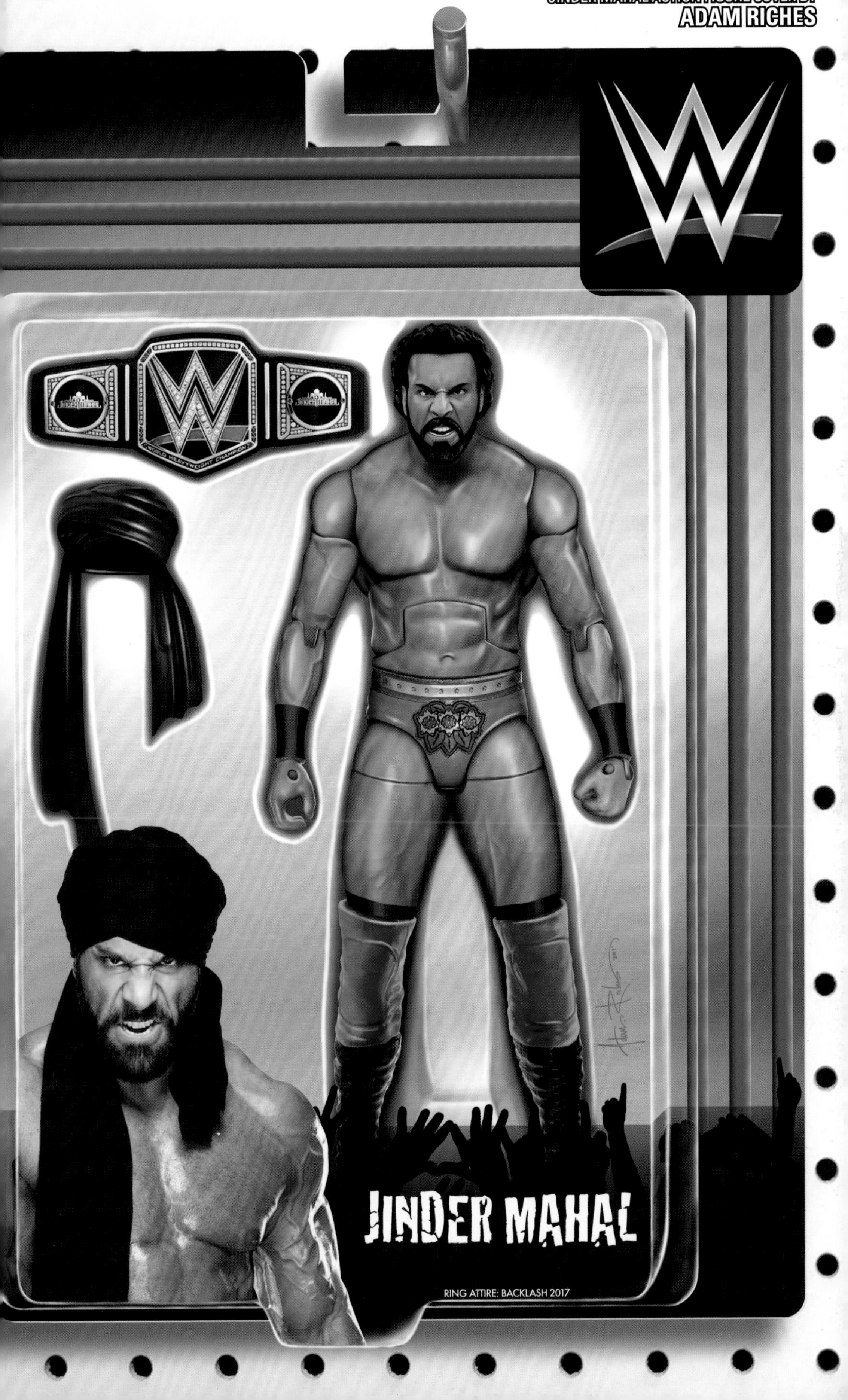
JINDER MAHAL
RING ATTIRE: BACKLASH 2017

WWE #15
DIAMOND DALLAS PAGE ACTION FIGURE COVER BY
ADAM RICHES

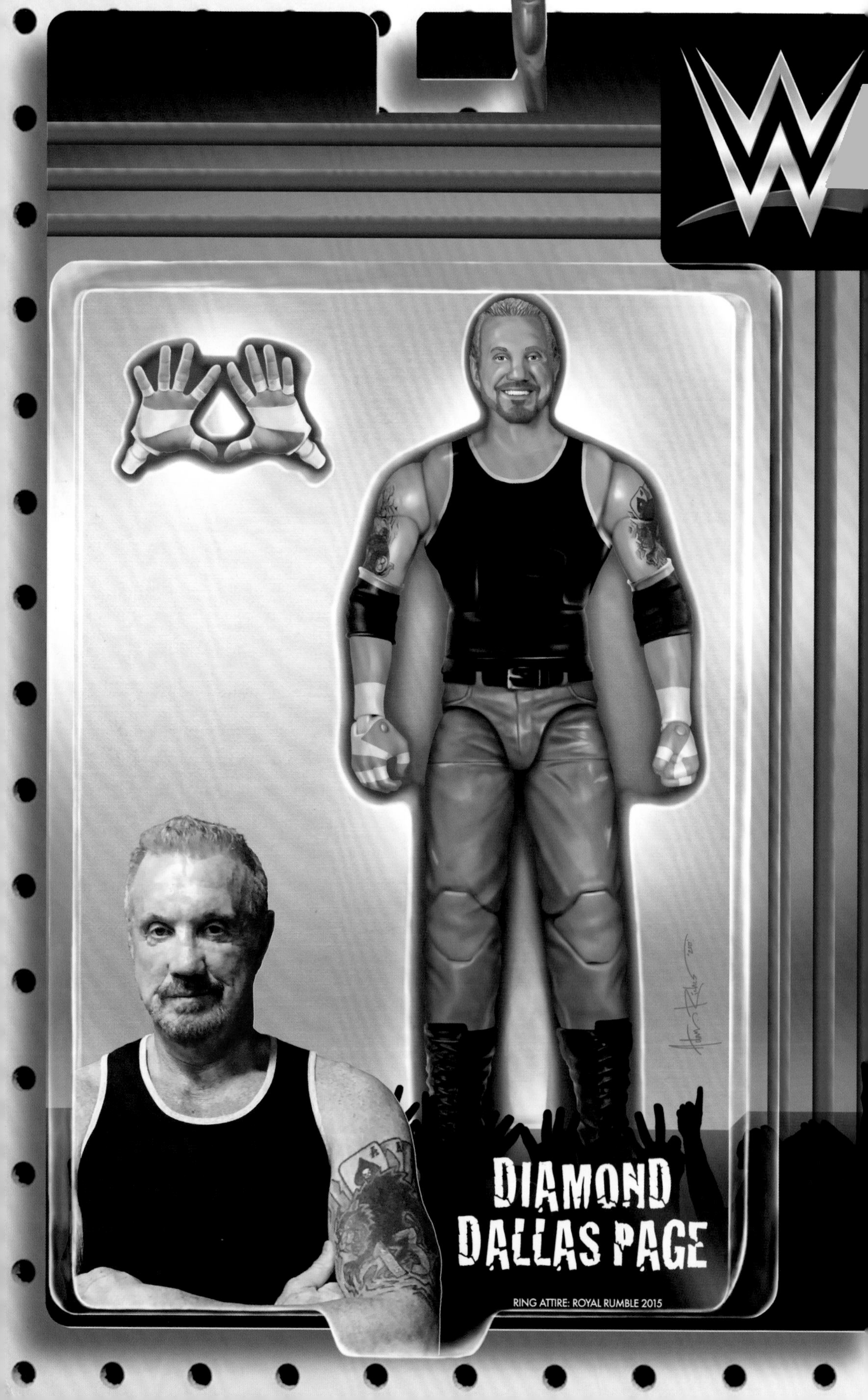
DIAMOND
DALLAS PAGE
RING ATTIRE: ROYAL RUMBLE 2015

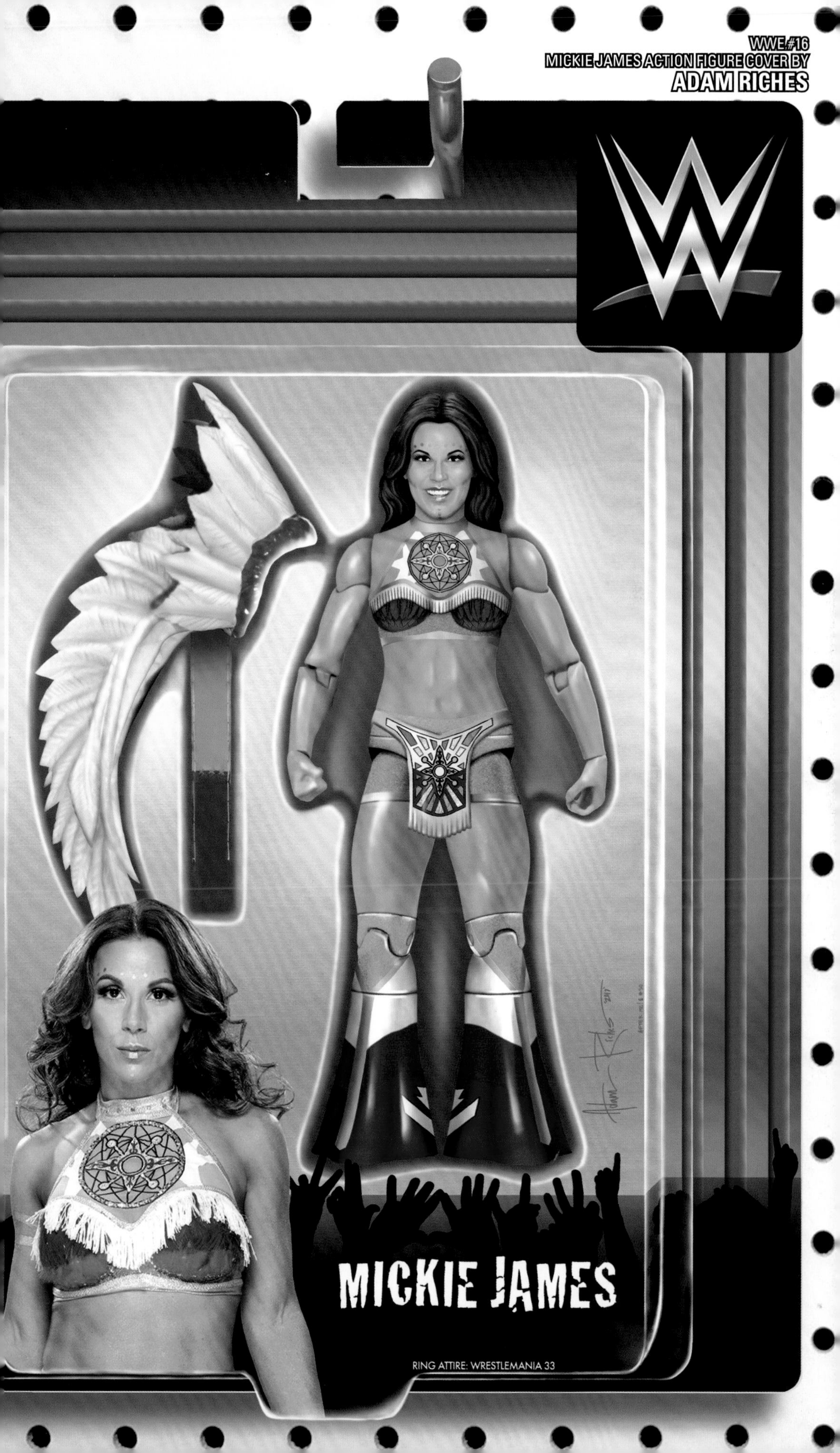
WWE #16
MICKIE JAMES ACTION FIGURE COVER BY
ADAM RICHES
MICKIE JAMES
RING ATTIRE: WRESTLEMANIA 33

WWE #17
XAVIER WOODS ACTION FIGURE COVER BY
ADAM RICHES

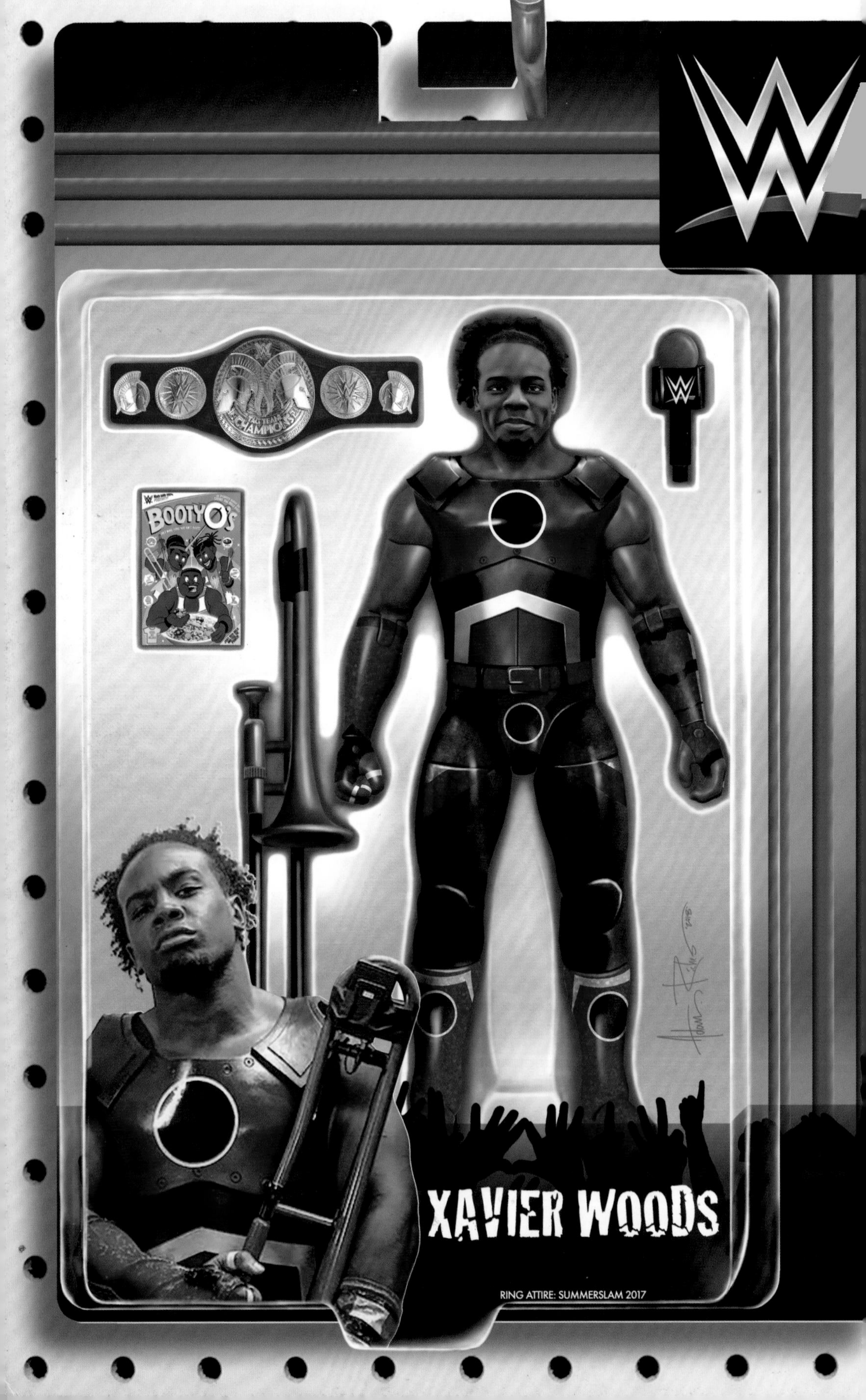
BOOTY O's
XAVIER WOODS
RING ATTIRE: SUMMERSLAM 2017

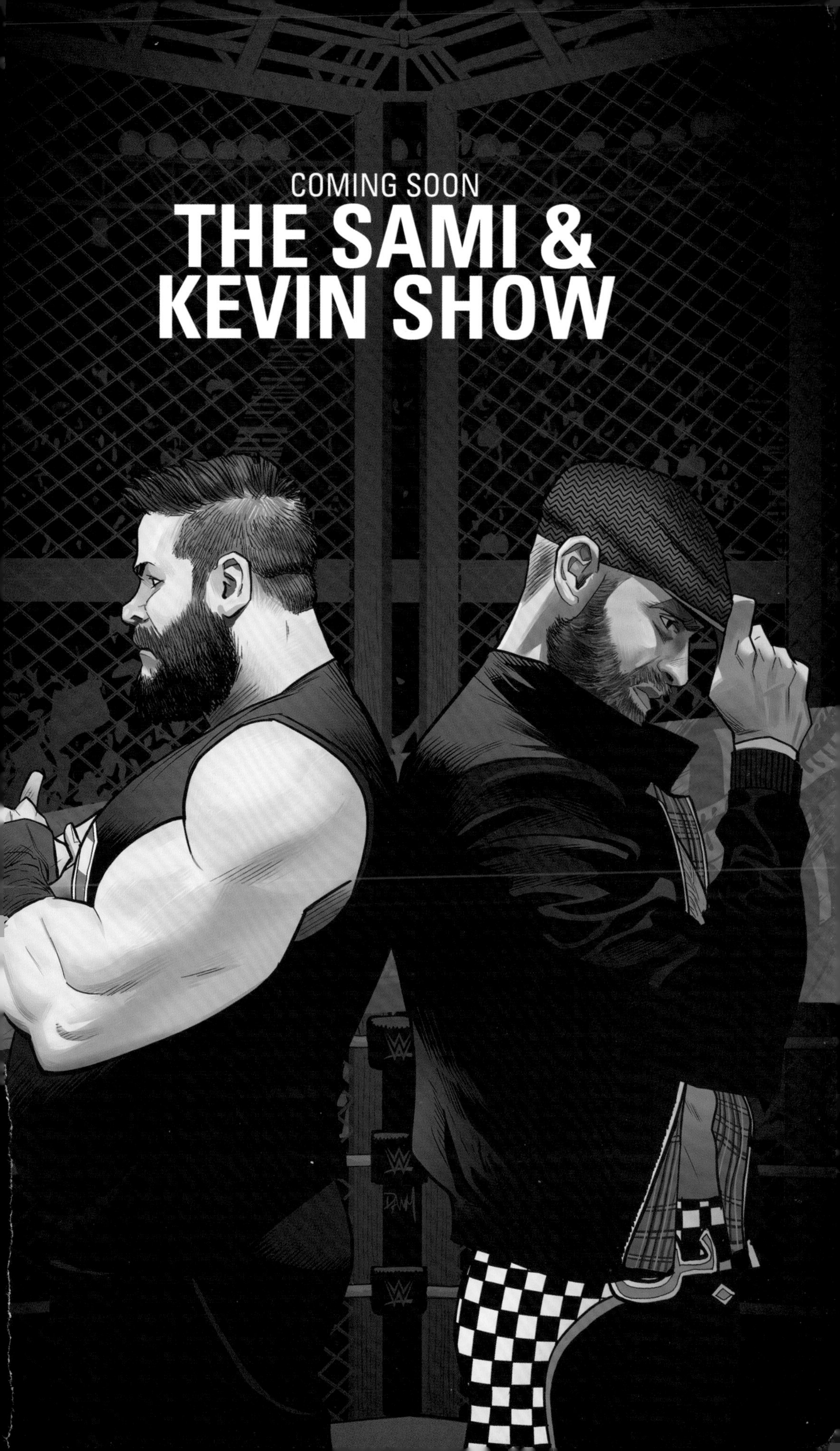
COMING SOON
THE SAMI &
KEVIN SHOW

DISCOVER
VISIONARY CREATORS

THE WOODS
JAMES TYNION IV • MICHAEL DIALYNAS
VOL. 1
THE ARROW

"The Spire is fantastic! My kind of genre free-for-all."
—BRIAN K. VAUGHAN (Saga)
THE SPIRE
SIMON SPURRIER
JEFF STOKELY
ANDRÉ MAY

MARK WAID • PETER KRAUSE
IRREDEEMABLE
AFTERWORD BY GRANT MORRISON

J.G. JONES
MARK WAID
STRANGE FRUIT
Foreword by
ELVIS MITCHELL

MICHAEL ALAN NELSON
DAN MORA
GABRIEL CASSATA
HEXED
THE HARLOT & THE THIEF VOLUME ONE

ABNETT & CULBARD
WILD'S END
FIRST LIGHT
"IT'S REALLY GREAT!"
JEFF LEMIRE

BOOM! STUDIOS

AVAILABLE AT YOUR LOCAL COMICS SHOP AND BOOKSTORE

To find a comics shop in your area, call 1-888-266-4226

WWW.**BOOM-STUDIOS**.COM

James Tynion IV

The Woods

Volume 1

ISBN: 978-1-60886-454-6 | $9.99 US

Volume 2

ISBN: 978-1-60886-495-9 | $14.99 US

Volume 3

ISBN: 978-1-60886-773-8 | $14.99 US

The Backstagers

Volume 1

ISBN: 978-1-60886-993-0 | $14.99 US

Simon Spurrier

Six-Gun Gorilla

ISBN: 978-1-60886-390-7 | $19.99 US

The Spire

ISBN: 978-1-60886-913-8 | $29.99 US

Weavers

ISBN: 978-1-60886-963-3 | $19.99 US

Mark Waid

Irredeemable

Volume 1

ISBN: 978-1-93450-690-5 | $16.99 US

Volume 2

ISBN: 978-1-60886-000-5 | $16.99 US

Incorruptible

Volume 1

ISBN: 978-1-60886-015-9 | $16.99 US

Volume 2

ISBN: 978-1-60886-028-9 | $16.99 US

Strange Fruit

ISBN: 978-1-60886-872-8 | $24.99 US

Michael Alan Nelson

Hexed The Harlot & The Thief

Volume 1

ISBN: 978-1-60886-718-9 | $14.99 US

Volume 2

ISBN: 978-1-60886-816-2 | $14.99 US

Day Men

Volume 1

ISBN: 978-1-60886-393-8 | $9.99 US

Volume 2

ISBN: 978-1-60886-852-0 | $9.99 US

Dan Abnett

Wild's End

Volume 1: First Light

ISBN: 978-1-60886-735-6 | $19.99 US

Volume 2: The Enemy Within

ISBN: 978-1-60886-877-3 | $19.99 US

Hypernaturals

Volume 1

ISBN: 978-1-60886-298-6 | $16.99 US

Volume 2

ISBN: 978-1-60886-319-8 | $19.99 US

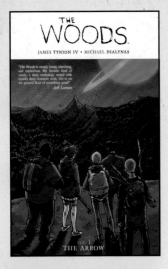

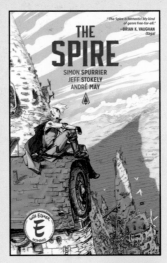

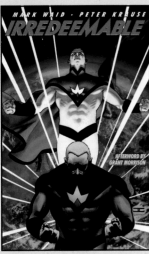

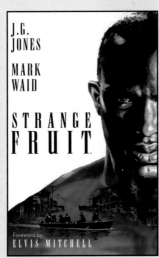

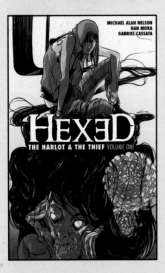

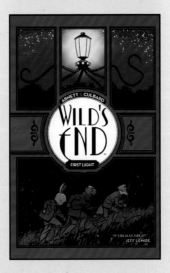

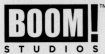